TAKING PLACE

Die Arbeiten von | The Works of Michael Elmgreen & Ingar Dragset

TAKING PLACE

Die Arbeiten von | The Works of Michael Elmgreen & Ingar Dragset

Herausgegeben von | Edited by

Kunsthalle Zürich
Danish Contemporary Art Foundation

Hatje Cantz Verlag

Vorwort
Preface 08

Beatrix Ruf
Taking Place 12

Coco Fusco
An Interview with Michael Elmgreen and Ingar Dragset
Transformierende Handlungen
Transformational Acts 36

Markus Brüderlin
Arbeit am White Cube
Work on the White Cube 74

Dan Cameron
The Road Always Taken 109

Biografie & Bibliografie
Biography & Bibliography 144

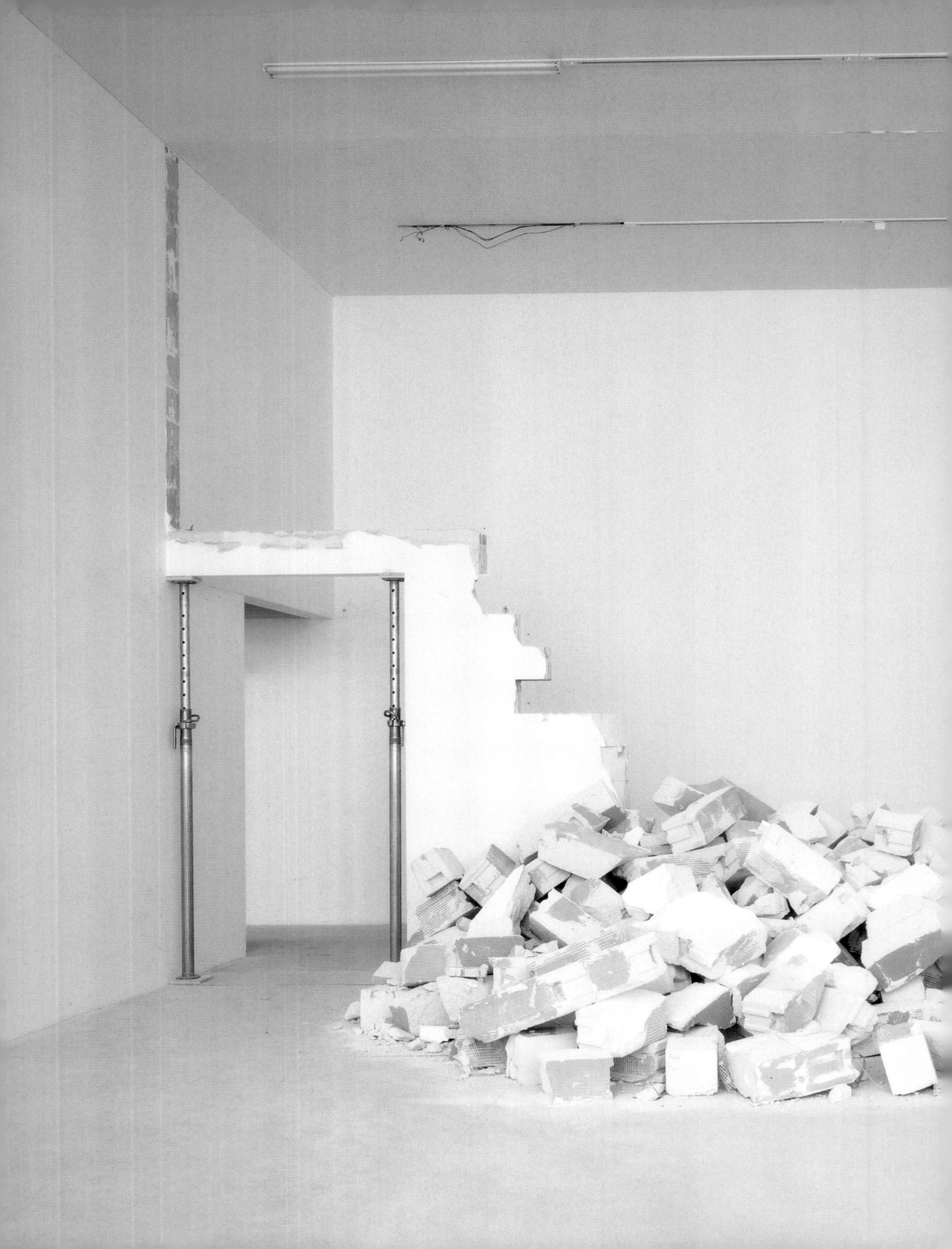

Vorwort | Preface

Seit Mitte der neunziger Jahre arbeiten Michael Elmgreen und Ingar Dragset als Künstler- und Lebenspartner an einem Werk, das Fragen nach den Strukturen und Wirkungsweisen der soziokulturellen Umfelder von Gesellschaft im Allgemeinen und der Kunst im Besonderen aufgreift. Ihre Arbeit umfasst Performances, Objekte, ortsbezogene Projekte und großangelegte Installationen.
Ihre von historischer Analyse, dadaistischer Paradoxie und politischer Schärfe geprägten und zur Ohnmacht geführten Formationen der Realität benutzen die scheinbare Neutralität eines minimalistischen Formenvokabulars in Architektur und Kunst und immer wieder die ebenso scheinbare Neutralität der Farbe Weiß. Ihre räumlichen Strukturen und Objekte decken die inhaltlichen Blindstellen der Zuschreibung formaler Autonomie und Neutralität listig auf, indem sie sexuelle und widersprüchliche Elemente einführen oder die Gegensatzpaare innen – außen, privat – öffentlich als sich nicht ideologisch gegenüberstehende, sondern als Inhalte in Bewegung aufscheinen lassen. Immer zielen die Arbeiten von Michael Elmgreen & Ingar Dragset auf eine komplexe, humorvolle und nicht ironische Hinterfragung gängiger Theorien, ideologischer Richtigkeit und bestehender Kategorien. Ihre Befragungen sind dabei nicht Anti-Kunst oder Auflösung der Kunst, sondern sie stellen Kunst und die Räume der Kunst in den gleichen existenziellen Lebensraum der Nutzung wie die Objekte und Räume des Alltags.
Taking Place, das Projekt, das die Künstler für die Kunsthalle Zürich realisiert haben, stellte wie zahlreiche ihrer Arbeiten einen Prozess ins Zentrum: Sie verwandelten die Kunsthalle in eine Baustelle, die die Arbeit an einer reorganisierten architektonischen Situation der Ausstellungs- und Publikumsräume zeigte. In *Taking Place* legten sie die Arbeit am White Cube als nie endendes Werk offen, das die Architektur, den Raum der Kunst als immer wieder neu zu befragenden symbolischen Ort gesellschaftlicher Bedeutungsproduktion thematisiert.

Since the mid-nineties, Michael Elmgreen and Ingar Dragset, partners in art and life, have been working on an oeuvre that addresses aspects of the structures and effects of socio-cultural contexts in society at large and particularly in art. Their art encompasses performances, objects, and large-scale installations.
Characterized by historical analysis, Dada-style paradox, and political incisiveness and pursued to the point of powerlessness, their formations of reality exploit both the seeming neutrality of a Minimalist formal vocabulary in architecture and art and the equally illusory neutrality of the color white. In some cases, their spatial structures and objects cunningly expose the substantive blind spots of the attribution of formal autonomy and neutrality through the inclusion of sexual elements and contradictory aspects. In others, they emphasize oppositions such as inside-outside or private-public, not as ideological opposites but as contents in motion. The works of Elmgreen & Dragset consistently seek to question generally accepted theories, concepts of ideological correctness, and existing categories in a highly complex, humorous yet non-ironic approach. The fruits of their inquires are not anti-art, nor do they negate art; instead, they place art and the spaces in which art appears in the same existential utilitarian context of life as the objects and spaces of everyday life.
Like many of the artists' works, Taking Place, *the project they have realized for the Kunsthalle Zürich, focused upon a process. They transformed the Kunsthalle into a construction site as a demonstration of work on the reorganization of the architectural situation in exhibition rooms and other spaces open to the public. In* Taking Place, *they openly presented their own investigations into the White Cube as a never-ending work concerned with the place of art as a symbolic setting for the social production of meaning which must continually be examined anew.*

The project involved an extended discourse regarding the use of a public art gallery for the diverse purposes required of it as a venue for the exhibition of art, a discussion of such questions as how the use of spaces can contribute to the development of its own form and what thematic approaches the representation of art as an open process is capable of initiating.

The theme of the 25th Bienal de São Paulo is the metropolis and urbanism as figure and discourse in contemporary art. DCA's choice of Michael Elmgreen & Ingar Dragset as the Danish representatives at the biennial was natural considering their working method, straddling the intersections of private and public, local and global—or, perhaps more accurately, operating in the passage, the dissonance, between these polar opposites.

As an artist duo, Elmgreen & Dragset work in a collective practice that plays down the creator-subjectivity and instead raises issues of sociality and context as significant factors in the reading of their work. Their continuing explorations of spatial and social structures, actions and problems of representation persistently trigger new questions about current mores of human behavior and control.

The two artists' installation for the Bienal de São Paulo, Prison Breaking/Powerless Structures, Fig. 333, *is a part of their* Powerless Structures *series. Many of these installations and social interventions are site specific, and the projects often contain a socio-political comment on the local situation in which they are shown.* Prison Breaking *consists of two prison cells that have been blown apart. The prison, so to speak, has broken in half, a passage opening up the sealed space and leaving two cleaved halves behind as autonomous architectural components. Metaphorically, the bound structures of all imprisonment are broken here. Yet, openings also imply vulnerability and, socially and politically speaking,*

Das Projekt umfasste einen lang angelegten Diskurs über den Gebrauch einer Kunsthalle für die vielfältigen Anforderungen, die Kunsträume heute für Ausstellungen zur Verfügung stellen sollten, eine Auseinandersetzung über Fragen danach, wie der Gebrauch von Räumen seine Form mit konstituieren kann, und darüber, welche Themenfelder die Repräsentation von Kunst als offener Prozess zu initiieren in der Lage ist.

Das Thema der 25. Biennale von São Paulo lautet »Großstadt und Urbanismus als Figur und Diskurs in der zeitgenössischen Kunst«. Dass Michael Elmgreen & Ingar Dragset von der Danish Contemporary Art Foundation ausgewählt wurden, Dänemark bei der Biennale zu vertreten, ist angesichts ihrer Arbeitsmethode nicht verwunderlich, die an den Schnittstellen zwischen privat und öffentlich, lokal und global, oder genauer gesagt, in dem Zwischenraum, der Dissonanz zwischen diesen polaren Gegensätzen operiert.

Als Künstlerpaar arbeiten Elmgreen & Dragset mit einem kollektiven Verfahren, das die Rolle des schöpferischen Subjekts relativiert und stattdessen Fragen des gesellschaftlichen Bezugs und des Kontextes zu entscheidenden Faktoren für das Verständnis ihrer Arbeiten macht. Ihre fortgesetzte Untersuchung von räumlichen und gesellschaftlichen Strukturen, Aktionen und Problemen der Darstellung werfen beständig neue Fragen auf hinsichtlich heutiger menschlicher Verhaltensweisen und der Formen gesellschaftlicher Kontrolle.

Ihre für die Biennale in São Paulo entwickelte Installation *Prison Breaking/Powerless Structures, Fig. 333* ist Teil ihrer Serie *Powerless Structures.* Viele dieser Installationen und sozialen Interventionen wurden speziell für den jeweiligen Ort konzipiert, und die Projekte enthalten oft einen gesellschaftspolitischen Kommentar zu der Situation an dem Ort, an dem sie gezeigt werden. *Prison Breaking* besteht aus zwei aufgesprengten Gefängniszellen. Das Gefängnis ist

sozusagen in zwei Teile zerbrochen, und ein Durchgang öffnet den hermetisch verschlossenen Raum und lässt zwei abgetrennte Hälften als autonome architektonische Komponenten zurück. In einem metaphorischen Sinne sind hier die gebundenen Strukturen jeglicher Gefangenschaft gesprengt. Doch Öffnungen implizieren auch Verletzlichkeit und, gesellschaftlich und politisch gesehen, die Forderung nach einem Konsens. Die Arbeiten von Elmgreen & Dragset fragen nach dem Freiheitspotenzial jedes Einzelnen, doch die Antworten hängen von unseren gemeinsamen Lebensbedingungen ab, die von der Gesellschaft bestimmt sind.
Wir freuen uns, diese umfangreiche Publikation als Katalog der Künstler zu ihrer Ausstellung in der Kunsthalle Zürich und zu ihrem Beitrag für die 25. Biennale von São Paulo sowie auch als selbstständige und erste umfassende Dokumentation des Werkes von Elmgreen & Dragset vorlegen zu können, in der entscheidende Aspekte ihrer Arbeit aus unterschiedlichen kunsttheoretischen Blickwinkeln beleuchtet werden.
Wir danken allen Autoren und Autorinnen, die zu diesem Band beigetragen haben, superfantastic in Berlin für die grafische Gestaltung und dem Hatje Cantz Verlag für die Leitung der Produktion und des Vertriebs.

Beatrix Ruf
Kunsthalle Zürich

Lars Grambye und Dorthe Abildgaard
Danish Contemporary Art Foundation

a demand for consensus. Elmgreen & Dragset's work raises questions about the potentials of freedom with each individual, but the answers are conditioned by our common conditions of life as shaped by society.
It is with great pleasure that we issue this comprehensive publication, both as a joint catalogue for Elmgreen & Dragset's exhibition at the Kunsthalle Zürich and their contribution to the 25th Bienal de São Paulo, and as independent documentation and illumination by art theory of significant parts of these two artists' production.
We wish to thank the many authors for their contributions, superfantastic in Berlin for the graphic design, and Hatje Cantz Publishers for handling the production and distribution.

Beatrix Ruf
Kunsthalle Zürich

Lars Grambye and Dorthe Abildgaard
Danish Contemporary Art Foundation

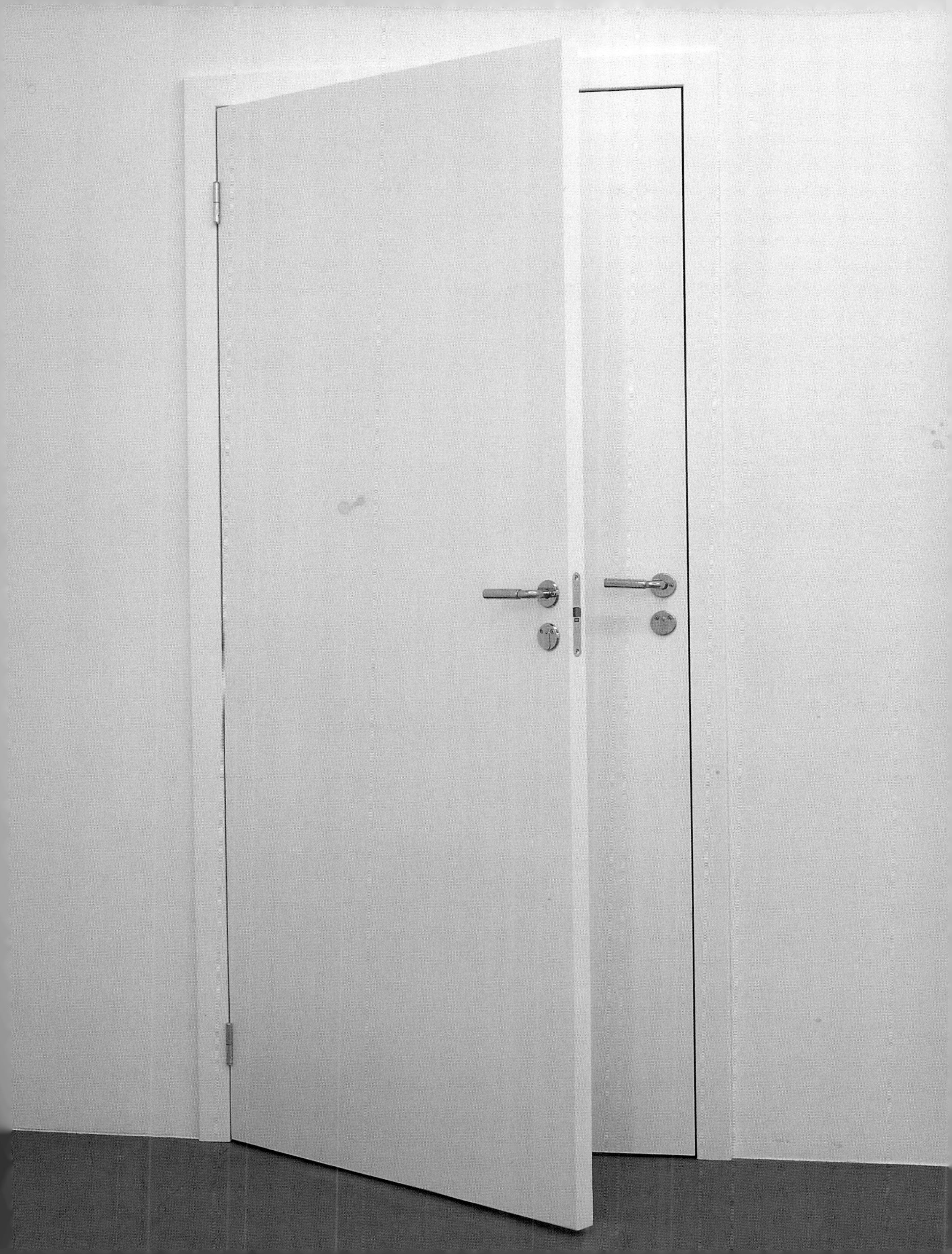

Taking Place

In einem breit angelegten Werk, das von Objekten über Performances zu raumgreifenden Installationen reicht, untersuchen Michael Elmgreen und Ingar Dragset als Paar seit 1995 soziokulturelle Strukturen, die sich in Kunst und Gesellschaft manifestieren. Seit 1997 entwickeln sie die fortlaufend nummerierte Werkserie der Powerless Structures, die um bekannte Phänomene der Produktion, des Vertriebes, der Präsentation und Rezeption von Kunst als Attribute ihrer Erkennbarkeit und um Phänomene ihrer gesellschaftlichen Bedeutungskonstruktionen kreist.

Die Konventionen und die scheinbare Neutralität eines minimalistischen Formenvokabulars und der Farbe Weiß werden von ihnen als solche Attribute benutzt. Und selbstverständlich steht der White Cube, der institutionalisierte Container für Kunst im Zentrum ihres Interesse – weil sie »Künstler« sind und weil dieser folglich der ihnen zugeschriebene öffentliche Raum gesellschaftlicher Präsenz darstellt.

Mit ihren auf den White Cube bezogenen Arbeiten stehen Elmgreen & Dragset in einer langen Tradition der Auseinandersetzung von Künstlerinnen und Künstlern mit den Prämissen der Kunst und der Kunstrezeption, die von Marcel Duchamps Kontextverschiebung von Objekten über die kritischen, die Institution der Kunst revolutionierenden und aus dem Museum heraus drängenden Ansätzen der sechziger und siebziger Jahre – Robert Barry, Daniel Buren, Michael Asher, Dan Graham sind nur einige der wichtigen Namen – zu den wiederum in der Institution angesiedelten Ansätzen der Kontextkunst und der Institutionellen Kritik der späten achtziger und der neunziger Jahre des 20. Jahrhunderts führt. 1976 hat der Künstler und Kunsttheoretiker Brian O'Doherty in der umfassenden Essayserie »Inside the White Cube« die gesellschaftliche »Ortlosigkeit« und die Erhebung der weißen Zelle der Kunst zur eigentlichen Ikone des 20. Jahrhunderts zum ersten Mal umfassend formuliert und

Since 1995, the duo of Michael Elmgreen and Ingar Dragset have been investigating the socio-cultural structures manifested in art and society in a multifaceted oeuvre covering a spectrum ranging from objects to performance to large-scale spatial installations. They began work on their sequentially numbered Powerless Structures in 1997. This series deals with familiar phenomena in the production, distribution, presentation, and reception of art as attributes of art's recognizability as such and with aspects of the construction of its meaning in a social context.

The artists make use of the conventions and the supposed neutrality of a Minimalist formal vocabulary and the color white as attributes of this kind. And of course they are also interested in the White Cube, the institutionalized container for art, because they are "artists" and because the White Cube accordingly represents the public space of social presence that is allotted to them.

With their works relating to the White Cube, Elmgreen & Dragset take a position within the long tradition of artists' examination of the premises of art and its reception—a tradition that has developed from Marcel Duchamp's experiments in altering the context of objects to the concepts of the 1960s and 1970s that revolutionized the institution of art and drove it outside the museum (Robert Barry, Daniel Buren, Michael Asher, and Dan Graham are only a few of the names that come to mind in this context) and on to the—once again institutional—approaches of contextual art and institutional criticism in the late 1980s and 1990s. In his extensive series of essays entitled "Inside the White Cube" , published in 1976, the artist and art theorist Brian O'Doherty provided the first extensive discussion and critique of the social "homelessness" of the White Cube and its elevation to the status of the true icon of the 20th century. In his later essay "Gallery as Gesture" (1981), he expanded his reflections to encompass

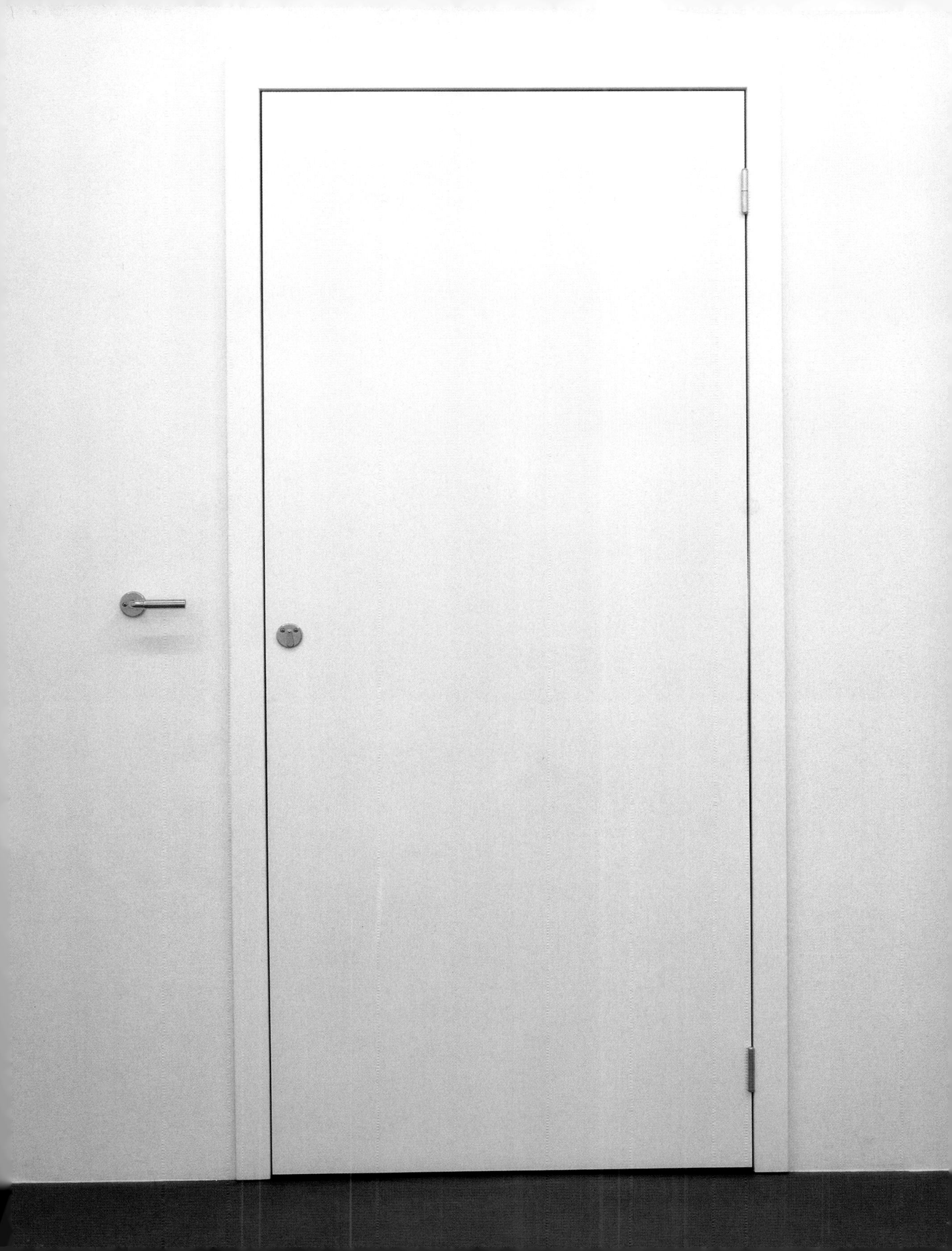

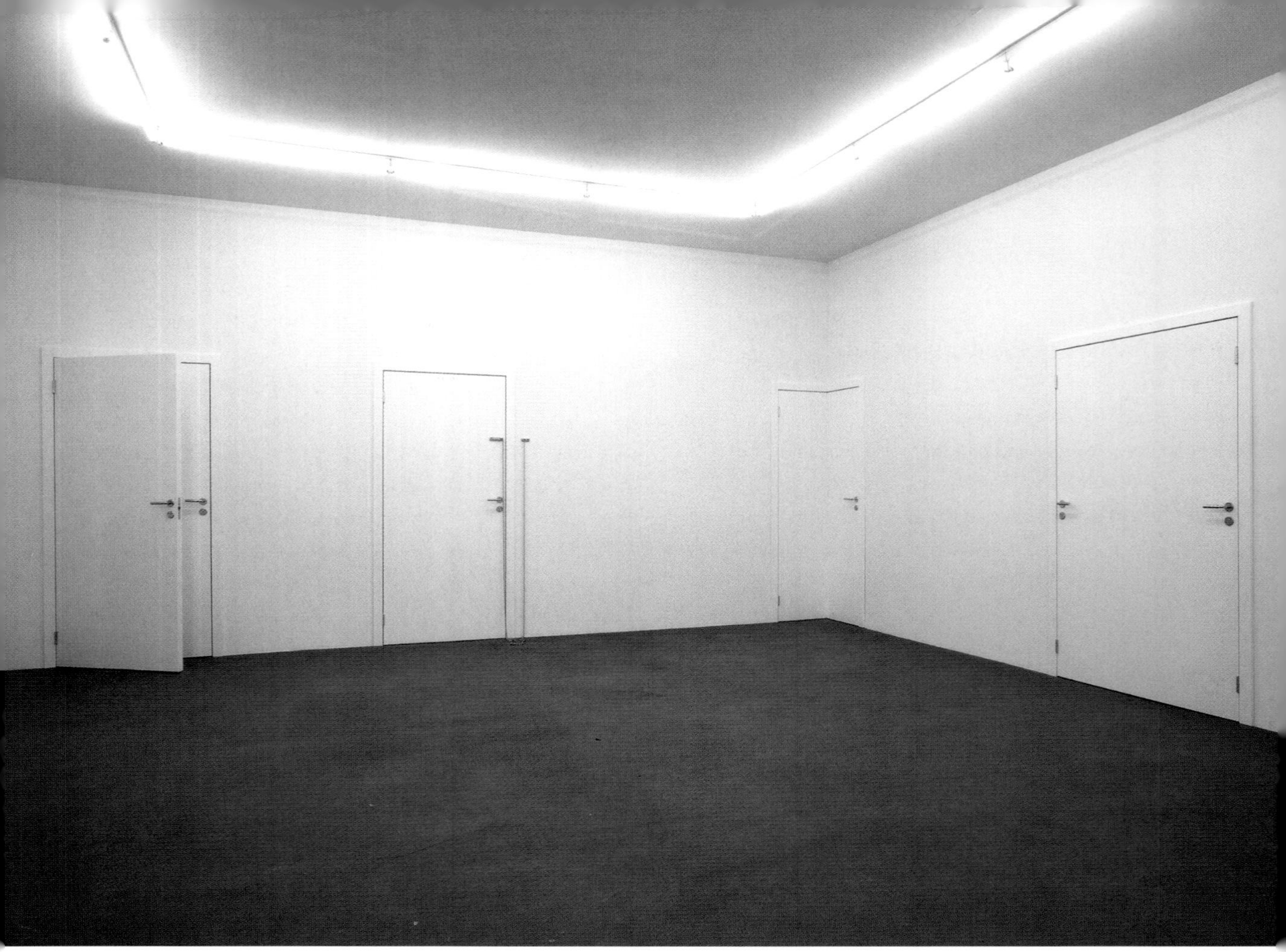

Postmodern questions and the opening of the White Cube to incorporate social contents.[1]
In the works of the first generation, the White Cube is presented conceptually and critically for discussion primarily as the setting for and the guarantor of the autonomy and neutrality of art viewed in terms of both form and content as an ideologically charged icon of social models of inclusion and exclusion. Artists of the second generation, such as Heimo Zobernig and Gerwald Rockenschaub, articulated important positions in which the space of art itself, with its Minimalist formal vocabulary, is represented as sculpture in spatial formulation.[2]
In the art of Michael Elmgreen & Ingar Dragset, historical aspects and formulations of artists' involvement with the space of art presentation, the White Cube, overlap and intersect in a discussion that sets concepts, contents, and forms in parallel and is "tainted" at every level: while the White Cube is subjected to critical examination as an essential construction of art, at the same time it is accepted on the artistic level as the societal context of the representation of art. Minimalist formal language is used as a characteristic feature of autonomous products of art, yet at the same time disavowed as aesthetic trash in both artistic and everyday design. Affirmation is seen as contamination and thus as a critical method for the dissolution of such categorical oppositions as art and life, public and private, neutral and ideological, which are applied strategically, appropriated in affirmation, and made available as moveable players in a new pattern in the discussion of objects and contents of the social construction of reality.
Michael Elmgreen & Ingar Dragset continue to pursue these questions about the place of art by inquiring in different ways into the conditions affecting art spaces as public spaces, and they cunningly expose the substantive blind spots in the

kritisiert und 1981 in dem Aufsatz »Gallery as Gesture« auf postmoderne Fragestellungen und einer Öffnung des White Cube hinsichtlich der Einführung von gesellschaftlichen Inhalten erweiternd reflektiert.[1]
In den Arbeiten der ersten Generation wird der White Cube vor allem als Erscheinungsort und Garant der Autonomie und Neutralität der Kunst inhaltlich und formal als ideologisch aufgeladene Ikone gesellschaftlicher Inklusions- und Exklusionsmodelle konzeptionell und kritisch zur Diskussion gestellt. In der Kunstproduktion der zweiten Generation formulieren Heimo Zobernig und Gerwald Rockenschaub etwa wichtige Positionen, die den Kunstraum mit seinem minimalistischen Formenvokabular als Skulptur der Raumformulierung selbst zur Repräsentation bringen.[2]
Bei Michael Elmgreen & Ingar Dragset überlagern sich die historischen Ansatzpunkte und Formulierungen der Auseinandersetzung mit dem Raum der Kunst, dem White Cube, zu einer Begriffe, Inhalte und Formen parallel setzenden und auf allen Ebenen »verunreinigten« Diskussion: Der White Cube wird als kunstimmanente Formulierung kritisch reflektiert, ist aber als gesellschaftlicher Ort der Repräsentation von Kunst künstlerisch akzeptiert. Minimalistisches Formenvokabular wird als Erkennungszeichen autonomer Kunsterzeugnisse benutzt und zugleich als ästhetischer Trash in Kunst- und Alltagsdesign desavouiert. Affirmation als Kontamination und damit als kritische Methode der Aufhebung kategorialer Gegensatzpaare wie Kunst und Leben, öffentlich und privat, neutral und ideologisch bestimmt, die strategisch eingesetzt, bestätigend zu Eigen gemacht als bewegliche Mitspieler in einem neuen Muster der Diskussion von Objekten und Inhalten gesellschaftlicher Realitätskonstruktion zur Disposition gestellt sind.
Michael Elmgreen & Ingar Dragset führen die Fragestellungen um den Ort der Kunst weiter, indem sie wieder und

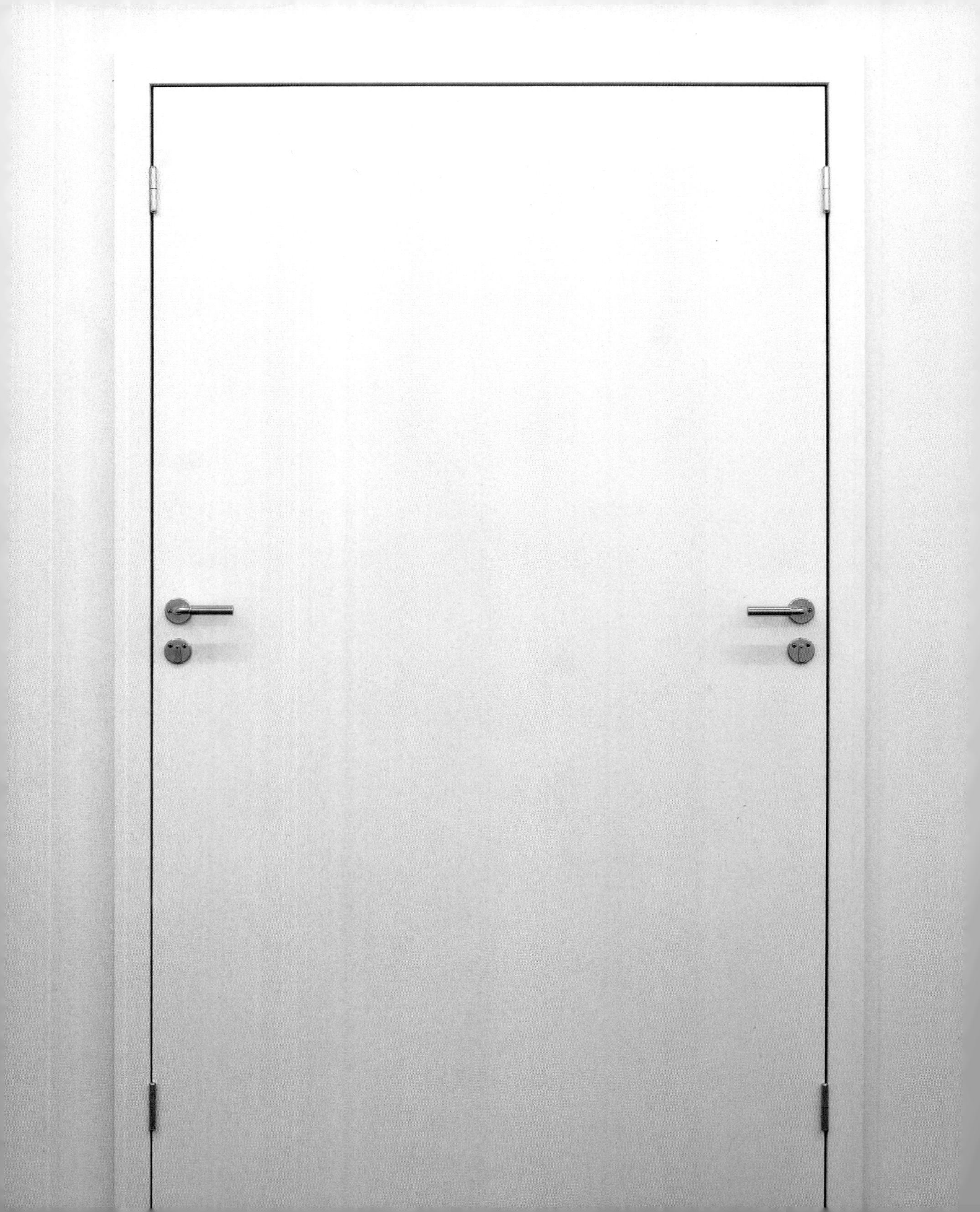

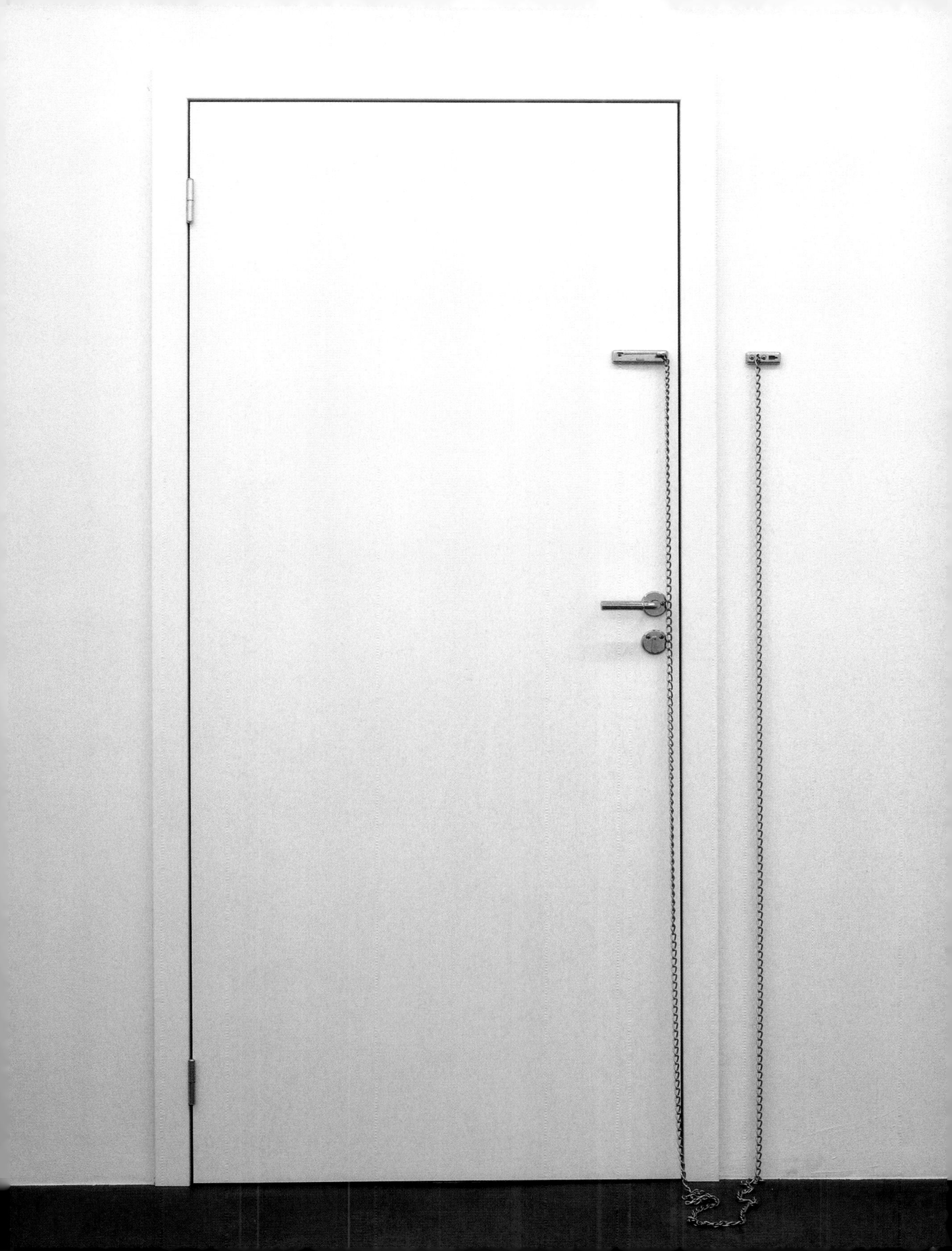

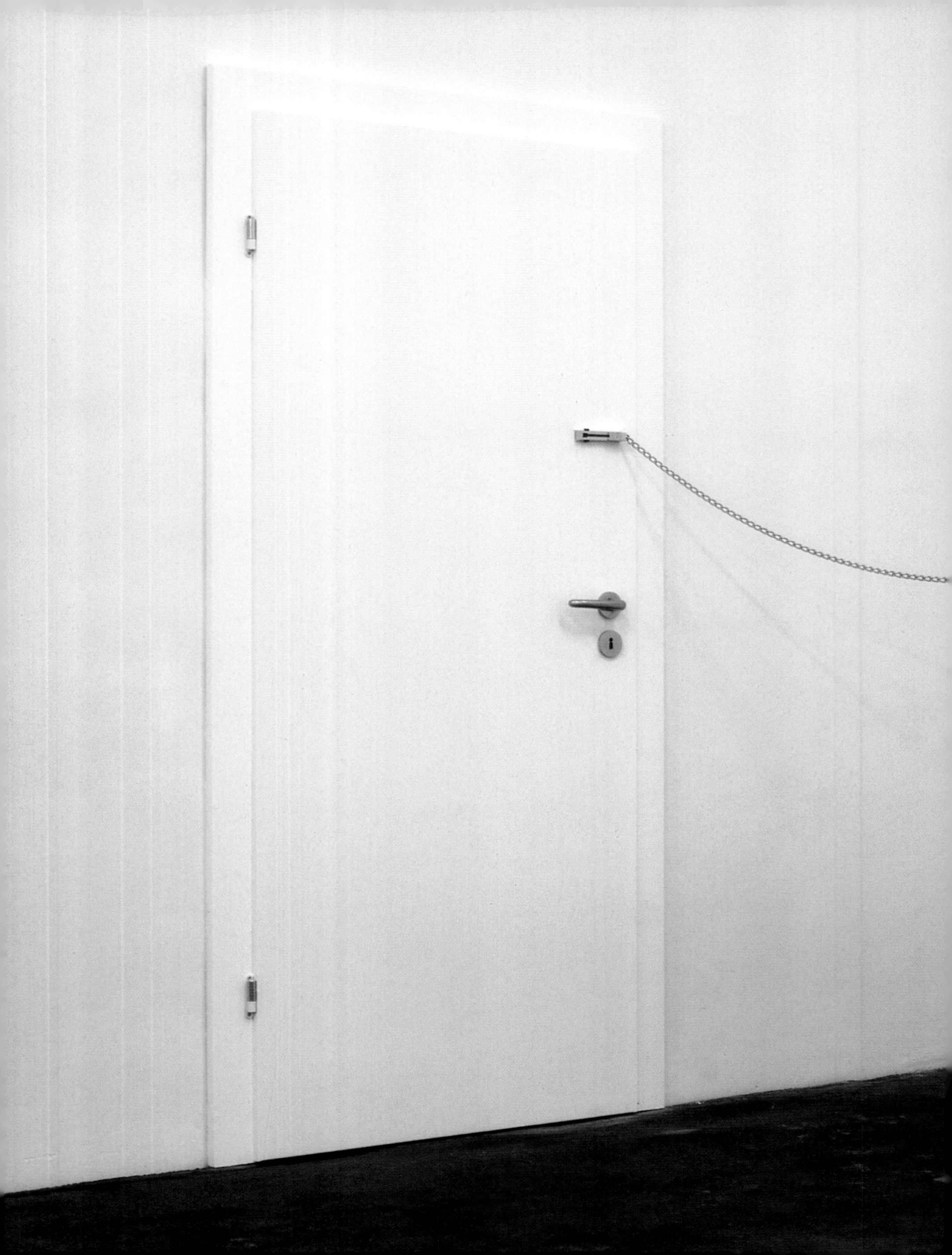

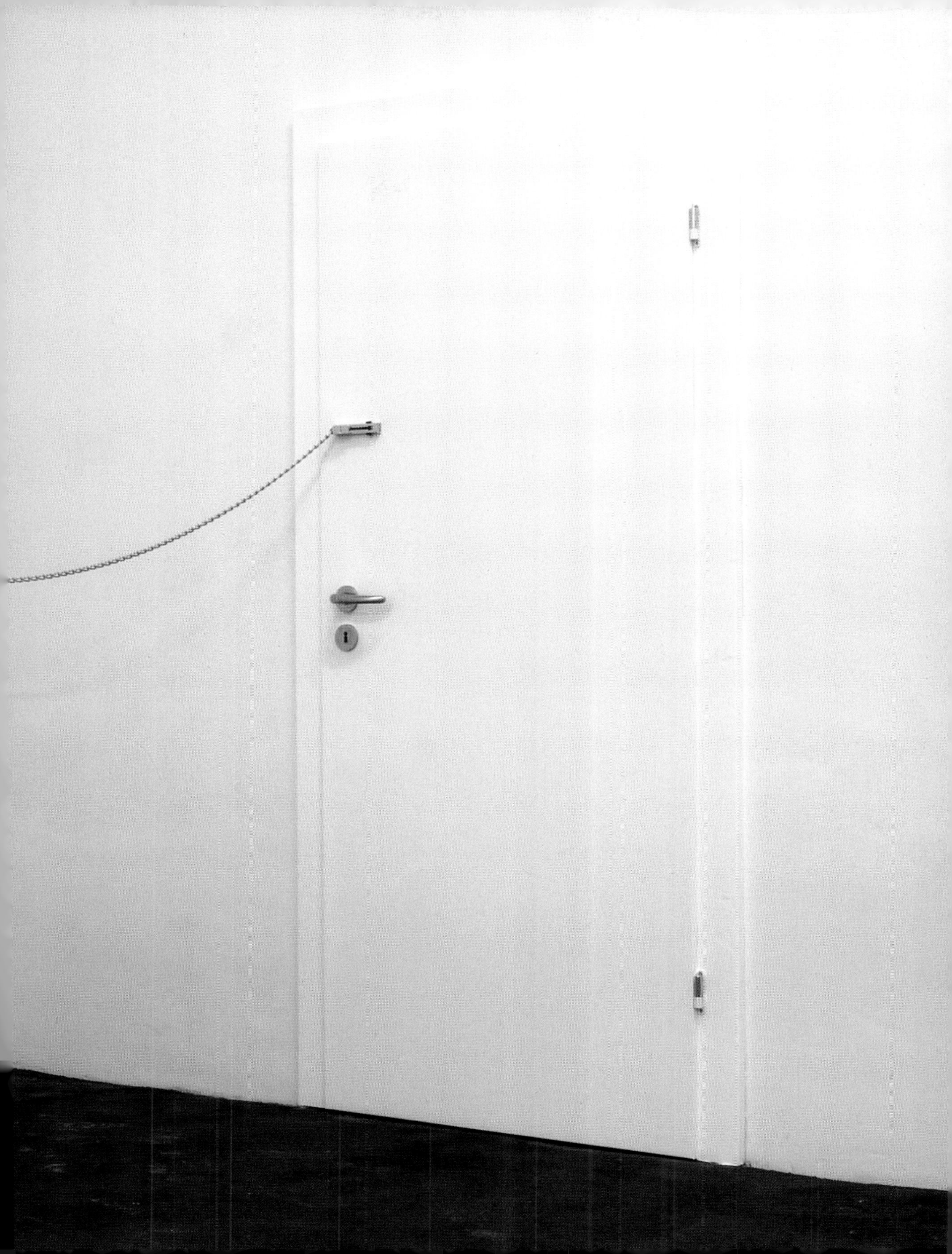

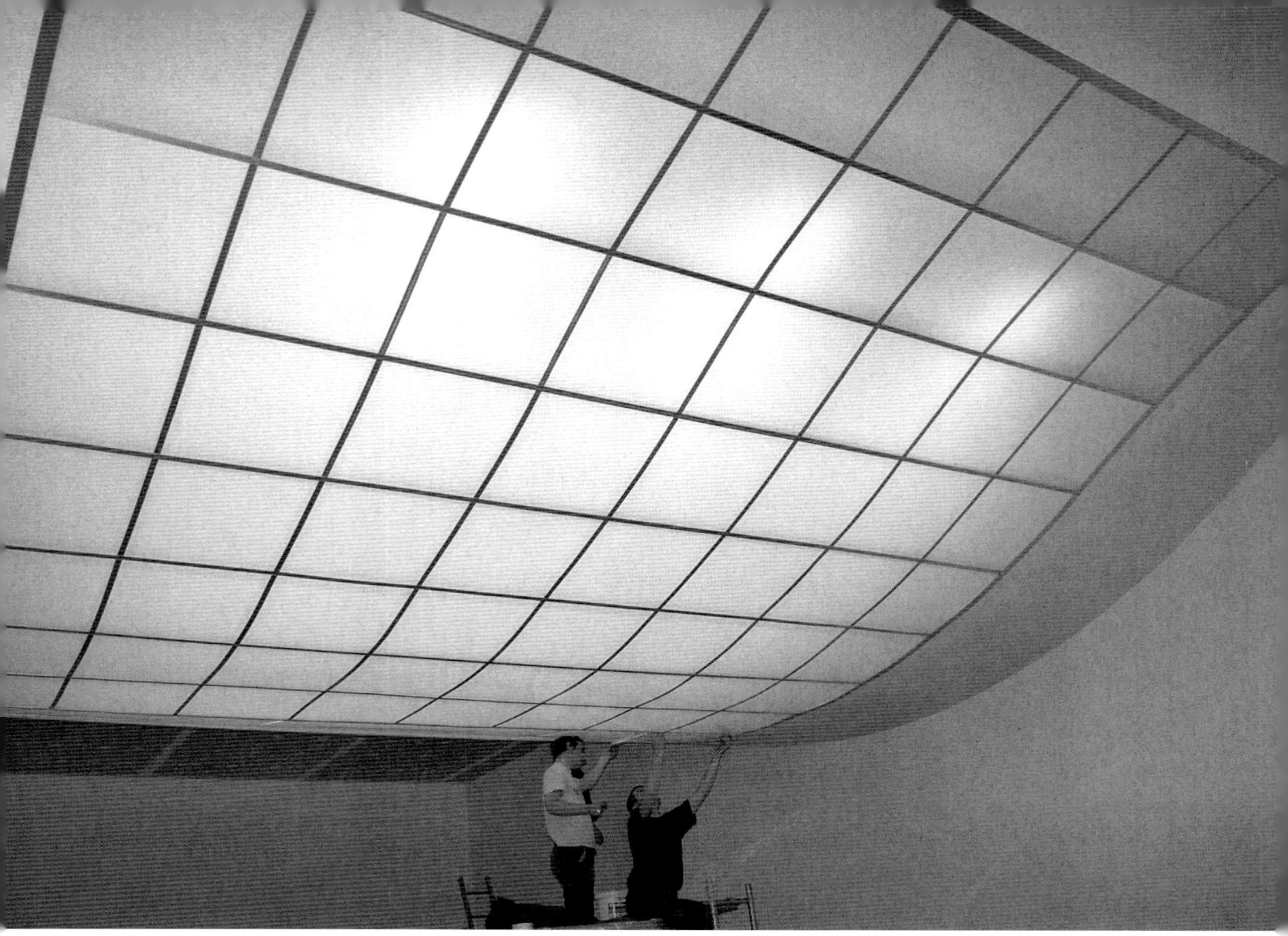

attribution of formal autonomy and neutrality through the inclusion of sexual elements and contradictory aspects. Their interest is not so much in the "building" itself, but in building as a process of developing meaning and discussing premises for both artists and users alike. They inquire into the heterogeneous but always specifically social realities that take possession of neutral space, emphasizing the individual's use of space: who uses what kinds of spaces under what conditions—and why?
Their art logically combines aspects of performance with the presentation of objects which in turn develop their own performative qualities as process- and action-oriented structures. Cruising Pavilion/Powerless Structures, Fig. 55 *(1998), for example, is a white container erected by the artists for use in a public park in Aarhus. Its labyrinthine interior structure suggests the presence of separate rooms, but the walls of these rooms are full of holes that permit visual and physical contact. Perceptible as a Minimalist "sculpture," the object was deliberately placed at a spot known as a meeting place for homosexual couples or individuals seeking contact, a circumstance which led to a collision of form and content that subverted accepted standards regarding the use of public places. The artists' plan to install the work again in an exhibition at Witte de With in Rotterdam in 2001 was rejected.* Powerless Structures, Fig. 88 *(2000) is a White Cube realized by the artists in a group exhibition at* Manifesta 3 *at the Museum of Modern Art in Ljubljana. They made their "exhibition piece" available to young curators from Ljubljana as a gallery space, thus drawing attention to questions of selection and the role of the market in art and to the interplay between high-profile international group exhibitions and the lack of commercial structures for art at the local level.*
For Zwischen anderen Ereignissen/Between Other Events *(2000), they hired two unemployed house painters who repeatedly renovated the exhibition spaces at the Galerie für*

anders nach den Bedingungen der Kunstorte als öffentliche Orte fragen, und sie decken inhaltliche Blindstellen der Zuschreibung formaler Autonomie und Neutralität listig auf, indem sie sexuelle und paradoxe Elemente einführen. Ihr Interesse richten sich dabei nicht so sehr auf das »Gebäude« an sich, sondern auf den Prozess des Bauens als Prozess der Entwicklung von Bedeutung und Diskussion der Prämissen sowohl für Künstlerinnen und Künstler wie für Benutzerinnen und Benutzer. Sie fragen nach den heterogenen, aber immer wieder spezifischen gesellschaftlichen Realitäten, die den neutralen Raum einnehmen, und stellen den Gebrauch durch das Individuum ins Zentrum: Wer benutzt welche Räume unter welchen Bedingungen und warum?
Ihr Werk verbindet folgerichtig performative Aspekte mit der Präsentation von Objekten, die als prozess- und handlungsorientierte Strukturen selbst performative Qualität entwickeln. *Cruising Pavilion / Powerless Structures, Fig. 55,* (1998) etwa ist ein weißer Container, den sie in einem öffentlichen Park in Århus zum Gebrauch aufstellten. Seine labyrinthische Innenraumstruktur gibt einzelne Räume vor, deren Wände aber von visuellen und physischen Kontakt ermöglichenden Löchern durchbrochen sind. Das als minimalistische »Skulptur« wahrnehmbare Objekt wurde gezielt in einer Gegend platziert, die als Treffpunkt homosexueller Paare oder Partnersuchenden bekannt ist, was zu einer Kollision von Form und Inhalt, einer Unterwanderung des gesellschaftlich akzeptierten Gebrauches der öffentlichen Anlagen führte. Eine erneute Installation in einer Ausstellung des Witte de With in Rotterdam 2001 wurde verboten. *Powerless Structures, Fig. 88 (2000)* ist ein White Cube, den die Künstler anlässlich der *Manifesta 3* im Museum of Modern Art in Ljubljana in einer Gruppenausstellung realisierten. Sie stellten ihr »Ausstellungsexponat« jungen Kuratorinnen und Kuratoren aus Ljubljana als Galerieraum zur Verfügung und thematisierten so Fragen nach Auswahl

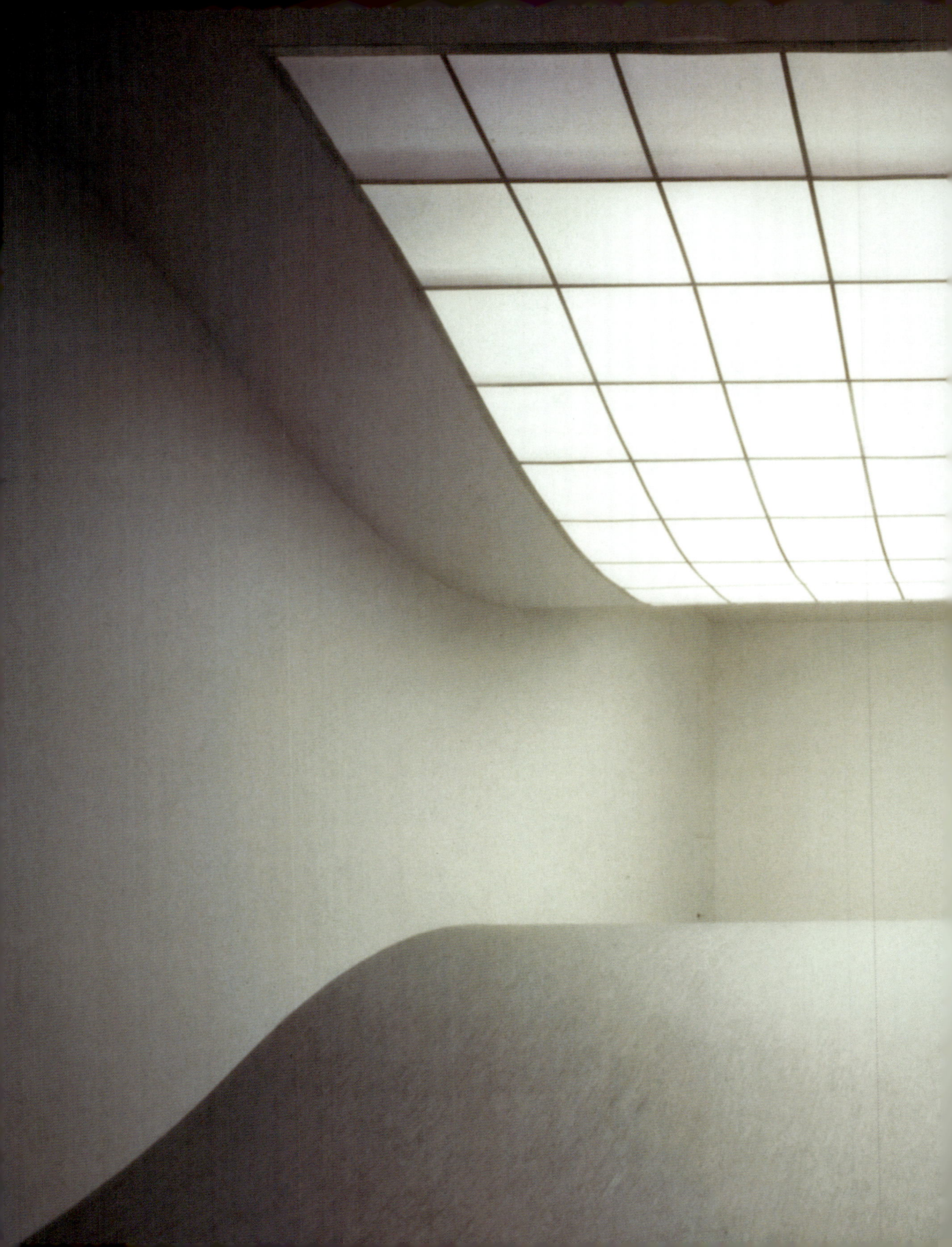

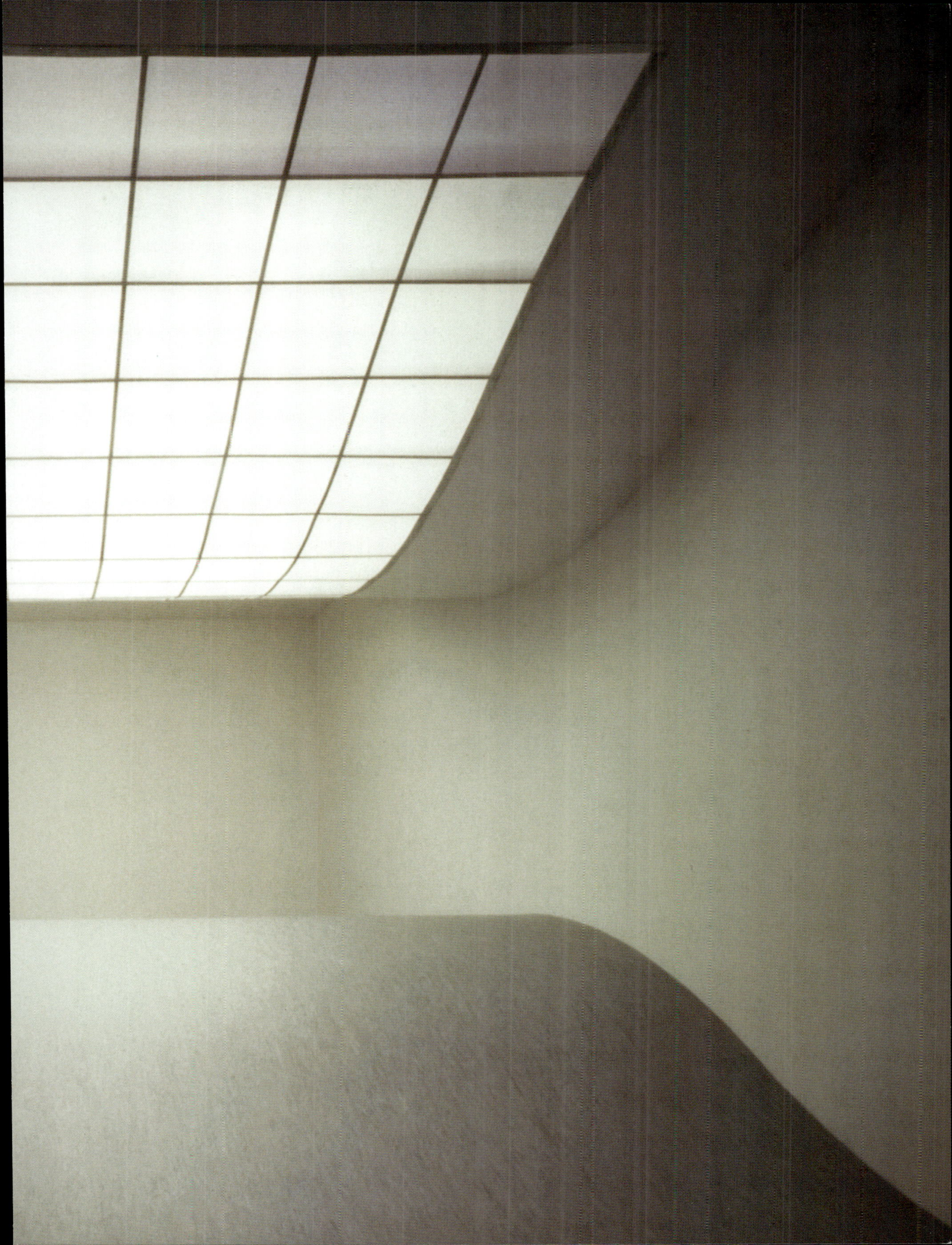

und Markt im Kunstbetrieb und das Zusammenspiel von hoch profilierten internationalen Gruppenausstellungen und fehlenden kommerziellen Strukturen für die Kunst vor Ort.
Für Zwischen anderen Ereignissen / Between Other Events (2000) engagierten sie zwei arbeitslose Anstreicher, die die Ausstellungsräume der Galerie für Zeitgenössische Kunst in Leipzig über den gesamten Zeitraum der Ausstellungsdauer permanent renovierten und durch 35 weiße Farbaufträge als Bereitstellung der Galerieräume für die nächste Ausstellung die Galerie erst renovierungsbedürftig machten. Zwischen anderen Ereignissen zeigte nicht nur das Dazwischen, das, was sonst vom Ausstellungsbetrieb nicht zu sehen ist, als Tautologie des White Cube und Paradox, sondern thematisierte auch gesellschaftspolitische Strukturen des Ortes der Galerie.
Den drei Arbeiten ist, wie vielen Arbeiten der Künstler, aber auch gemeinsam, dass sie die Präsentation, Präsenz und Repräsentation von Strukturen als Pause formulieren, die eine Neudefinition, eine individualisierte Definition ihres Gebrauches ermöglichen kann. Und: Dass sie die Präsenz des individuellen Benutzers offen stellen.
Hier war jemand, hier wird jemand sein, hier war etwas, hier wird etwas sein..., artikulieren ihre Objekte und Installationen. Und von *Back in a Minute/Powerless Structures, Fig. 87*, 2000 (ein Bauhelm, Malerwerkzeug, eine Jeans und eine weiße Farbspur, deren beiläufiger Strich sich in Nuancen vom Weiß der Wand abhebt), über zahlreiche Kunstverpackungskisten, die mehr oder weniger glücklich, mehr oder weniger sicher am Ort ihrer Bestimmung gelandet sind (und uns natürlich an Marcel Broodthaers erinnern), bis zu zerbrochenen Krügen, die von Sockeln gefallen sind, leeren Jeans und Unterhosen, die über geschlossenen Türen hängen oder am Boden zu liegen kommen, sprechen die Objekte nicht nur von der Exklusion oder Inklusion des Betrachters, der

Zeitgenössische Kunst in Leipzig over the entire course of the exhibition, adding thirty-five coats of white paint in preparation for the next exhibition and thereby making it necessary to renovate the gallery when they were done. Between Other Events presented not only what lies in between—the aspects of exhibition work that are ordinarily not seen—as a tautology of the White Cube and a paradox, but also emphasized socio-political structures that affect the gallery as a place.
A shared aspect of these three and many of the artists' other works is the fact that they formulate the presentation, presence, and representation of structures as a stopping point, a break which offers an opportunity for redefinition or individualized definition of their use. What is more, they prompt curiosity about the presence of the individual user.
Someone was here, someone will be here, something was here, something will be here: these ideas are articulated in their objects and installations. And from Back in a Minute/ Powerless Structures, Fig. 87 *of 2000 (a construction worker's hard hat, painter's tools, a pair of jeans, and a white trace of paint, a random stroke of color that stands out in nuances against the white wall) to the many packing crates for art that have landed more or less fortunately, more or less safely at their destinations (reminding us, of course, of Marcel Broodthaers), to smashed pitchers that have fallen from pedestals, and empty jeans and underpants hung over closed doors or lying on the floor: all of these objects speak not only of the viewer's exclusion from or inclusion in the process or the reality of art, but also of the exclusion or inclusion of the producers of art when it comes to the conventions of artistic formulation.*
Both exclusion and inclusion always denote the fragmentation of experience and perception, the incompleteness and non-verifiability of others who can only be imagined. These are themes Elmgreen & Dragset have articulated in many

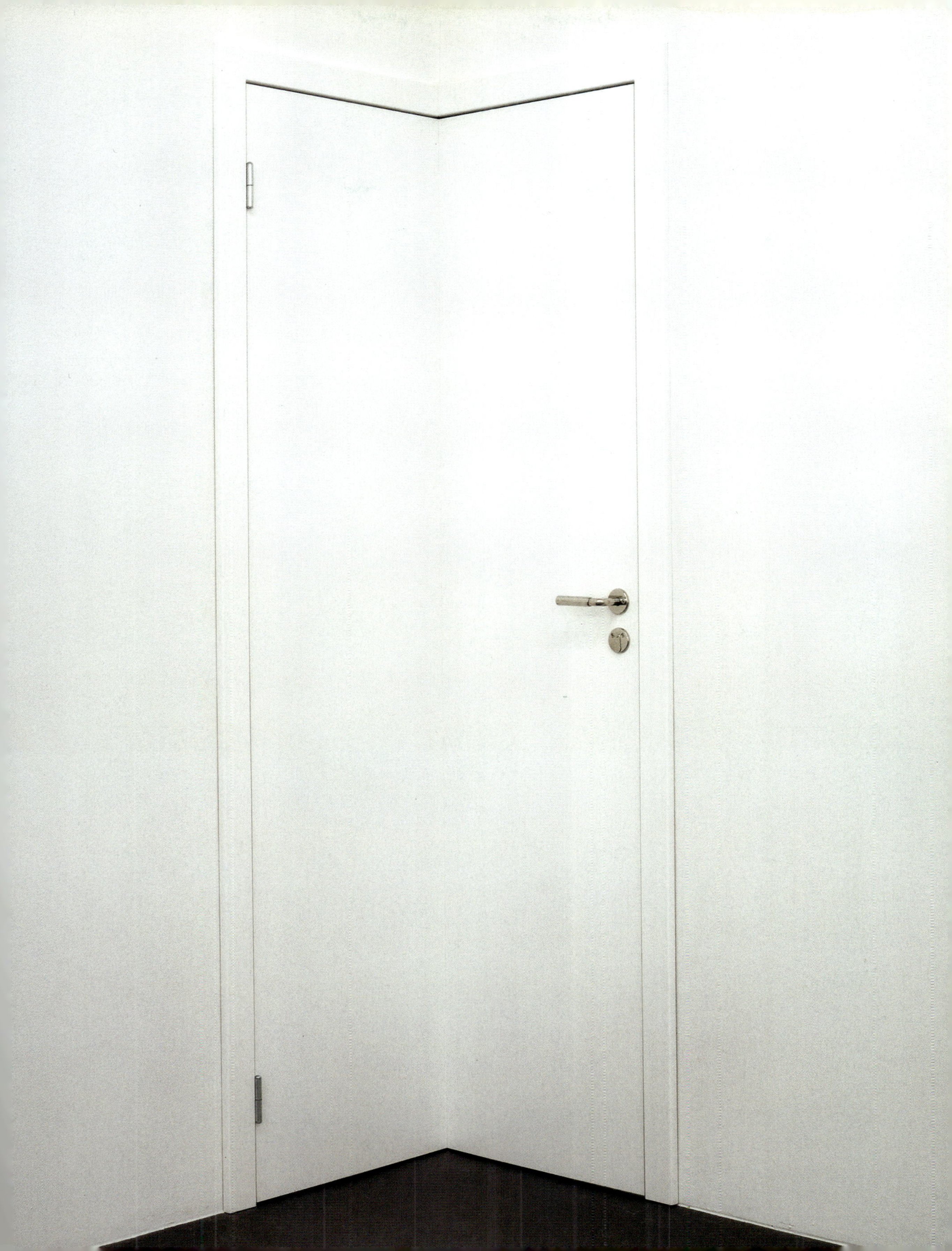

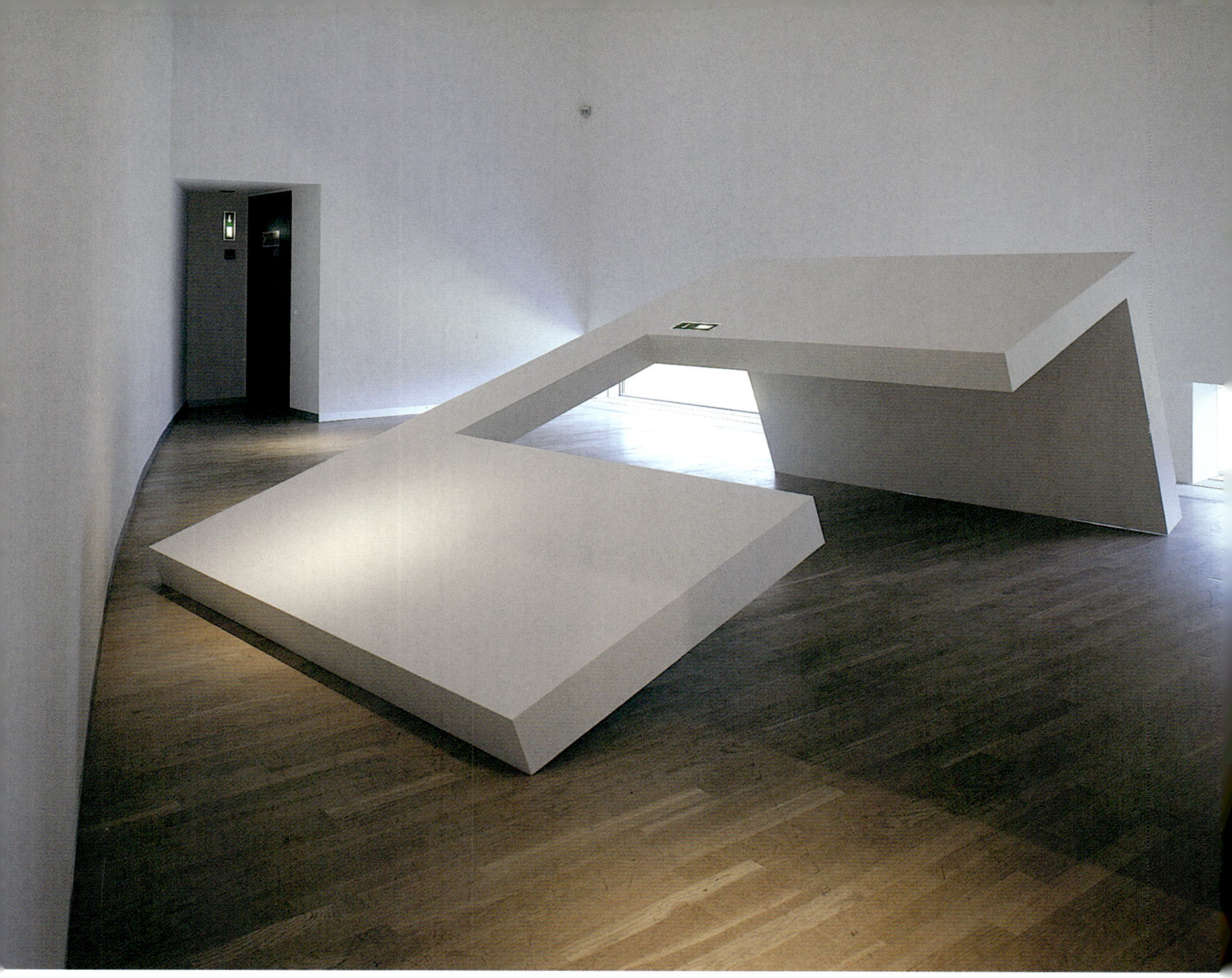

different works concerned with the space of art. An entire series of installations is devoted to the implantation and presentation of nothing but doors, which in an irritating manner play on themes of entry and exit (and naturally call to mind Marcel Duchamp's paradoxical door in 11, rue Larrey *of 1927 as well). The* Powerless Structures *of everyday life are not only dysfunctional themselves (they cannot be opened, they are hung with chains or incorrectly labeled), they also transform the reality of the exhibition space into fiction by turning the real space inside out: we enter where we are told to exit—but in the art space itself we are held captive by the potential of possibility and by the absence of real space.*
The volume of the interior of the Galerie Klosterfelde in Berlin determined the shape of the outer shell of the object the artists realized as Linienstrasse 160 *(2001) on the occasion of the gallery's move into a new building. They placed the much smaller original gallery inside the new, much more spacious exhibition rooms—an object most visitors nearly overlooked because it was perfectly integrated into the first room compartment of the new gallery. The exhibition room, the space in which artists' work can be present in a commercial environment, became an exhibited work in its own right, one that displays the conditions of presentation and the public space available to the artists and their colleagues. Displayed in the distinctly larger space, it raises questions about the meaning of representative presence and work opportunities.*
Powerless Structures, Fig. 111 *(2001), the installation realized at Portikus in Frankfurt am Main, renders the aesthetic and ideological restrictions imposed by architecture and the space of art physically palpable. Inside the classical box of the White Cube with a skylight ceiling, the artists created two waves. The floor bulged upward in a massive spatial wave*

Betrachterin in den Prozess oder die Realität der Kunst, sondern auch von Exklusion oder Inklusion ihrer Produzenten hinsichtlich der Konventionen künstlerischer Formulierungen. Exklusion sowie Inklusion bedeuten aber immer auch Fragmentierung von Erfahrung und Wahrnehmung, Bruchstückhaftigkeit und das nicht überprüfbare nur imaginierbare Andere. Themen, die Elmgreen & Dragset in unterschiedlichsten Arbeiten mit dem Raum der Kunst formulieren. Eine ganze Serie von Installationen implantiert und zeigt im Ausstellungsraum nichts anderes als Türen, die irritierend mit der Thematik des Eingangs und Ausgangs spielen (und uns natürlich an Marcel Duchamps paradoxe Türe *11, rue Larrey* von 1927 erinnern). Die *Powerless Structures* des Alltags sind nicht nur in ihrer Funktionalität verkehrt (sie sind nicht zu öffnen, mit Ketten verhangen oder seitenverkehrt beschriftet), sondern sie verkehren auch die Realität des Ausstellungsraumes in Fiktionalität, da sie das Innen und Außen des Realitätsraumes umstülpen: Wir treten da ein, wo nur auf das Austreten verwiesen wird – aber im Kunstraum selbst sind wir gefangen in der Potenzialität der Möglichkeit und dem Fehlen des realen Raums.
Das Innenraumvolmen der Galerie Klosterfelde in Berlin bestimmt die Außenhülle des Objekts, das die Künstler zum Einzug der Galerie in neue Räume als *Linienstraße 160* (2001) realisierten. Die viel kleinere erste Galerie stellten sie in die neuen viel größeren Ausstellungsräume, ein Objekt, das von den meisten Besucherinnen und Besuchern beinahe übersehen wurde, da es sich perfekt in das erste Raumkompartiment der neuen Galerie integrierte. Der Ausstellungsraum, der Raum, in dem die Arbeit der Künstler im kommerziellen Umfeld präsent werden kann, wurde zum Ausstellungsexponat, das die Bedingungen und den zur Verfügung stehenden öffentlichen Raum der Künstler und

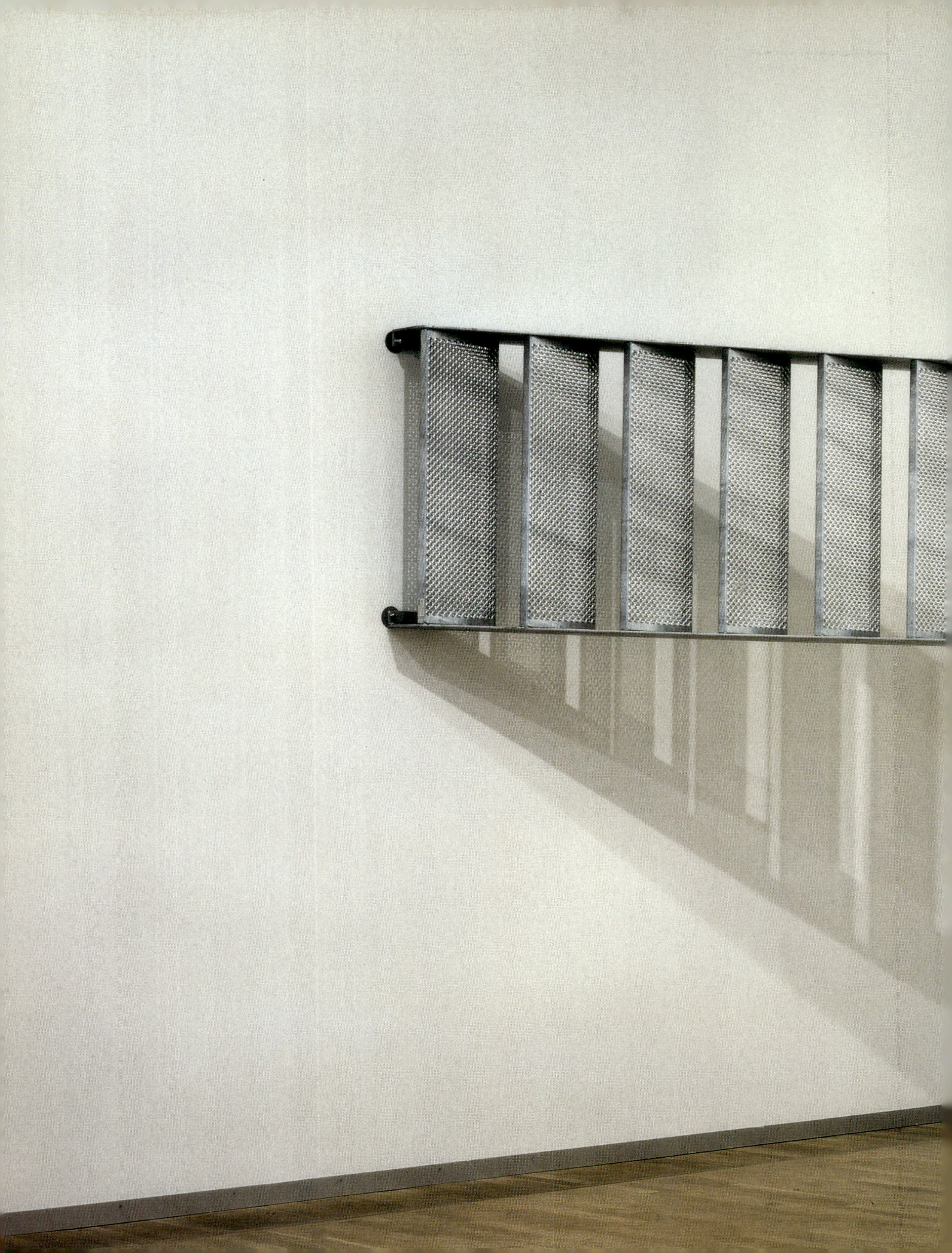

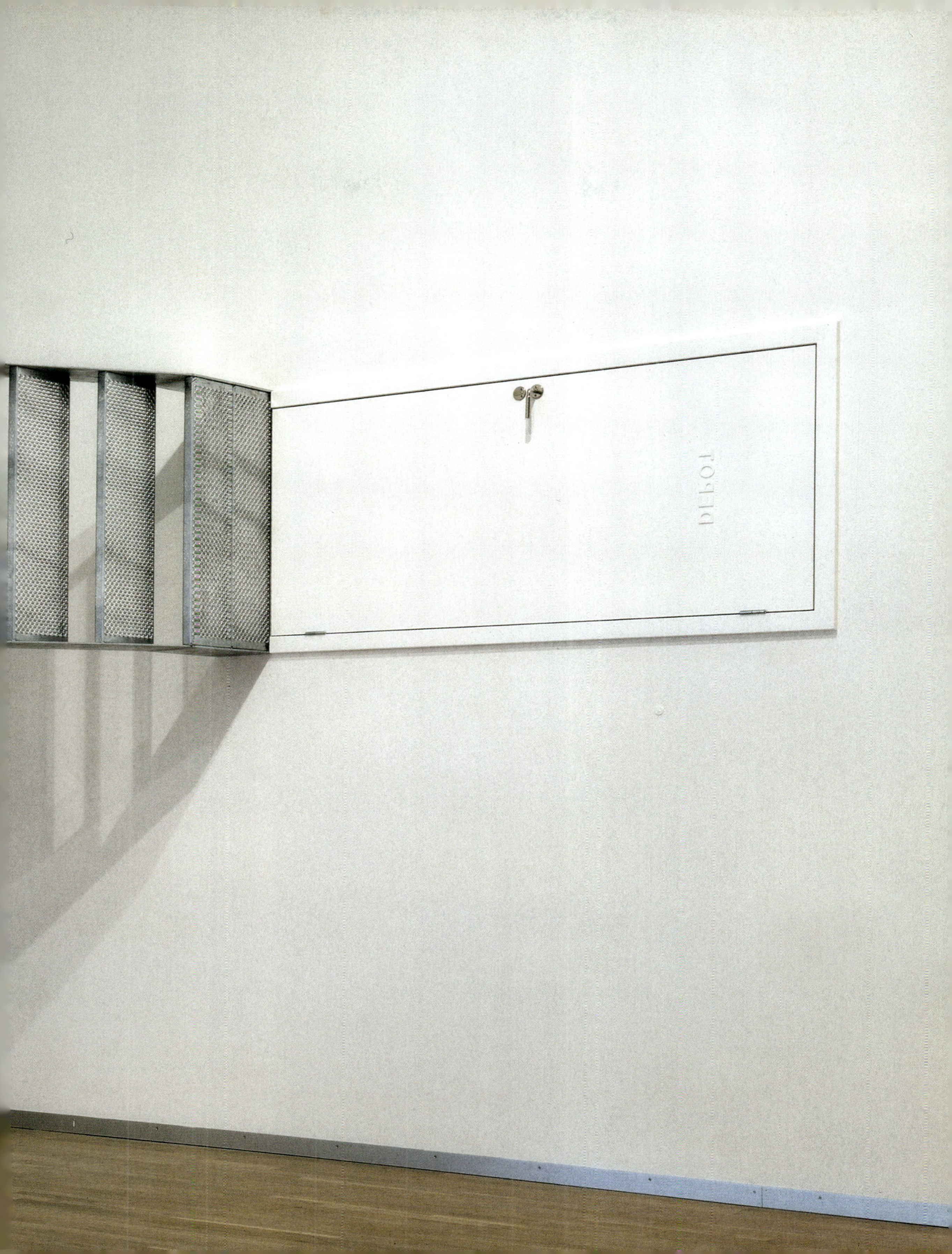
DEPOT

ihrer Kollegen und Kolleginnen vorführt und im nun ungleich größeren Raum Fragen nach der Bedeutung von repräsentativer Präsenz und Arbeitsmöglichkeiten aufwirft.
Die ästhetische und ideologische Einengung durch Architektur und den Kunstraum im Besonderen macht *Powerless Structures, Fig. 111* (2001), die Installation für Portikus in Frankfurt am Main, physisch erfahrbar. In die klassische Box des White Cubes mit Oberlichtdecke ließen die Künstler zwei Wellen legen. Der Boden wölbte sich in einer großen Raumwelle nach oben, die Decke ebenso nach unten. Die Dreidimensionalität des Raumes war als perfektes flaches Bild perspektivisch inszeniert. Und was Brian O'Doherty in seinem bereits erwähnten Essay in Bezug auf die fotografische Repräsentation des White Cubes als perfekte Ikone des 20. Jahrhunderts mit der Bemerkung kritisiert: »Das Auge ist der einzige Bewohner der sterilen Ausstellungsfotos. Der Betrachter ist nicht anwesend.« [3], wird hier physisch erlebbar. Betrat man den Raum und stieg gegen das Zentrum, kehrte sich die Konvention visueller Wahrnehmung in das physische Erleben der Surrealität des Kunstraums. Aufrechtes Stehen war unmöglich, die visuelle Erscheinung von physischer Begehung Lügen gestraft, es blieb nur das Beugen vor den realen Verhältnissen, die Raum und Bild unterschieden.
Vor dem Hintergrund dieser Arbeiten erscheint das für die Kunsthalle Zürich realisierte Werk und die bislang größte »Installation« der Künstler mit dem Titel *Taking Place* (2001) programmatisch. Taking Place ist die Aneignung eines »echten« Umbaus der Kunsthalle als Arbeit und die Ausstellung des Prozesses der Konstruktion einer »permanenten Installation« als zukünftige Displaysituation für andere Künstlerinnen und Künstler. Als Künstler stellen sie aber auch ihre Einzelausstellung, ihre Repräsentationszeit im Museum, dem Ort der Kunst selbst zur Verfügung.

mirrored by an identical wave in the ceiling, and the three-dimensionality of the space was presented in perspective as a perfect flat image. Thus, precisely the phenomenon Brian O'Doherty criticizes in the essay cited above with reference to the photographic representation of the White Cube as a 20th-century icon—"The eye is the only inhabitant of the sterile exhibition photos. The viewer is absent." [3] *—could be experienced here in a physical sense. When one entered the room and ascended toward the center, conventional visual perception was transformed into a physical experience of the surreal character of the art space. It was impossible to stand upright; the visual appearance of the physical act of moving about inside the object was shown to be an illusion; all that remained was to bow to the real relationships that distinguished space from the image.*
Viewed against the background of these earlier works, the piece entitled Taking Place *(2001), which was realized for the Kunsthalle Zürich and is their largest "installation" to date, assumes a programmatic quality. Taking Place appropriates a "genuine" renovation of the Kunsthalle as work and the exhibition of the process of constructing a "permanent installation" as a future setting for the display of art by other artists. As artists, however, they are also making their own solo exhibition, the time during which they are represented at the museum, available to the place of art itself.*
In Taking Place*, the art space was exposed as a work of art which takes place and then formulated as the creation of space specifically for the presentation of art. For the duration of the exhibition, the artists provided visitors with a look behind the scenes. They also opened inside and outside, public and private, traditionally accessible and non-accessible areas of the Kunsthalle architecture to view. They showed*

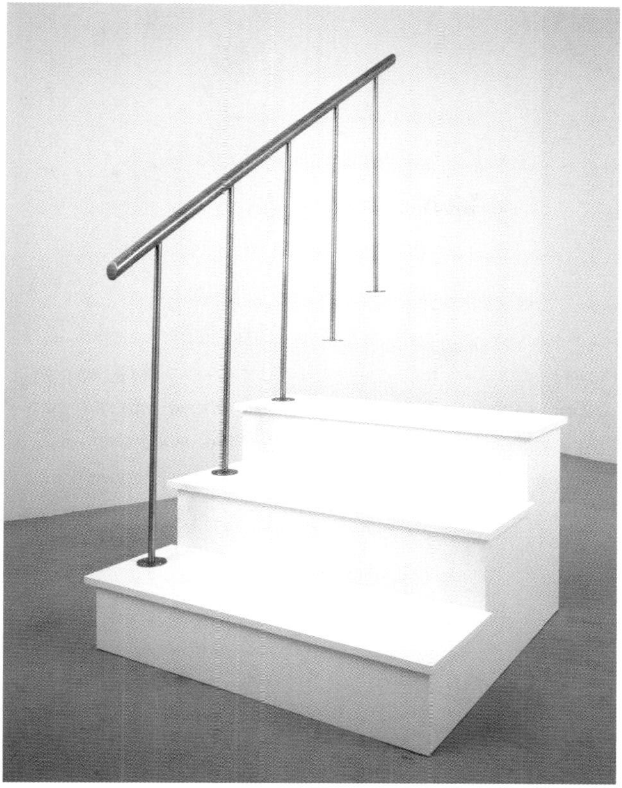

offices being moved, the processes of tearing down and rebuilding walls, details of renovation work, and the suspended state of reorganization of non-public areas dedicated to the administration of art and of public areas in which art is presented.
For the opening of the exhibition, the artists created an "image" representing this process which showed the space of art as a picturesque, romantic-looking "ruin," as a trashy, sentimental fragment of its own identity.
A precisely developed image of the process of destruction that encompassed both the form of the demolished and rebuilt places and the colors of the materials used in the work presented a picture of decadence and luxury, but also of the potential inherent in our designable architectural and social environments.
As a "ruin," the Kunsthalle questioned the validity of many aspects of our construction of reality and more than a few

In *Taking Place* wurde der Raum der Kunst als Werk offen gelegt, das sich ereignet und dann formuliert als spezifische Platzschaffung für die Präsentation von Kunst. Während der gesamten Ausstellungsdauer öffneten sie dem Publikum die Tore für das Hinter-den-Kulissen. Sie öffneten auch innen und außen, öffentliche und private, traditionell zugängliche und nicht zugängliche Bereiche der Kunsthallenarchitektur. Sie zeigten die Umlagerung der Büros, den Abriss und Aufbau von Wänden, die Detailarbeiten, den schwebenden Zustand der Reorganisation der Bereiche von nichtöffentlichen Räumen der Administration von Kunst und dem öffentlichem Raum der Kunstpräsentation.
Zur Ausstellungseröffnung entwarfen sie ein »Bild« der Repräsentation dieses Prozesses, das den Kunstraum als malerische romantisch anmutende »Ruine«, als trashig-sentimentales Fragment seiner eigenen Identität zeigte.
Ein präzise entwickeltes Bild der Zerstörung, das sowohl die Form der Abbruch- und Aufbaustellen wie die Farbgebung der Arbeitsmaterialien umfasste, präsentierte die Dekadenz und der Luxus, vor allem aber die Potenzialität unserer gestaltbaren architektonischen und gesellschaftlichen Umgebungen.
Die Kunsthalle als »Ruine« ließ viele Elemente unserer Wirklichkeitskonstruktion und nicht wenige Begriffe ins Wanken geraten: Der »echte« Umbau der Kunsthalle präsentierte die Künstlichkeit einer Situation, da das Eröffnungsbild eine genaue Unterscheidung von authentisch zum Umbau gehörend oder künstlich erzeugte Situation nicht definitiv entscheiden ließ.[4] Ein Theater des Authentischen wurde ausgebreitet, das sowohl die Wahrnehmungen und Erfahrungen der Kunst wie des Alltags hinterfragbar erscheinen ließ und einen Prozess der Reorganisation symbolischer Formen vielleicht

erst im nachträglichen Gebrauch in Gang zu setzen vermag: Welche Räume braucht die Kunst? Wer entscheidet über ihre Gestalt? Wer nutzt sie? Was ist eine Installation? Was Arbeit? Und was ist eine Ausstellung?

Beatrix Ruf

1 Siehe dazu den ausführlichen Artikel von Markus Brüderlin in diesem Katalog
2 Dazu ebenfalls Markus Brüderlin
3 Brian O'Doherty, *In der weißen Zelle / Inside the White Cube,* Hrsg. von Wolfgang Kemp, Berlin 1996, S. 43.
4 Das Verwirrspiel von echt und unecht erfährt eine Fortsetzung, denn die Künstler werden mit echtem Bauschutt der Kunsthalle eine Installation für die Kwangju Biennale 2002 realisieren. Ob es sich dabei um eine scharfe Kritik der unökologischen Eurotransportpraxis durch die selbst praktizierte Perversion aber überhöhte Form durch Kunst handelt oder aber um eine weitere Verschachtelung der Aneignungsprozesse der Künstler in Form von gestaltetem Material und der Diskussion um Orte der Kunst, bleibt zu diskutieren.

concepts. The "genuine" renovation of the Kunsthalle demonstrated the artificiality of a situation, as the opening image did not permit one to distinguish definitively between an authentic renovation situation and an artificially created one.[4] A theater of the authentic expanded before the viewers' eyes, exposing both the perceptions and experiences of art and everyday life to critical questioning and perhaps triggering a process of reorganization of symbolic forms within the context of later use. What kind of spaces does art need? Who decides what form they take? Who uses them? What is an installation? What is work? And what is an exhibition?

Beatrix Ruf

1 *On O'Doherty, see the in-depth essay by Markus Brüderlin in this catalogue.*
2 *See also Markus Brüderlin.*
3 *Brian O'Doherty,* In der weißen Zelle / Inside the White Cube, *ed. Wolfgang Kemp, Berlin 1996, p. 43.*
4 *This puzzling interplay of the authentic and the non-authentic will be continued in a sequel. The artists plan to realize an installation using genuine construction rubble for the Kwangju Biennial in 2002. Whether their work—in the form of the perversion they practice themselves, albeit in overstated form through art—represents strong criticism of ecologically dubious European transportation practice or—in the form of shaped material and the discussion concerning the places of art—a further compartmentalization of the artists' process of appropriation, remains a matter for discussion.*

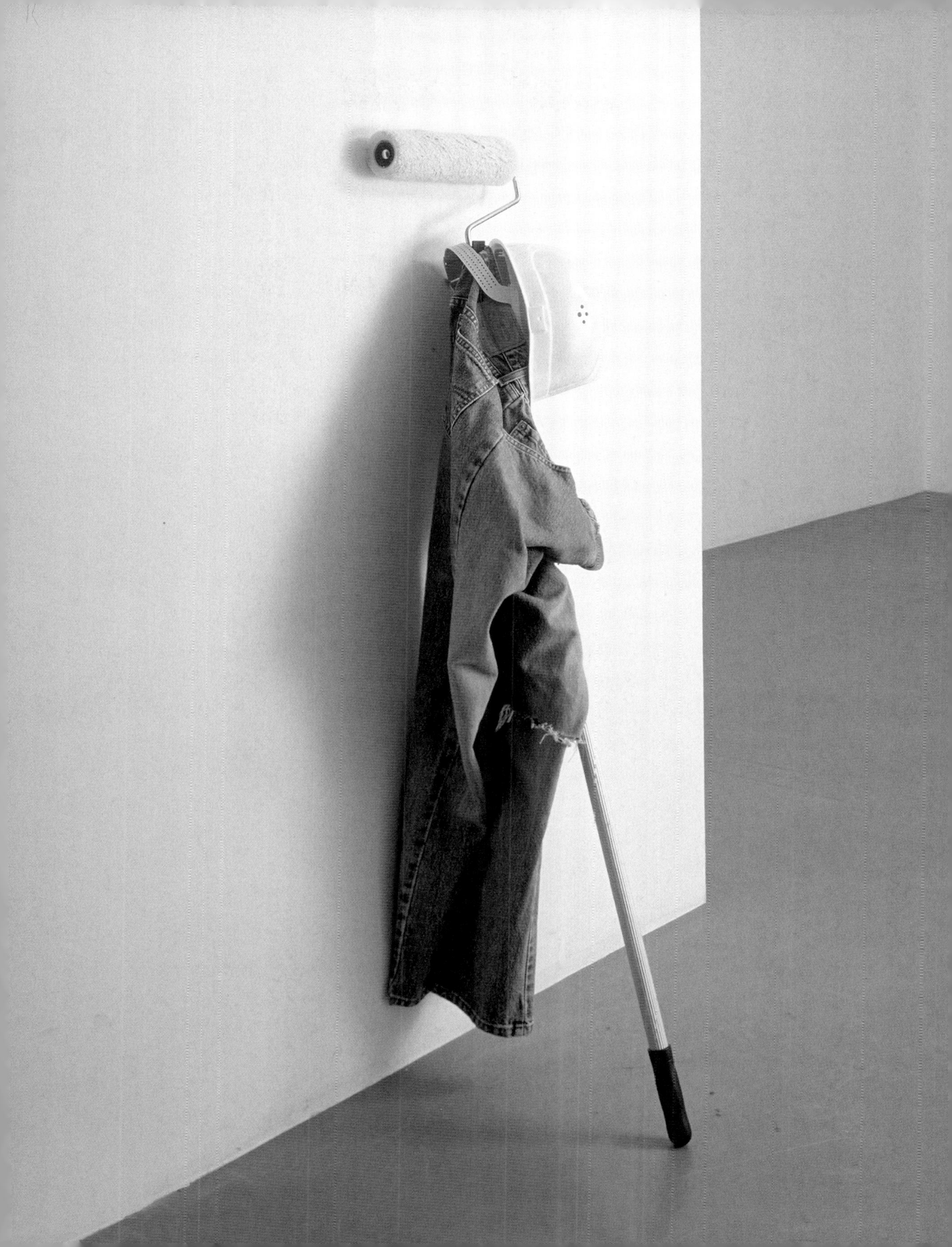

umschlag-innenseite | inside cover

Powerless Structures, Fig. 161, 2001
Holz, Kunststoff, Acryl / Wood, plastic, acrylic
109 x 79 x 129 cm
Tanya Bonakdar Gallery, New York
Photo: Oren Slor
Sammlung / Collection: Bernardo Nadal-Ginard and Laura Steinberg, Chestnut Hill, MA

seite | page 06–07

Taking Place, 2001
Ortsbezogenes Projekt / Site-specific project: Umbau der Ausstellungsräume / Remodelling of the exhibition space
Ausstellungsansicht / Installation view, Kunsthalle Zürich
Photo: Burkhard Meltzer
Courtesy Tanya Bonakdar Gallery, New York; Klosterfelde, Berlin; Galleri Nicolai Wallner, København

seite | page 11

Powerless Structures, Fig. 124, 2001
MDF, Holz, Farbe, Türklinken, Türangeln / MDF, wood, paint, door handles, hinges
217.5 x 98 x 50.5 cm
Galleri Nicolai Wallner, København
Photo: Bent Ryberg / Planet Foto
The Speyer Family Collection, New York

seite | page 13

Powerless Structures, Fig. 131, 2001
MDF, Holz, Farbe, Türklinken, Türangeln / MDF, wood, paint, door handles, hinges
217.5 x 103.5 cm
Galleri Nicolai Wallner, København
Photo: Bent Ryberg / Planet Foto
Courtesy Galleri Nicolai Wallner, København

seite | page 14

Ausstellungsansicht / Installation view
Galleri Nicolai Wallner, København, 2001
Photo: Bent Ryberg / Planet Foto
Courtesy Galleri Nicolai Wallner, København

seite | page 16

Powerless Structures, Fig. 123, 2000
MDF, Holz, Farbe, Türklinken, Türangeln / MDF, wood, paint, door handles, hinges
217.5 x 133.5 cm
Galleri Nicolai Wallner, København
Photo: Bent Ryberg / Planet Foto
Sammlung / Collection: Thomas H. Bjarnason, Toronto

seite | page 17

Powerless Structures, Fig. 126, 2001
MDF, Holz, Farbe, Stahlkette, Türklinke, Türangeln / MDF, wood, paint, steel chain, door handle, hinges
217.5 x 103.5 cm
Galleri Nicolai Wallner, København
Photo: Bent Ryberg / Planet Foto
Private Collection / Privatsammlung, London

seite | page 18–19

Powerless Structures, Fig. 122, 2000
MDF, Holz, Farbe, Stahlkette, Türklinken, Türangeln / MDF, wood, paint, door handles, steel chain, hinges
Je / each 217.5 x 103.5 cm
neugerriemschneider, Berlin
Sammlung / Collection: Scott Lorinsky, New York

seite | page 20

Powerless Structures, Fig. 111
Ausstellungsaufbau / During installation, Portikus, Frankfurt/M., 2001

seite | page 22–23

Powerless Structures, Fig. 111, 2001
Sperrholz, Plexiglas, Aluminium, Vinyl, Fluoreszenzlicht / Plywood, Perspex, aluminum, vinyl, fluorescent lighting
480 x 750 x 1500 cm
Ausstellungsansicht / Installation view, Portikus, Frankfurt/M.
Photo: Wolfgang Günzel
Courtesy Tanya Bonakdar Gallery, New York; Klosterfelde, Berlin; Galleri Nicolai Wallner, København

seite | page 25

Powerless Structures, Fig. 129, 2001
MDF, Holz, Farbe, Türklinke, Türangel / MDF, wood, paint, door handle, hinges
217.5 x 57 x 57 cm
Galleri Nicolai Wallner, København
Photo: Bent Ryberg / Planet Foto
Douglas B. Andrews Collection, Italia

seite | page 26

Tilted Wall/Powerless Structures, Fig. 150, 2001
MDF, Holz, Farbe, »Ausgang«-Schild / MDF, wood, paint, exit sign
245 x 390 x 138 cm
Statens Museum for Kunst, København
Photo: SMK Foto
Private Collection / Privatsammlung, Frankfurt/M.

seite| page 28–29

Depot/Powerless Structures, Fig. 127, 2001
MDF, Holz, Stahl, Farbe, Türangeln, Türklinke, Acrylbuchstaben / MDF, wood, steel, paint, hinges, door handle, acrylic letters
100 x 360 x 285 cm
Statens Museum for Kunst, København
Photo: SMK Foto
Private Collection / Privatsammlung, Italia

seite | page 31

Powerless Structures, Fig. 202, 2001
MDF, Farbe, Stahl / MDF, paint, steel
190 x 80 x 150 cm
Klosterfelde, Berlin
Photo: Jens Ziehe
Sammlung / Collection: Marjory Jacobson, Boston

seite | page 33

Back in a Minute/Powerless Structures, Fig. 87, 2000
Malerrolle mit Stiel, weißer Schutzhelm, Jeans / Paint roll on stick, white hard hat, jeans
Größe variabel / Dimensions variable
Galleri Nicolai Wallner, København
Photo: Bent Ryberg / Planet Foto
Sammlung / Collection: Burt Minkoff, New York; Scott Lorinsky, New York; Nicolai Wallner, København

Transformierende Handlungen
Transformational Acts

Coco Fusco im Gespräch mit Ingar Dragset und Michael Elmgreen zum Thema Performance, Oktober 2001

Coco Fusco: Die Performance scheint das Medium zu sein, das euch als Künstler zusammengebracht hat. Welche Bedeutung hatte diese Kunstform ursprünglich für euch? Hat sich eure Vorstellung von der Performance seit Beginn eurer Zusammenarbeit verändert, und wenn ja, inwiefern?
Ingar Dragset: Ich habe in Norwegen Theaterwissenschaften studiert. Die Performance war damals meine erste Begegnung mit künstlerischen Ansätzen, die radikaler und stärker politisch aufgeladen waren als die anderen Formen von Theaterarbeit, die ich im Rahmen meines Studiums kennen lernte. Da ich aus einer Stadt kam, in der es praktisch kein Forum für moderne oder zeitgenössische Kunst gab, war ich wie umgewandelt, als ich Texte über das Living Theater, Allan Kaprow und Carolee Schneemann las. Die Performance erschien mir als eine neue Welt, die unbegrenzte Möglichkeiten bot. Als ich dann ein paar Jahre später Michael traf, kämpfte ich gerade darum, eine kleine experimentelle Theatergruppe zusammenzuhalten, und war ein wenig desillusioniert, weil ich nichts von dem visionären Geist der Performance gefunden hatte, von dem in den Geschichtsbüchern die Rede war. Als ich dann die Kunstszene in Kopenhagen kennen lernte, war das eine sehr befreiende Erfahrung. Dort gab es Anfang der neunziger Jahre eine sehr starke unabhängige Kunstszene, mit Künstlern, die ihre eigenen Ausstellungsräume hatten und in der ganzen Stadt Ausstellungen und Projekte kuratierten. Sie hatten dem ignoranten Establishment mehr oder weniger den Rücken gekehrt. Es gab nicht viele Performances im engeren Sinn, aber viele interaktive Arbeiten und gesellschaftlich engagierte Projekte. Allgemein gesehen, befasste sich die Kunstszene sehr viel mehr mit zeitgenössischen Themen und Sprachformen als die Theaterszene.

Coco Fusco Interviews Ingar Dragset and Michael Elmgreen on Performance, October 2001

Coco Fusco: Performance seems to be the medium that catalyzed your collaboration as artists. What did performance art mean to each of you when you began? Did your views of performance change after you worked together, and if so, how?
Ingar Dragset: I studied theater history at university in Norway. At that time performance art served as my introduction to art practices which were more radical and politically charged than the other dramatic work I was learning about. Coming from a city with practically no forum for modern or contemporary art, I was completely transformed when I read about the Living Theater, Allan Kaprow, and Carolee Schneemann. I saw performance as a new world with infinite possibilities. When I met Michael a few years later, I was struggling to keep a small experimental theater group together and was slightly disillusioned because I had not found the visionary performance spirit I had been reading about in the history books. When I finally encountered the visual art scene in Copenhagen, it was a very liberating experience. In the early nineties there was a very strong independent art scene there, with artists who ran their own spaces and curated exhibitions and projects throughout the city. They had more or less turned their backs on an ignorant establishment. There was not much actual performance around, but there was a lot of interactive work and many socially engaged projects. In general, the visual art scene was far more concerned with contemporary issues and languages than the theater world was.
Michael Elmgreen: When Ingar and I met, I had already been a part of the local art scene in Copenhagen for several years. Our first collaborations emerged from this context, but I admit that our first works together were due just as much to

our being in love as to our wanting to say something serious using the performance medium. Although I was familiar with performance practices, I had never thought of doing a performance myself until I met Ingar. I had not considered the possibilities of putting myself in front of an audience. I felt absolutely no relationship to contemporary theater whatsoever. But when we got together, the creative decisions were not just about me anymore, they were about us, and ultimately also about being a gay couple in a predominantly heterosexist environment.
C.F.: In what way does the "staging" of your interaction as a duo help you clarify your creative process as a partnership? Did performance help you fuse your individual sensibilities?
M.E.: As I was saying before, in the beginning of our relationship our collaborative projects were a pretext we used to spend more time together. We could get some invitations to travel together, and we created a platform for sharing some of our experiences. But as our work began to occupy a greater part of our time, the collaboration began to influence our entire way of living. Today I cannot imagine being with someone with whom I couldn't discuss a project over breakfast. It's such a luxury to have a life companion who has a natural interest in what you're saying. It would be terrible to sit there with your morning coffee and your brain exploding with some new ideas and then only hearing the reply, "Oh, really? Interesting!" But of course we've still kept our individual characters, which add a certain dynamics to our working process. As a team we know each other well and can still be different from each other. Our final artistic statements are never the result of one of us, but of something between us. This is not about a compromise, but rather about the gap between us. Our collaborations are the small fragments that emerge from the secret universe that exists in between the lines. On a pragmatic level our being two makes us stronger in terms of our dealing with the art scene. When you are a team, it is

Michael Elmgreen: Als Ingar und ich uns kennen lernten, gehörte ich schon seit einigen Jahren zur Kopenhagener Kunstszene. Unsere ersten gemeinsamen Arbeiten sind aus diesem Kontext hervorgegangen, aber ich gebe zu, dass sie ebenso sehr aus unserer Verliebtheit heraus entstanden sind wie aus dem Wunsch, mit dem Medium der Performance etwas Ernsthaftes zu sagen. Die Performance war mir als Kunstform zwar vertraut, aber bevor ich Ingar traf, war ich nie auf die Idee gekommen, selbst eine Performance zu machen. Ich hatte noch nicht über die Möglichkeit nachgedacht, vor ein Publikum zu treten. Ich hatte keinerlei Beziehung zum zeitgenössischen Theater. Doch als wir uns zusammentaten, betrafen die künstlerischen Entscheidungen nicht mehr nur mich selbst, sondern sie drehten sich um uns beide und schließlich auch darum, dass wir ein schwules Paar in einer vorwiegend heterosexistischen Umgebung sind.
C.F.: Inwiefern hilft euch die Inszenierung eurer Interaktion als Duo, Klarheit über den bei euch stattfindenden schöpferischen Prozess als Partnerschaft zu gewinnen? Hat die Performance euch geholfen, euer beider Sensibilität zu verschmelzen?
M.E.: Wie gesagt, zu Beginn unserer Beziehung waren unsere gemeinsamen Projekte für uns ein Vorwand, um mehr Zeit miteinander verbringen zu können. Wir bekamen dadurch Einladungen zu gemeinsamen Reisen, und wir hatten uns eine Plattform geschaffen, auf der wir einen Teil unserer Erfahrungen teilen konnten. Aber als unsere Arbeit mehr und mehr Zeit in Anspruch nahm, fing unsere Zusammenarbeit an, unsere ganze Lebensweise zu beeinflussen. Ich kann mir heute gar nicht mehr vorstellen, mit jemandem zusammen zu sein, mit dem ich nicht beim Frühstück ein Projekt besprechen kann. Es ist so ein Luxus, einen Lebensgefährten zu haben, den das, was man sagt, wirklich interessiert. Es wäre schrecklich, wenn man morgens beim Kaffee säße und einem der Kopf überkochen würde vor neuen

Ideen und man von seinem Partner nur die Antwort bekäme: »Ach, wirklich? Wie interessant!« Aber jeder von uns hat natürlich nach wie vor seinen eigenen Charakter, was eine bestimmte Dynamik in unseren Arbeitsprozess bringt. Als Team kennen wir einander sehr gut und können trotzdem jeder anders sein als der andere. Unsere künstlerischen Statements gehen nie nur auf einen von uns zurück, sondern auf etwas zwischen uns beiden. Dabei geht es nicht um einen Kompromiss, sondern eher um die Kluft zwischen uns. Unsere gemeinsamen Arbeiten sind die kleinen Bruchstücke, die aus dem geheimen Universum auftauchen, das zwischen den Zeilen existiert. Auf einer pragmatischen Ebene macht die Tatsache, dass wir zu zweit sind, uns stärker – was unseren Umgang mit der Kunstszene betrifft. Wenn man ein Team ist, ist es leichter, für das einzutreten, woran man glaubt. Wenn wir als Arbeitsteam auftreten, lassen wir uns nicht so leicht von fragwürdigen Organisatoren herumschieben oder manipulieren. Es hat uns schon mehrmals wirklich geholfen, ein Team zu sein. Andererseits müssen wir, weil wir zu zweit sind, sehr viel präziser sein. Wir müssen uns eine gemeinsame Instanz schaffen, die unsere Aussagen vermittelt und die wir beschützen und der wir treu sein müssen. Wenn wir für unsere Integrität als Zweierteam kämpfen, dann kämpfen wir nicht für die persönliche Integrität jedes Einzelnen von uns, sondern für das, was uns gemeinsam ist. Daher passiert es nicht so leicht, dass wir anfangen, über Grundbegriffe oder Grundvoraussetzungen zu diskutieren, oder dass wir Angst bekommen, wenn es um die Realisierung unserer Ideen geht. Ich finde es immer ein bisschen albern, wenn Künstler oder Künstlerinnen behaupten, sie hätten ihre Projekte in erster Linie für sich selbst gemacht, aber Ingar und ich sind einander wirklich ein ziemlich qualifiziertes Publikum. Ich habe kein großes Bedürfnis, etwas zu machen, das bei einem breiten Publikum ankommt. Unsere Arbeiten existieren für

easier to stand up for what you believe in. We are less likely to be pushed around or manipulated by insincere organizers when we present ourselves as a working team. On a few occasions being a team has really worked to our advantage. On the other hand, being two also requires that we be much more precise. Between the two of us we have to create a common purveyor of our messages who we have to protect and be loyal to. When we are fighting for our integrity as a team of two, we are not fighting for each one's own personal integrity, but for what we share, what we have in common. As a result we are less likely to start negotiating about basic concepts and conditions or to be scared when it comes to realization of our ideas. I've always found it a bit pathetic if an artist claims that he or she did projects primarily to satisfy him- or herself, but it's true that Ingar and I find a pretty qualified audience in each other. I don't feel such a strong need to do something that has wide popular appeal. Our work exists for us before it is appreciated by any other spectator and before it is interpreted by any art critic. It exists in the communication between the two of us, and this communication has become, I must say, the most important thing in my life.

C.F.: What did you want to show your audiences with your performances, beyond the specific details of the performances themselves?

I.D.: In some of our performances we've been more concerned with spatial issues than with performative issues. Those performances have been linked to certain materials that are symbolically charged and resonate in relationship to specific aspects of visual art traditions. Some of the objects we make also related to the performative. In the same way, our installations often suggest a potential activity that could take place in them.

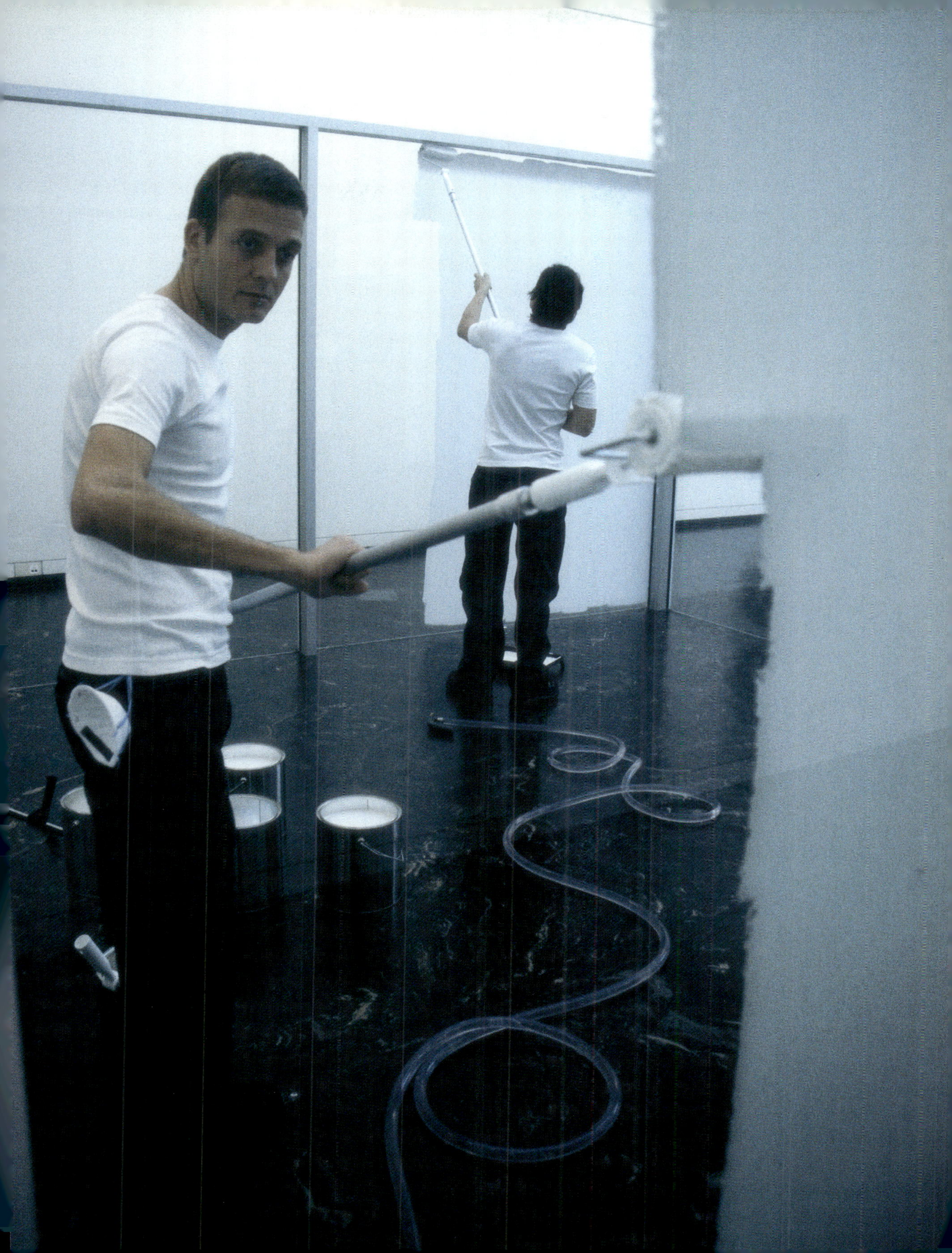

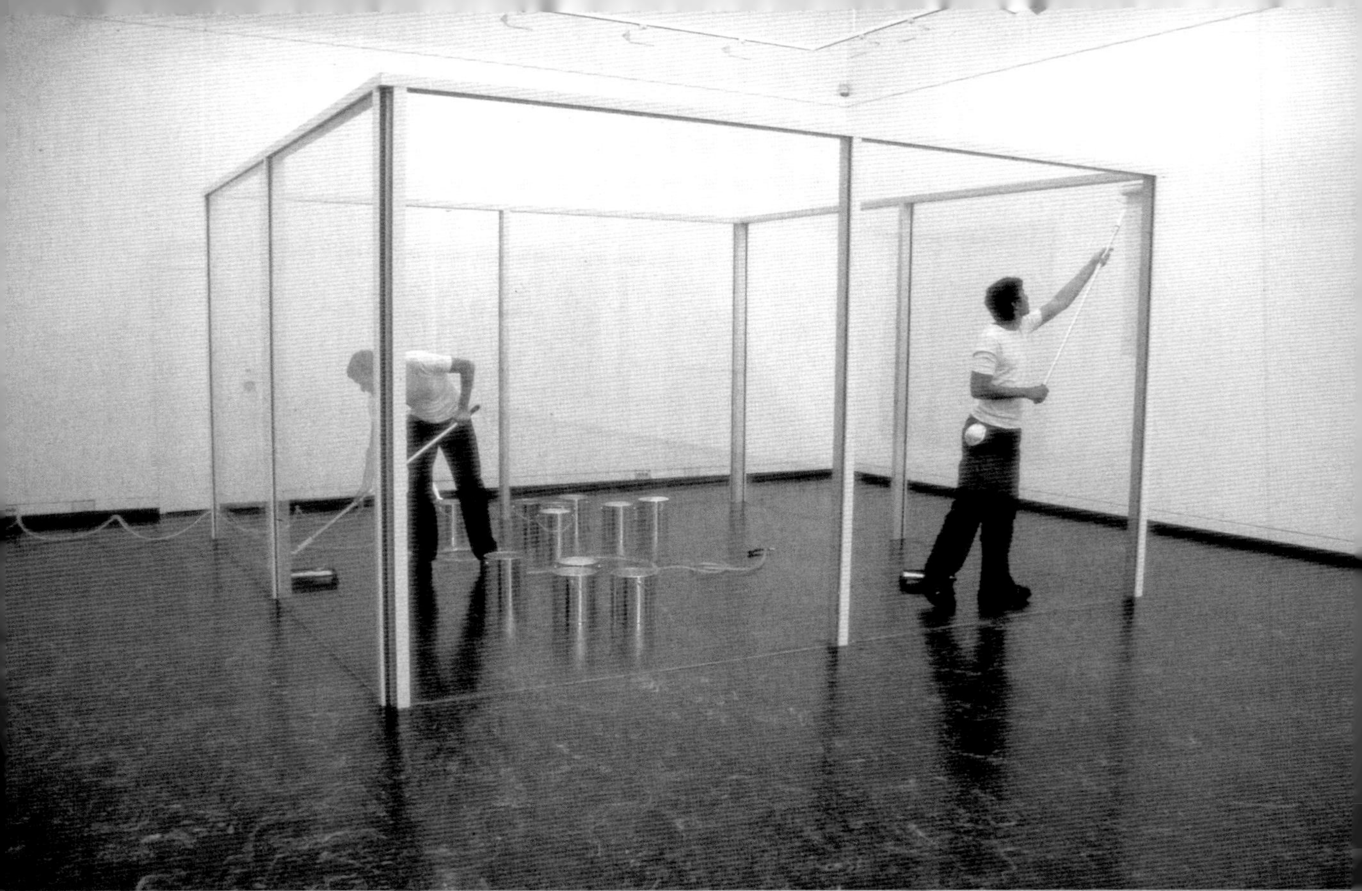

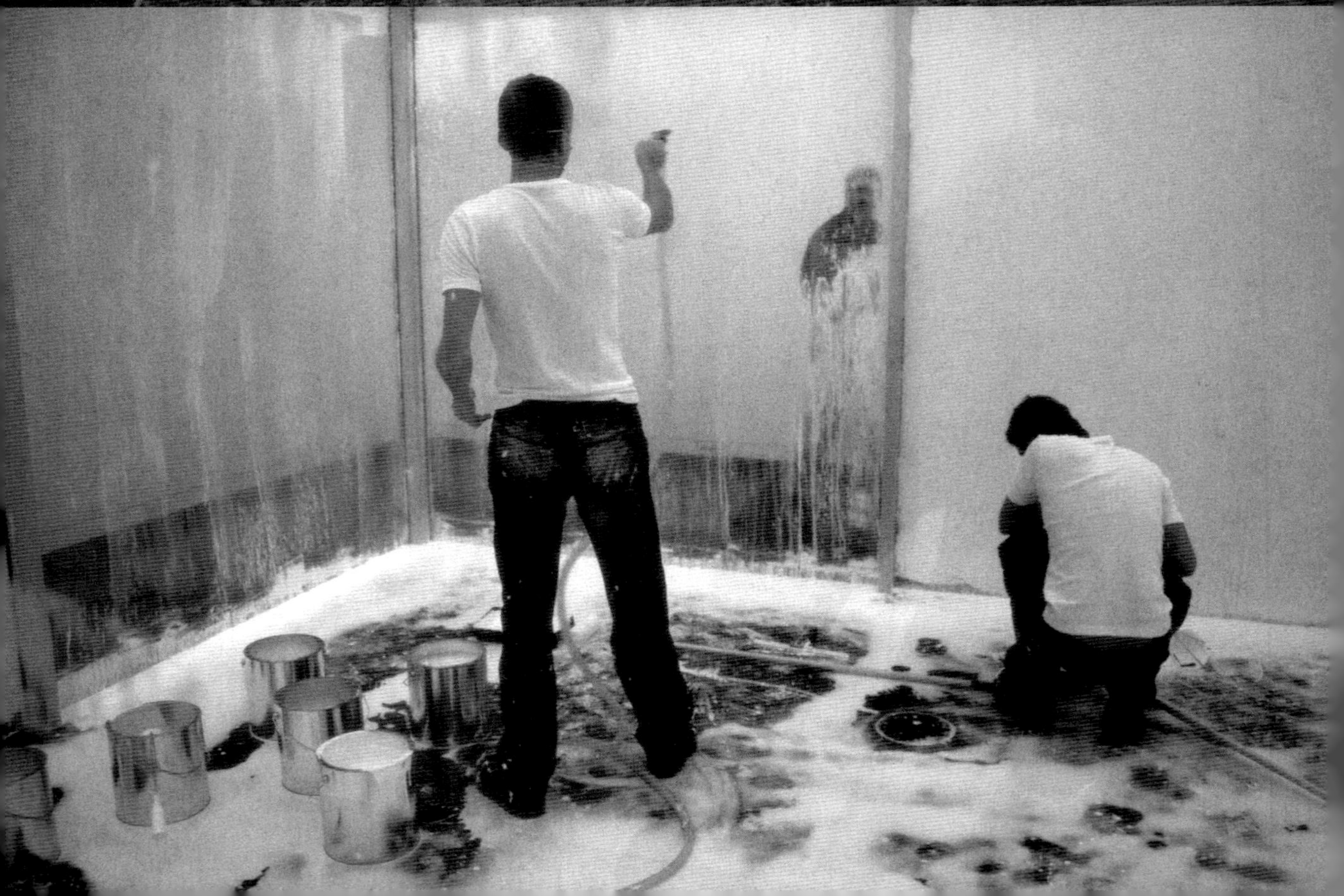

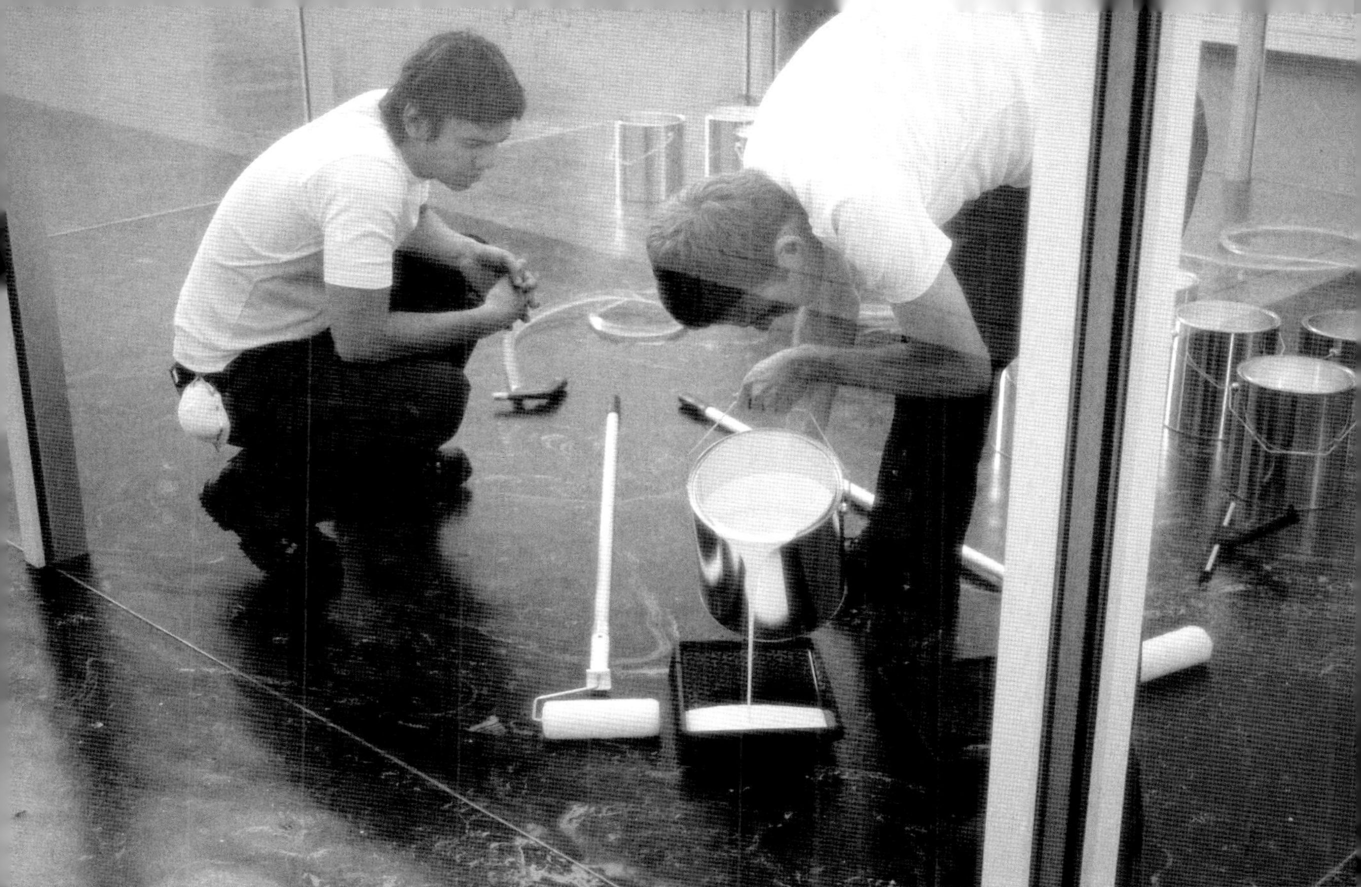

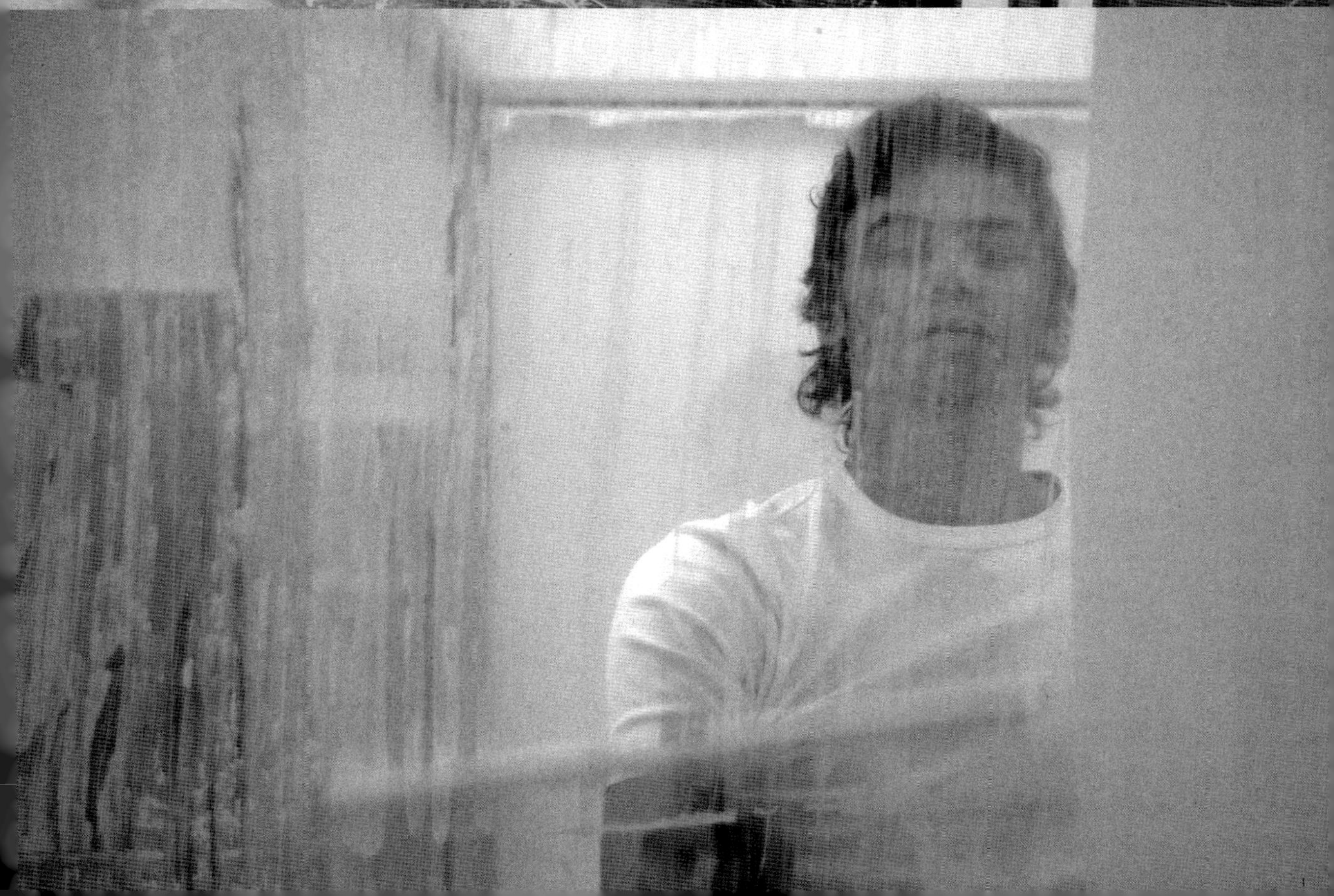

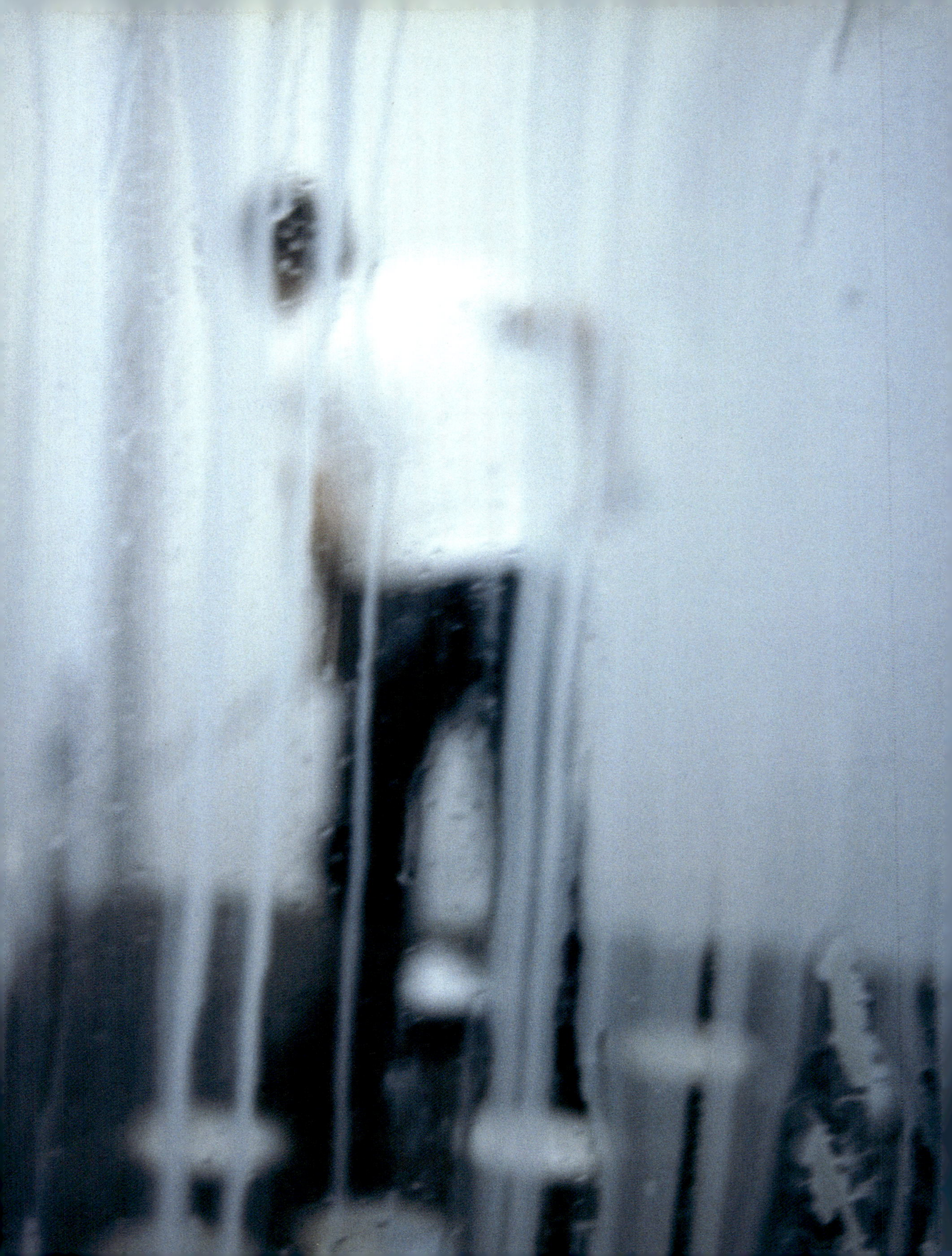

M.E.: Most of the live actions we've done so far have included very few expressive elements, and it has been a conscious choice for us to work in this impersonal way. We've been less focused on the issues of the body and subjectivity. With all due respect to the history of performance art, we've been thrilled by the idea of developing a performance language that did not position itself in opposition to object-based visual art. Hans Ulrich Obrist once pointed out that our installations and sculptural works are somehow more performative than most of our performances. In the series of painting performances that we have done different versions of since 1997, the material, the white paint, and the painting tools are the protagonists. We're just there to keep the activity going. These performances—or live installations, as we prefer to call them—show the fragility of the architectural environment in which they take place. As soon as one introduces the most minute human activity into a space, the character of that space will be transformed. By adding even more layers of white paint to the walls of a white cube and washing down the paint again, the very strict physical features of the gallery become completely blurred. In our live installation Twelve Hours of White Paint *we painted a typical gallery room white from noon until midnight. We used almost two hundred liters of white paint that we repeatedly washed down again and again. As the thick layers of paint slid down the walls and dripped onto the floor, the space started to insist on its own identity and thus broke out of its anonymous role as a neutral backdrop for art presentation. It started to live its own wild life. In this live installation we ourselves aren't of any importance. We could easily be replaced with anybody else, although it's a job that involves exposure to toxic chemicals, so I doubt that anyone else would find it a very attractive prospect to have to paint for twelve hours.*

C.F.: Do you think that your early performances—such as the one in which you knitted body coverings and unraveled

uns, bevor sie ein anderer Zuschauer wahrnimmt und bevor sie ein Kunstkritiker interpretiert. Sie existieren in dem Austausch zwischen uns beiden, und ich muss sagen, dieser Austausch ist für mich das Wichtigste in meinem Leben geworden.

C.F.: Was wolltet ihr dem Publikum mit euren Performances zeigen, über die konkreten Einzelheiten hinaus?

I.D.: In einigen Performances haben wir uns mehr mit räumlichen Themen als mit performativen Gesichtspunkten beschäftigt. Diese Performances waren mit Materialien verbunden, die symbolisch aufgeladen sind und mit bestimmten Aspekten von Traditionen der bildenden Kunst in Verbindung stehen. Andererseits haben auch einige unserer Objekte mit dem performativen Aspekt zu tun. So erwecken auch unsere Installationen oft die Vorstellung einer potenziellen Aktivität, die in ihnen stattfinden könnte.

M.E.: Die meisten der Live-Aktionen, die wir bisher gemacht haben, enthielten nur sehr wenige expressive Elemente, und es war eine bewusste Entscheidung, auf diese unpersönliche Weise zu arbeiten. Wir haben uns weniger auf das Thema des Körpers und das der Subjektivität konzentriert. Bei allem Respekt gegenüber der Geschichte der Performance hat uns doch die Vorstellung gereizt, eine Sprache der Performance zu entwickeln, die sich nicht als Gegensatz zu der auf Objekten basierenden Kunst verstand. Hans Ulrich Obrist hat einmal bemerkt, unsere Installationen und skulpturalen Arbeiten hätten in gewisser Hinsicht eher performativen Charakter als die meisten unserer Performances. In der Reihe von Mal-Aktionen, die wir seit 1997 in verschiedenen Versionen durchgeführt haben, sind das Material – die weiße Farbe – und die Malutensilien die Protagonisten. Wir selbst sind nur da, um die Aktivität in Gang zu halten. Diese Performances – oder Live-Installationen, wie wir sie lieber nennen – zeigen die Fragilität der architektonischen Umgebung,

in der sie stattfinden. Sobald man in einen Raum eine noch so geringfügige menschliche Aktivität hineinbringt, verändert sich der Charakter dieses Raumes. Indem man die Wände eines White Cube mit weiteren weißen Farbschichten versieht und die Farbe dann wieder abwäscht, werden die sehr strengen materiellen Merkmale der Galerie völlig verschwommen. In unserer Live-Installation *Twelve Hours of White Paint* haben wir von Mittag bis Mitternacht einen typischen Galerieraum weiß gestrichen. Wir haben fast zweihundert Liter weiße Farbe verbraucht, die wir immer wieder abgewaschen haben. Als die dicken Farbschichten die Wände hinunterrannen und auf den Boden tropften, begann der Raum, auf seiner eigenen Identität zu bestehen, und brach aus seiner anonymen Rolle als neutraler Hintergrund für die Präsentation von Kunstwerken aus. Er fing an, sein eigenes, ungeregeltes Leben zu führen. In dieser Live-Installation sind wir selbst nicht wichtig. Man könnte uns leicht durch jemand anderen ersetzen – allerdings ist das eine Arbeit, bei der man toxischen Chemikalien ausgesetzt ist, und ich bezweifle, dass jemand anderes die Aussicht, zwölf Stunden lang Wände streichen zu müssen, sehr attraktiv fände.
C.F.: Haben eure frühen Performances – wie etwa die, bei der ihr Kleider gestrickt und wieder aufgetrennt habt – in gewisser Hinsicht etwas mit Performance-Traditionen zu tun, die in Skandinavien dominant waren, wie etwa Fluxus?
I.D.: In Dänemark hat es in den siebziger Jahren eine starke Fluxus-Szene gegeben und in den Achtzigern eine Welle von expressiven Post-Punk-Performances. Von diesen beiden Traditionen hat uns die Erstere sicher mehr inspiriert. Doch als wir in den neunziger Jahren mit unseren Performances anfingen, kam niemand auf die Idee, diese Live-Aktionen mit irgendeiner bestimmten skandinavischen Richtung zu vergleichen. Wir haben nicht einmal daran gedacht. Von der Kunstgeschichte kleiner Länder wie Dänemark geht

them—relate in some way to performance traditions that have been dominant in Scandinavia, such as Fluxus?
I.D.: There was a strong Fluxus scene in Denmark in the seventies and a wave of expressive post-punk performances in the eighties. The first tradition is definitely more inspiring to us than the latter. Nonetheless, when we started doing our performances in the nineties, no one thought of comparing these live acts to any specific Scandinavian practice. We didn't even think of it. Sadly, a lot of the art history of a small country like Denmark gets lost. So little of what has happened artistically has been documented there or written about unless it fit into the most conventional institutional frameworks. Only recently have younger art critics and historians such as Lars Bang Larsen been trying to retrieve some of the material and spirit that was about to be lost forever. Of course, we do know about some infamous happenings such as Bjørn Nørgaard slaughtering a horse and putting it into jars in protest against the Vietnam war or Lene Adler walking through the stock exchange naked. But our main historical sources were really the Americans of that period: Vito Acconci, Carolee Schneemann, Dan Graham, Allan Kaprow, and so on.
C.F.: Was performing as a duo a means of "coming out"? Did you in some way seek to redefine a gay sensibility through your performance practice?
M.E.: I wouldn't use the term "coming out." We were already open in public about our gay identities when we met. However, we did indeed intend to redefine a gay sensibility, especially at the beginning of our collaboration. Artists making work about gay sexual identity have been inaccurately labeled as more soft core, more sensitive, or more feminine than their heterosexual male colleagues. These categories might be true in relation to some artists' working methods. For example, among prior generations of gay male artists

there had been a tendency to adapt a feminist vocabulary in their visual expressions, but things have changed since this early stage of "gay aesthetics." Homosexual identity has changed, and so has the art about it. An older generation such as Gilbert and George or even Félix González-Torres or Robert Gober were up against different kind of authorities in the art scene when they started exhibiting. Not that homophobia or sexism in general has disappeared from the art scene, but it has some new manifestations, and so our problems are different than those of ten years ago.

C.F.: What would you say that your problems are then?

M.E.: Some have criticized us for not being gay enough, or for being too macho. They are referring to the performances that feature what has traditionally been regarded as macho labor and to our bigger environmental installations. There is a danger of defining gay identity in such limited ways that there is no room for one's masculine side. To me it seems a bit strange to exclude your masculinity from your artwork just because it has got a bad reputation. Large-scale works or works showing a masculine activity cannot be considered necessarily or essentially repressive, nor should a more vulnerable or ephemeral art expression be seen as necessarily more progressive. After all, who is to judge what it is to be gay? Advertising uses stereotypically gay icons to sell T-shirts in magazines like The Face, *but these images don't really represent the totality of what gay identity is today.*

C.F.: It is understandable that you would argue for a more flexible, less literal view of the symbolic charge of certain styles or methods or content in your artwork, but are you calling for a complete separation of artistic gestures from social contexts and histories? If aesthetic expression is not essentially or necessarily rooted in the history of its manifestations, what is the relationship for you? There are plenty of formalist critics and artists out there who posit that any attempt to link

leider viel verloren. Nur sehr wenig von dem, was dort in künstlerischer Hinsicht passiert ist, wurde dokumentiert, und es wurde weniger darüber geschrieben, außer wenn es sich in die konventionellsten institutionellen Strukturen einfügte. Erst in letzter Zeit haben jüngere Kunstkritiker und Kunsthistoriker wie Lars Bang Larsen versucht, einiges von dem Material und dem Geist zu retten, die kurz davor waren, für immer verloren zu gehen. Wir wissen natürlich von einigen berüchtigten Happenings wie etwa dem von Bjørn Nørgaard, der als Protestaktion gegen den Vietnamkrieg ein Pferd geschlachtet und in Gefäße gefüllt hat, oder dem von Lene Adler, die nackt durch die Börse gegangen ist. Aber unsere wichtigsten historischen Quellen waren eigentlich die Amerikaner aus jener Zeit: Vito Acconci, Carolee Schneemann, Dan Graham, Allan Kaprow usw.

C.F.: War als Duo aufzutreten für euch eine Art Coming-out? Wolltet ihr durch eure Performances in gewisser Hinsicht eine neue schwule Sensibilität definieren?

M.E.: Ich würde dabei nicht von Coming-out reden. Als wir uns kennen lernten, gingen wir mit unserem Schwulsein in der Öffentlichkeit bereits ganz offen um. Doch wir wollten wirklich eine neue schwule Sensibilität definieren, vor allem zu Beginn unserer Zusammenarbeit. Künstler, die sich in ihren Arbeiten mit einer schwulen sexuellen Identität beschäftigen, sind fälschlicherweise als weniger aggressiv, als empfindsamer, als femininer bezeichnet worden als ihre heterosexuellen männlichen Kollegen. Im Hinblick auf die Arbeitsweisen einiger Künstler mögen diese Kategorien ja zutreffen. So gab es zum Beispiel bei früheren Generationen schwuler Künstler die Tendenz, dass diese in ihren Arbeiten ein feministisches Vokabular übernahmen, doch seit dieser Frühzeit einer »schwulen Ästhetik« hat sich viel geändert. Die homosexuelle Identität hat sich gewandelt und damit auch die Kunst, die sich mit ihr befasst. Ältere Generationen

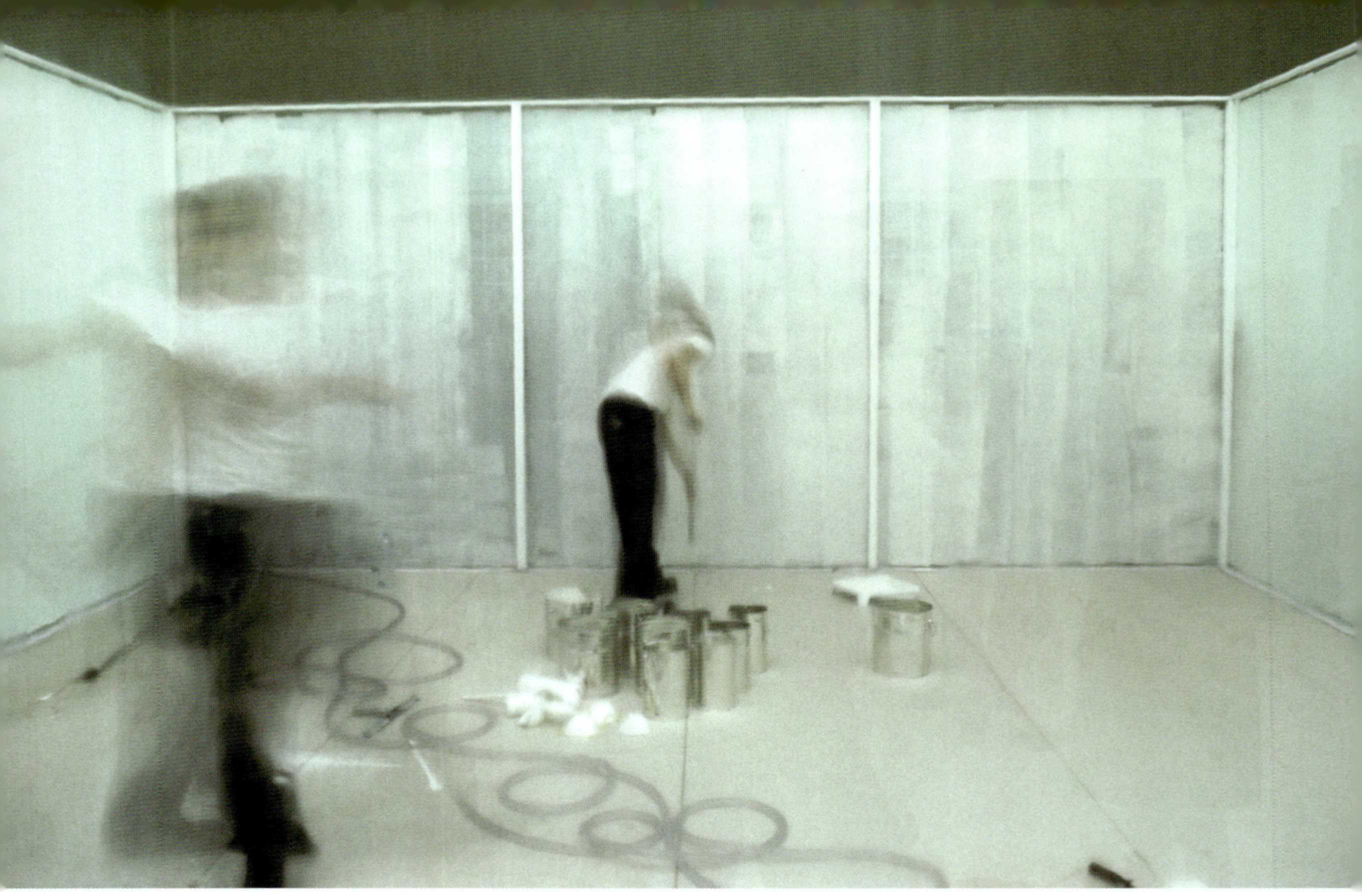

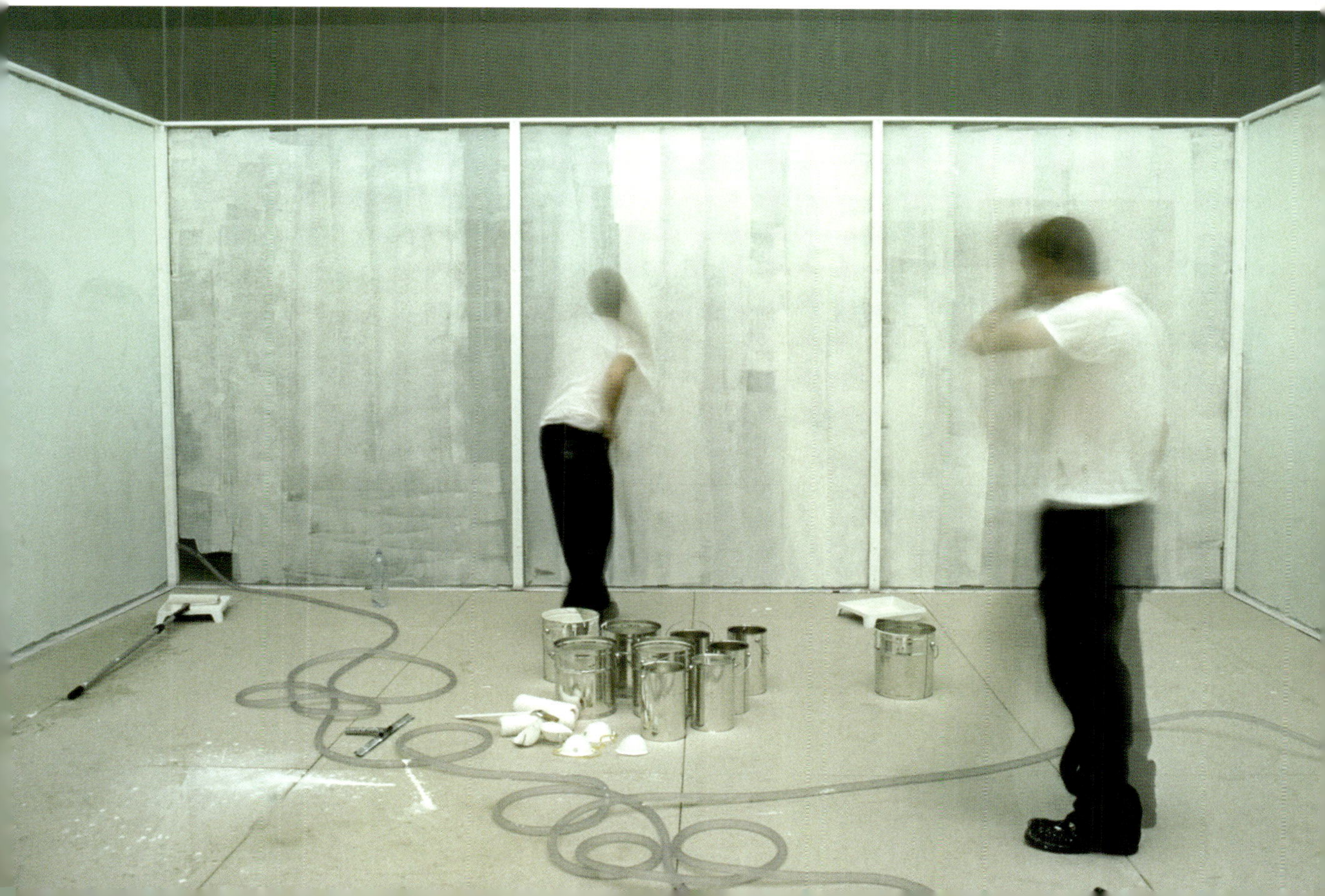

wie etwa die von Gilbert & George oder sogar die von Félix González-Torres oder Robert Gober hatten es, als sie anfingen auszustellen, in der Kunstszene mit einer anderen Art von Autoritäten zu tun. Nicht dass es in der Kunstszene heute keine Homophobie oder keinen Sexismus mehr gibt, aber sie schlagen sich auf andere Weise nieder, und so sind auch unsere Probleme andere als die der Künstler vor zehn Jahren.

C.F.: Was würdet ihr denn sagen, wo eure Probleme liegen?

M.E.: Manche Leute haben uns dafür kritisiert, dass wir nicht schwul genug seien oder zu machohaft. Damit beziehen sie sich auf die Performances, die sich um eine Form von Arbeit drehen, die traditionell als Machoarbeit gilt, und auf unsere größeren Environments. Es besteht die Gefahr, dass man die schwule Identität auf so begrenzte Weise definiert, dass die eigene maskuline Seite darin keinen Platz mehr hat. Ich finde es ein wenig merkwürdig, wenn man seine Männlichkeit aus seiner Kunst ausschließt, nur weil sie einen schlechten Ruf hat. Großformatige Arbeiten oder solche, die eine männliche Aktivität zeigen, sind darum noch nicht unbedingt oder im Wesentlichen repressiv, und genauso wenig sollte man eine eher verletzliche oder ephemere künstlerische Ausdrucksweise unbedingt als progressiver ansehen. Wer kann denn sagen, was es heißt, schwul zu sein? In der Werbung, in Zeitschriften wie *The Face*, werden stereotype schwule Ikonen benutzt, um T-Shirts zu verkaufen, aber diese Bilder repräsentieren nicht die Totalität dessen, worin die schwule Identität heute besteht.

C.F.: Es ist verständlich, dass ihr für eine flexiblere, weniger buchstäbliche Auffassung des symbolischen Gehalts bestimmter Stile oder Methoden oder Inhalte in eurer Kunst plädiert, aber wollt ihr denn eine völlige Trennung der künstlerischen Geste vom gesellschaftlichen Kontext und von der Geschichte? Wenn der künstlerische Ausdruck nicht

the two is repressive. And there are many artists who have come to prominence in the nineties who insist that their particular identities—as non-Europeans, or as gays or lesbians—have nothing to do with their work, and that their expressions have nothing to do with any specific cultural reference. The problem I have with these assumed positions is that they invariably rely on Modernist myths about universality and Romantic notions of creativity as singular and intuitive. Furthermore, their deployment by the art market serves as a way to mask the subtle marketing of most of these artists as refined exotics, and of "peripheral" locales, whether they are cities like Istanbul or the back rooms of gay bars, as touristic spectacles.

M.E.: To me, any artistic expression must be considered a representation! From Michelangelo to Donald Judd, you would be assuming a very conservative or Romantic art-historical standpoint if you denied that there is a direct link between the political, cultural, social, and sexual background of an artist and his or her visual statements. To exclude any of these aspects in your working method is also a highly political choice. I've never been a true believer of notions of artistic transcendence such as the sublime—I never experienced sublime moments standing in front of a Mark Rothko painting, for example, but I've experienced joy in reading the messages and codes in a work of art. You can, of course, have different strategies. Some prefer to present political matters in a rather direct way, some work with more open statements and an underlying critique. What I meant by saying that no one can actually make a strict definition of gay identity today was not a call for leaving out the identity issue from the artistic expression. After all we've done pieces with titles such as Queer Bar, Cruising Pavilion, *and so on. But what I would like to see is the establishment of a more complex image of our sexual identity. It has been urgent for us to*

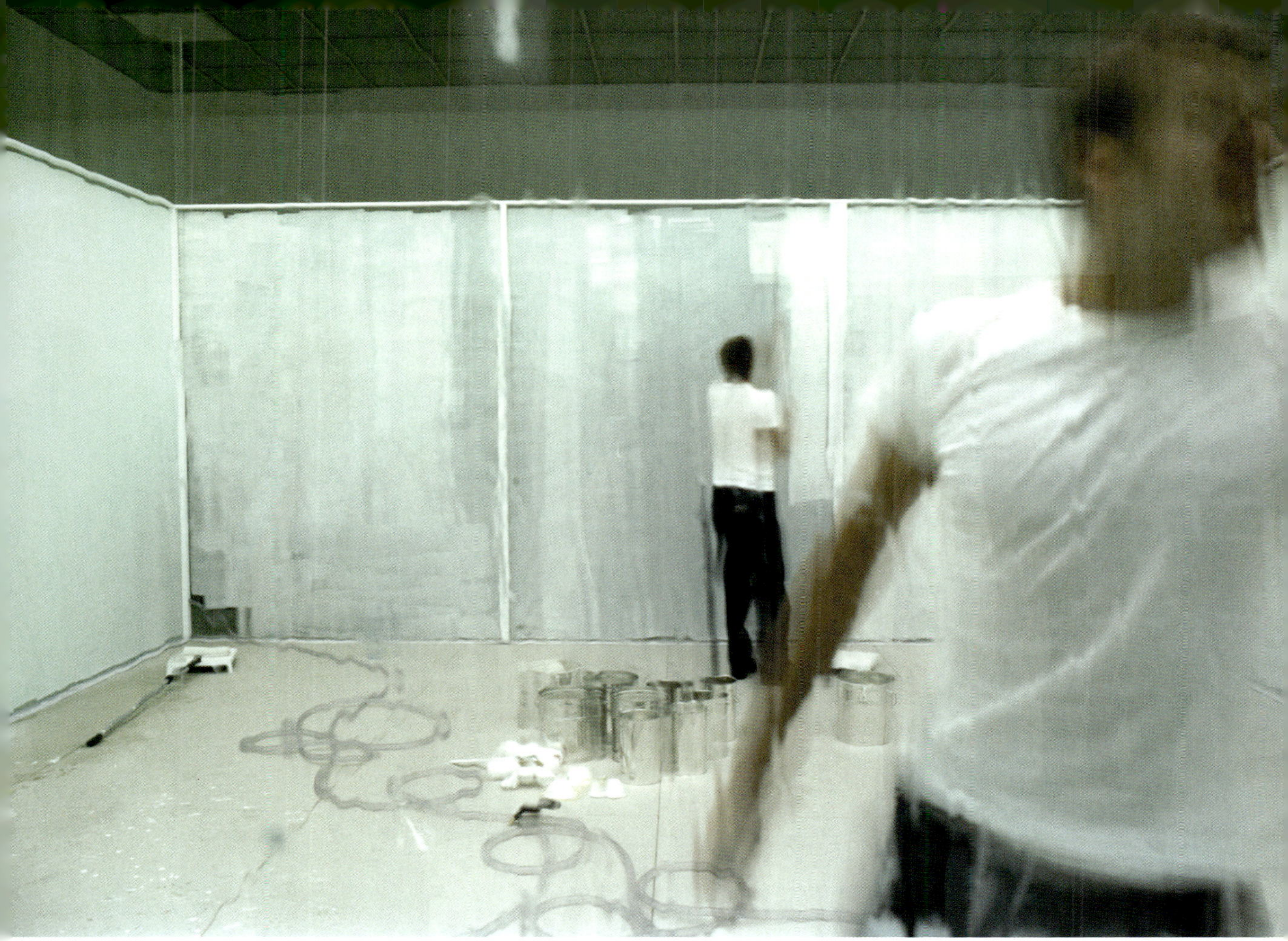

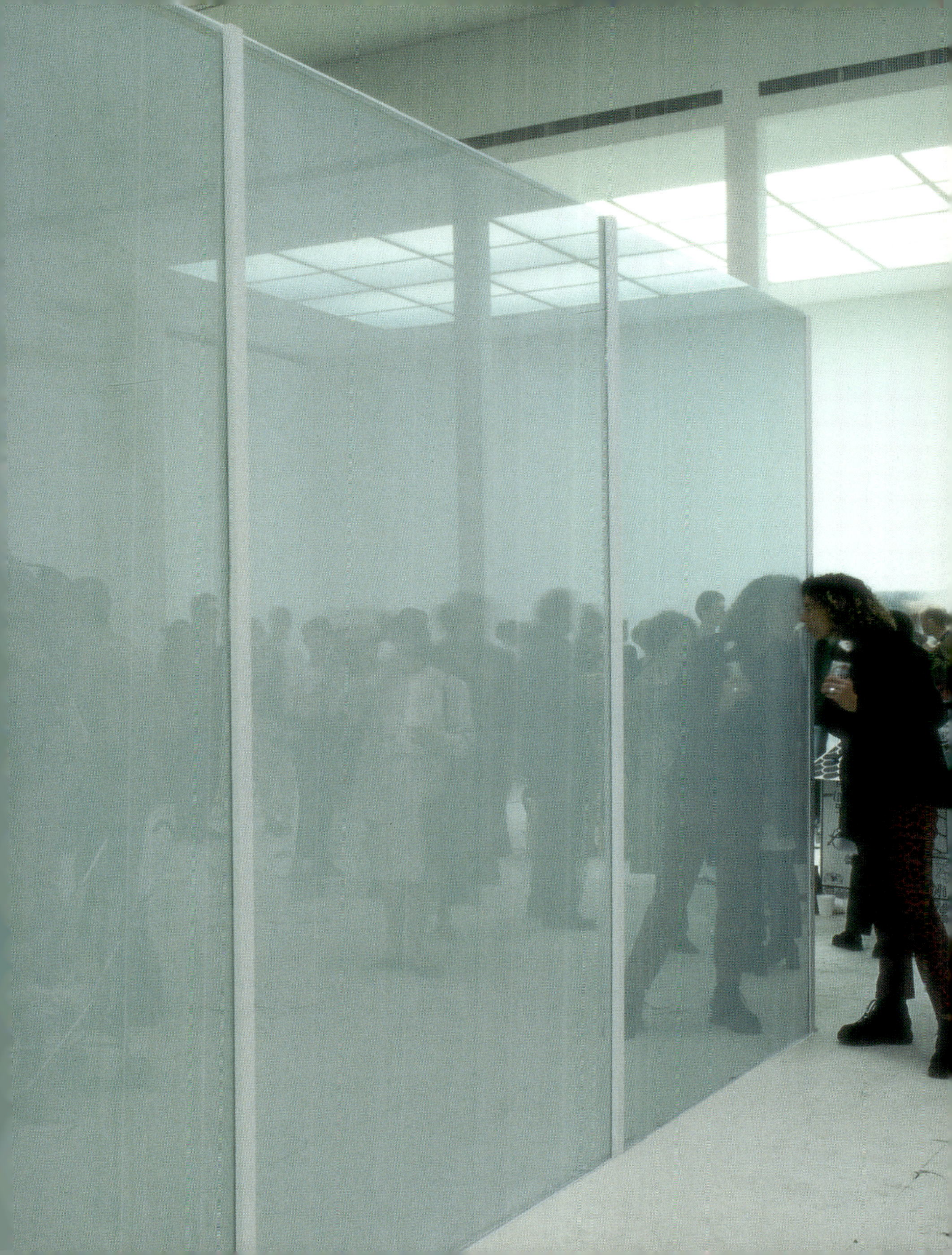

essenziell oder notwendig in der Geschichte seiner Manifestationen verwurzelt ist, worin besteht dann für euch diese Beziehung? Es gibt unzählige formalistische Kritiker und Künstler, die behaupten, jeder Versuch, die beiden zu verbinden, sei repressiv. Und viele Künstler, die in den neunziger Jahren bekannt geworden sind, bestehen darauf, dass ihre Identität – als Nichteuropäer oder als Schwule oder Lesben – nichts mit ihrer Arbeit zu tun hat und dass ihre Werke unabhängig sind von jedem bestimmten kulturellen Bezug. Das Problem, das ich mit diesen ostentativ vertretenen Standpunkten habe, ist, dass sie alle auf modernen Universalitätsmythen und auf romantischen Vorstellungen von Kreativität basieren, nach denen diese einzigartig ist und intuitiv. Und auf dem Kunstmarkt dienen sie dazu, die subtile Vermarktung der meisten dieser Künstler als verfeinerte Exoten zu kaschieren und »periphere« Orte – seien es Städte wie Istanbul oder die Hinterzimmer von Schwulenlokalen – als Touristenattraktionen zu verkaufen.

M.E.: Nach meiner Ansicht hat jeder künstlerische Ausdruck Darstellungscharakter! Von Michelangelo bis Donald Judd gilt, dass man einen sehr konservativen oder romantischen kunsthistorischen Standpunkt einnehmen würde, wenn man leugnet, dass es eine direkte Verbindung gibt zwischen dem politischen, kulturellen, gesellschaftlichen und sexuellen Hintergrund eines Künstlers und seinen visuellen Statements. Einen dieser Aspekte von seiner Arbeit auszuschließen ist eine hochpolitische Entscheidung. Ich habe nie so richtig an solche Vorstellungen von künstlerischer Transzendenz wie das Erhabene geglaubt – so habe ich zum Beispiel noch nie vor einem Bild von Mark Rothko einen erhabenen Moment erlebt, aber es hat mir Freude gemacht, die Botschaft und die Codes in einem Kunstwerk zu lesen. Man kann natürlich verschiedene Strategien anwenden. Manche Künstler präsentieren politische Themen lieber auf ziemlich

try to avoid blindly taking over those gay icons that are established conventions—namely the misinterpretation of gay life as being based on glamour, kitsch, Gloria Gaynor, and gyms only—or the new mainstream homosexual movement on the other hand, where you experience gay men replicating petit-bourgeois values and fighting for getting the legal rights to marry. You still meet heterosexuals who have the best intentions of being free minded and because of their eagerness to flatter you, they burst out with bullshit like, "Gay men have so good taste, gays are so artistically talented, gays have such interesting lives, or gay couples are such an important group of consumers as they normally are better off than other social groups in society." New York is filled with homeless homosexuals. Gay men don't just live in fancy designed homes in Santa Monica—millions of gays are living in poor neighborhoods, and they get shitty educations just like anybody else. But a great part of the homosexual culture sustains this annoying fairy-tale, Cinderella-like image of itself, and that's what we want to work against. If you're consciously dealing with representation, it's quite important to check out that you are not part of creating some new prejudices, that you are not just excluding another group of people because their identity does not fit into the public picture you're drawing of them. It doesn't help much—if you are a graffiti-painting punk kid without any education—that society's acceptance of homosexual behavior is based on a twisted version of Christian nuclear-family values. An obvious case of that is Giuliani, the ex-mayor of New York, who claimed he was doing the gay community a big favor by closing down the sex venues and the dirty bars in the city. I got very upset when I saw him participating in the Gay Pride Parade in 1999. Another matter is the art market's use of so-called minority artists to play the role as "exotica," as you mention: artists getting an invitation to spice up the boring main dish.

For decades you've seen a tendency for these artists to be displayed as a mixed chorus behind the white, male, and heterosexual master singer. Those expressions which have their starting point outside European art history are only there to confirm the central position of this tradition; these "other" artists are present in order to frame and contextualize the takeovers of the dominant tradition. Therefore it makes sense to me to borrow from Modernist aesthetics, to make the changes from within the system. And these aesthetics are also the ones I've been growing up with, the ones I've had to deal with through my entire life. Minimalism and Functionalism are right there in your everyday life, when you come from Scandinavia.

C.F.: You have said that your use of Minimalist vocabulary works against the cliché of gay art as kitsch and camp. What do your very methodical, low-key, repetitive labors as performance artists contribute to this process of redefining gay aesthetics?

I.D.: It is true that gay visual culture is still predominantly based on kitsch and camp aesthetics. On the other hand the gay scene, as well as the urban youth cultural scene in general, has been "Wallpapered" or "loungified" over the last few years. Restaurants, bars, clubs, and shops are increasingly dominated by a version of a Minimalist aesthetic that has turned into Minimalist kitsch; Minimalism as pop, as style and glamour. For us it has been important to play with Minimalism and twist its reductive strategies. To recharge Minimalist surfaces by imposing representational layers onto them. For instance, in works such as Cruising Pavilion/ Powerless Structures, Fig. 55, *and* Queer Bar/Powerless Structures, Fig. 21, *we have combined slick, white, "straight" features with elements adapted from "low culture" venues, like bars or sex venues. In a performance like* Powerless Structures, Fig. 44, *where we continuously paint a glass box*

direkte Weise, andere arbeiten mit offenen Statements und einer unterschwelligen Kritik. Wenn ich sage, dass niemand heute eine klare Definition von schwuler Identität geben kann, dann meine ich damit nicht, dass die Frage der Identität beim künstlerischen Ausdruck keine Rolle spielen soll. Schließlich haben wir ja Arbeiten mit Titeln wie *Queer Bar, Cruising Pavilion* usw. gemacht. Doch würde ich gerne sehen, dass sich ein komplexeres Bild unserer sexuellen Identität durchsetzt. Es war für uns sehr wichtig, zu vermeiden, die schwulen Ikonen, die etablierte Konventionen sind, blind zu übernehmen – dieses Missverständnis, dass das Leben des Schwulen nur auf Glamour, Kitsch, Gloria Gaynor und Fitness-Studios basiert – oder auch die neue homosexuelle Mainstream-Bewegung, in der schwule Männer kleinbürgerliche Wertvorstellungen kopieren und darum kämpfen, das gesetzliche Recht zum Heiraten zu bekommen. Man trifft immer noch Heterosexuelle, die sich ernsthaft bemühen, keine Vorurteile zu haben, und die in ihrem Eifer, einem zu schmeicheln, mit solchem Schwachsinn herausplatzen wie: »Schwule haben so einen guten Geschmack, Schwule sind künstlerisch so begabt, Schwule haben so ein interessantes Leben, oder schwule Paare sind eine sehr wichtige Konsumentengruppe, weil sie finanziell meistens besser gestellt sind als andere Gesellschaftsgruppen.« In New York gibt es massenweise obdachlose Schwule. Schwule wohnen nicht nur in schicken, durchgestylten Häusern in Santa Monica – Millionen Schwule leben in Armenvierteln und bekommen eine genauso beschissene Ausbildung wie andere auch. Doch ein Großteil der homosexuellen Kultur unterstützt dieses ärgerliche aschenputtelhafte Märchenbild von sich selbst, und dagegen wollen wir angehen. Wenn man bewusst mit der Darstellung arbeitet, dann muss man aufpassen, dass man sich nicht daran beteiligt, neue Vorurteile zu schaffen, dass man nicht einfach eine andere Gruppe von Menschen

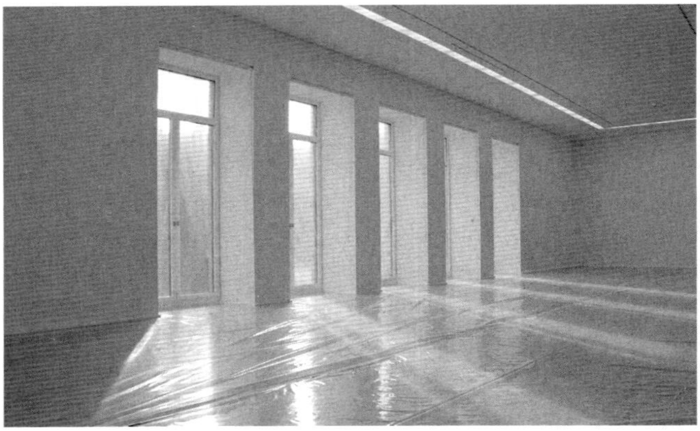
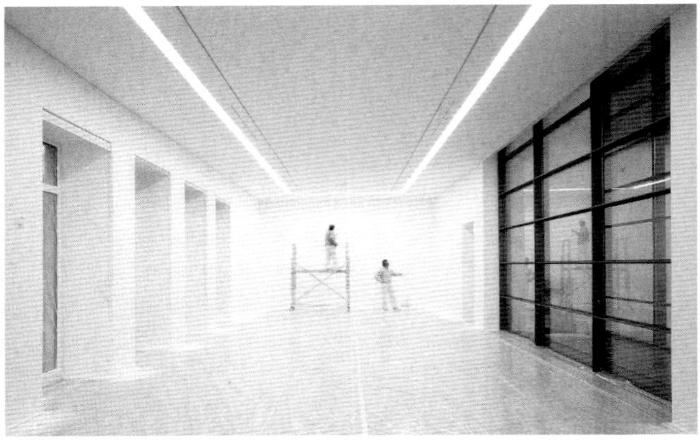
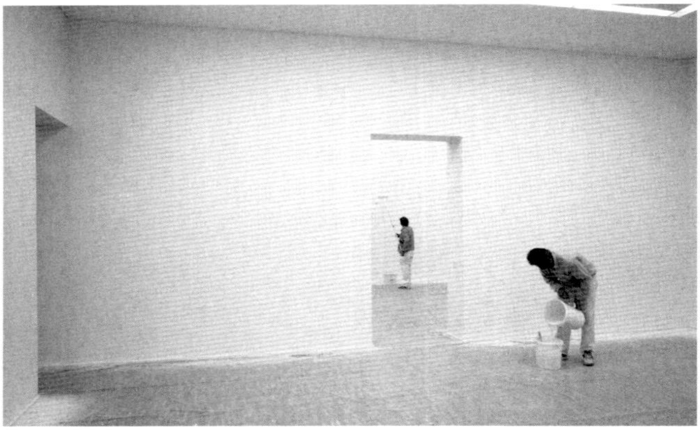
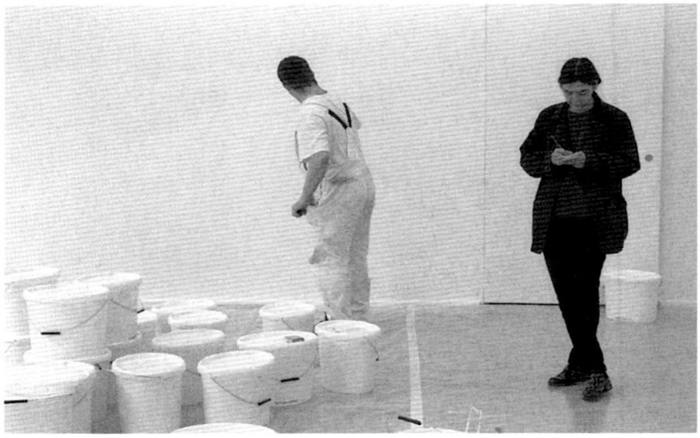
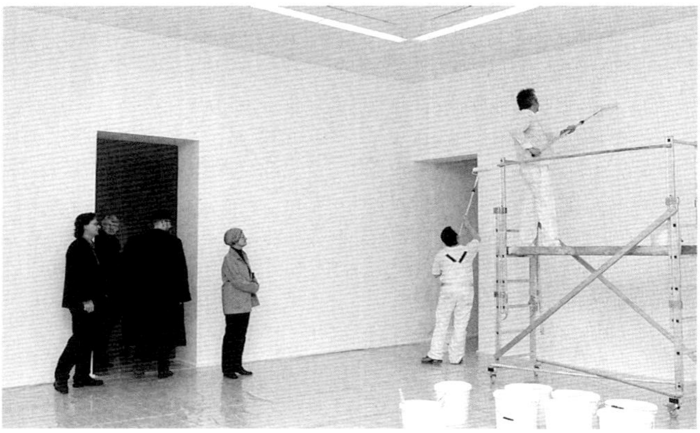
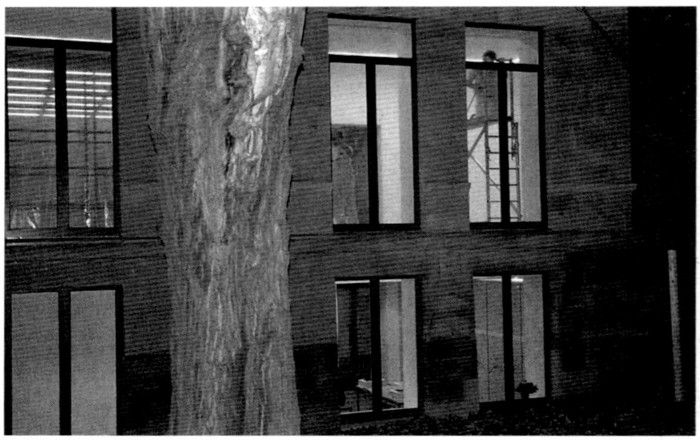
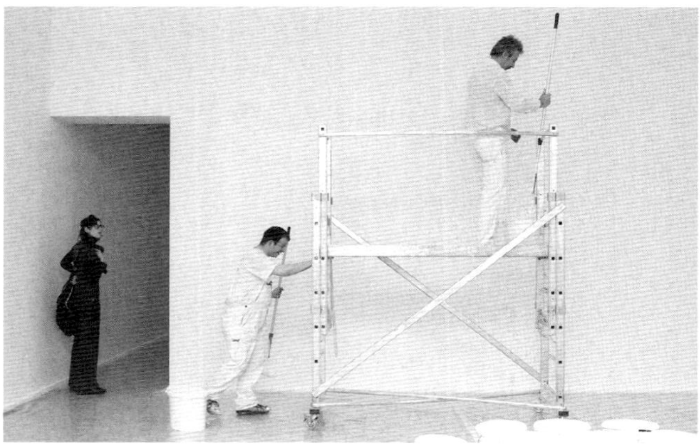
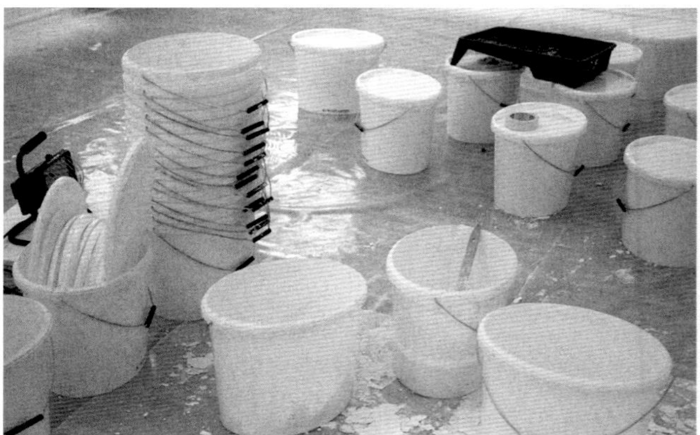

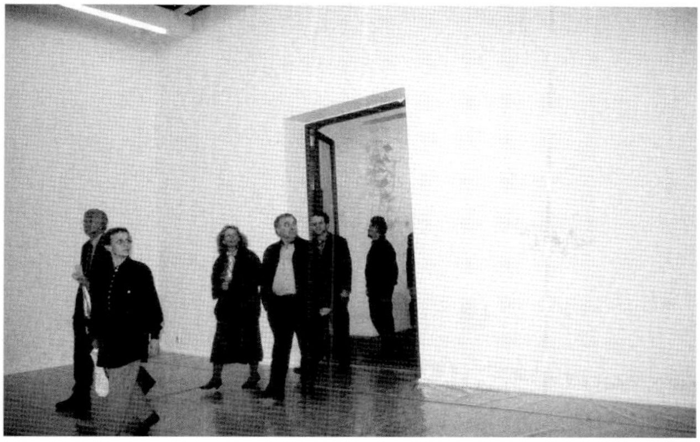
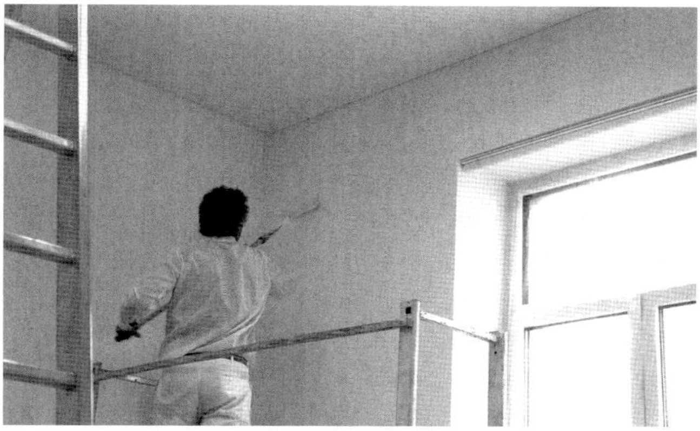
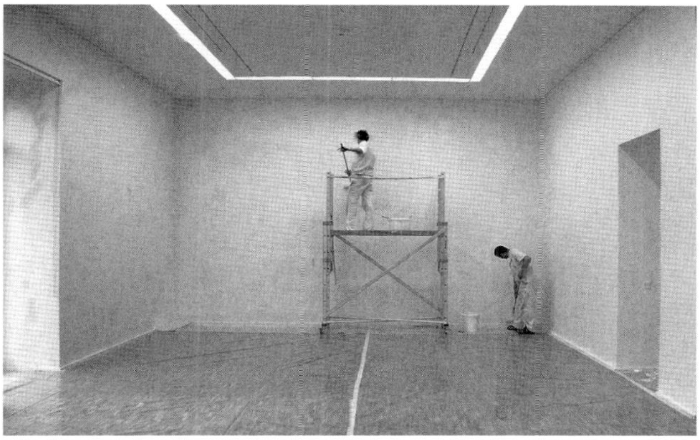
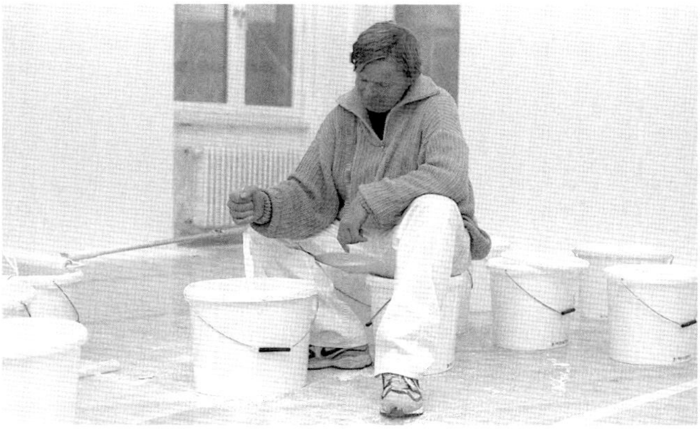
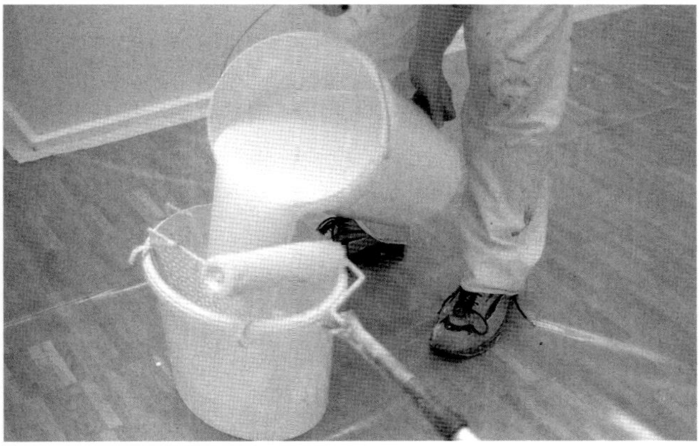
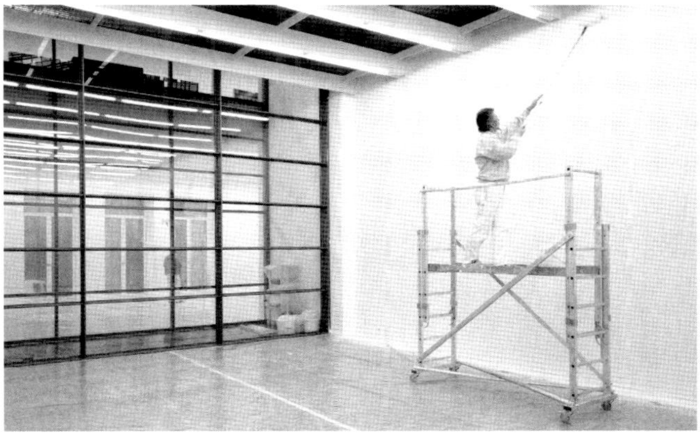
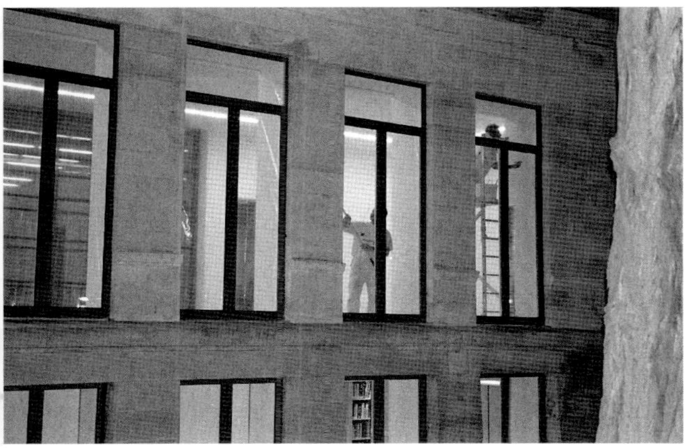
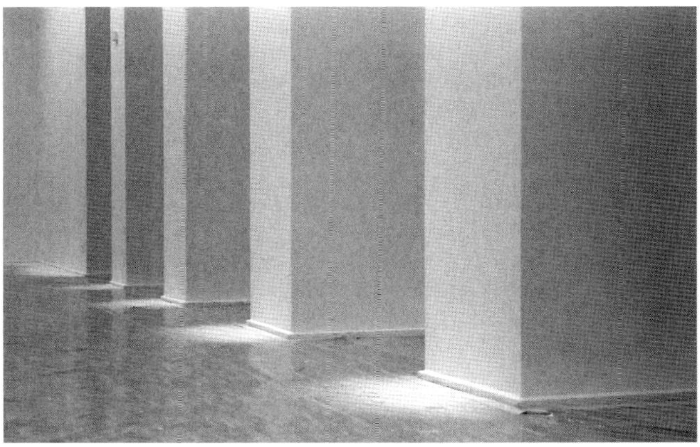

ausschließt, weil ihre Identität nicht in das öffentliche Bild passt, das man von ihnen zeichnet. Wenn man ein mittelloser Jugendlicher ohne Ausbildung ist, der Graffiti malt, hilft es einem nicht viel, dass die Gesellschaft homosexuelles Verhalten auf der Basis einer verdrehten Version christlicher Kleinfamilienwerte akzeptiert. Ein gutes Beispiel hierfür ist Giuliani, der Ex-Bürgermeister von New York, der behauptete, den Schwulen einen großen Gefallen damit zu tun, dass er die Sex-Treffs und die schmutzigen Bars in der Stadt schließen ließ. Ich habe mich furchtbar geärgert, als ich ihn 1999 an der Gay Pride Parade habe teilnehmen sehen. Eine andere Sache ist, dass der Kunstmarkt so genannte Minderheitenkünstler als Exotika benutzt, wie du gesagt hast: Künstler, die eingeladen werden, um dem langweiligen Hauptgericht mehr Würze zu geben. Seit Jahrzehnten besteht die Tendenz, diese Künstler als einen gemischten Chor hinter dem weißen, männlichen, heterosexuellen Meistersänger zu präsentieren. Kunstwerke, die ihren Ursprung außerhalb der europäischen Kunstgeschichte haben, sind nur dazu da, die zentrale Stellung dieser Tradition zu bestätigen. Diese »anderen« Künstler sollen nur den Rahmen und den Kontext für die Machtergreifung der dominanten Tradition abgeben. Darum erscheint es mir sinnvoll, auf die Ästhetik der Moderne zurückzugreifen: um die Veränderungen aus dem System heraus herbeizuführen. Und diese Ästhetik ist auch die, mit der ich aufgewachsen bin, mit der ich mein ganzes Leben lang zu tun hatte. Wenn man aus Skandinavien kommt, gehören Minimalismus und Funktionalismus zum Alltag.
C.F.: Du hast gesagt, eure Verwendung des Vokabulars des Minimalismus richte sich gegen das Klischee, dass schwule Kunst kitschig und tuntig sei. Was tragen eure sehr methodischen, unaufdringlichen, repetitiven Anstrengungen als Performance-Künstler zu diesem Prozess einer Neudefinition einer schwulen Ästhetik bei?

from the inside, the pristine setting at some points during the performance reminds you of a white cube, but at other times it looks completely trashy. A very simple set-up is combined here with a very simple activity, but together, as a statement, it becomes pretty complex. You have different situations created simultaneously: the artists trapped inside their own work—framed by a glass façade. This façade divides them from the audience, but at the same time the glass mirrors the audience and also the space (white cube,) in which it is situated. The audience finds itself trapped in between an ever-changing, reflexive space and the familiar, conforming exhibition space. Mainly, the performance questions—on different levels—the conception of the neutrality of the white cube. But it is also open to other readings. Bill Arning has extended the post-Pollock theory of the painterly drip being an equivalent to the male ejaculation into allegorizing this performance with a gay jack-off party. Hopefully, our contribution to redefining gay aesthetics might be that of offering a path of transition, of suggesting possibilities of change. We are looking for strategies that do not hold people in place and that suggest that any aesthetics might potentially be gay.
C.F.: In some of your pieces you borrow from the vocabulary of women's work (that is, domestic labor), a strategy that was also used extensively by feminist artists in the seventies. You also revive the repetitive gestural strategies of seventies body art, now infused in your pieces with more obvious social content. What is it about these tactics that draws you to them?
I.D.: There is something very fascinating about the early feminist strategy of bringing domestic work and work traditionally rendered feminine to the altars of high art. They were infusing with value what had been thought of as second-rate labor, activities and things that were thought of as useless and worthless. These artists were, in a sense, allowing

certain things to "take place." We are now also referring to the title of this very book and our show at the Kunsthalle Zürich, Taking Place. In a similarly subversive way, with the emergence of body art the body itself was claimed as a fully useful material, a language, a medium for expressing one's ideas artistically. It is exactly this act of transforming "worthless" into "valuable" within a system that has been relevant to us.

C.F.: Regarding the performance Twelve Hours of White Paint *and its evolution into* Between Other Events*, how is the work transformed by your giving away the performance to local workers? I have commented on this piece in another essay in which I point out that your doing this in Leipzig adds a level of social commentary to your work on the labor situation there, the role of global art events in presenting spectacles of wealth and plenitude in places where local economies are quite depressed. What is your view about this?*

I.D.: In Between Other Events *we wanted to avoid any reference to the discourse connected to the artist-as-subject and the artist's body being present in the work. In* Twelve Hours of White Paint *we were in the work as ourselves, as two artists and as a gay couple. This live installation and the related* Powerless Structures, Fig. 44, *in which we continuously painted the inside of a glass box white and wash it down again, have since been included in painting exhibitions. We gave the agency of this process of painting a space over and over again away to two unemployed professional house painters so the actual act of painting would never be read into the field of painting as an artistic expression.*

C.F.: But doesn't putting working-class men on display in a gallery make them and their painting into an aesthetic spectacle? There certainly is a history of aestheticizing manual labor within art, ranging from its glorification by Social Realists to the mimicry of the working man's persona by

I.D.: Es stimmt, dass die visuelle Kultur der Schwulen größtenteils immer noch auf einer Kitsch-und-Tunten-Ästhetik basiert. Andererseits ist die Schwulenszene, wie die städtische Jugendkulturszene überhaupt, in den letzten Jahren ziemlich edel geworden. In Restaurants, Bars, Klubs und Läden macht sich zunehmend eine Form von minimalistischer Ästhetik breit, in der diese zu einem minimalistischen Kitsch geworden ist – Minimalismus als Pop, als Stil und Glamour. Für uns war es wichtig, mit dem Minimalismus zu spielen und seine reduktiven Strategien zu verkehren. Auf minimalistische Oberflächen Schichten mit Darstellungscharakter aufzutragen und sie dadurch wieder aufzuladen. So haben wir zum Beispiel in Arbeiten wie *Cruising Pavilion/Powerless Structures, Fig. 55* und *Queer Bar/Powerless Structures, Fig. 21* Elemente, die glatt, weiß und straight sind, mit solchen verknüpft, die aus der Subkultur stammen wie Bars oder Sex-Treffs. In einer Performance wie *Powerless Structures, Fig. 44*, in der wir die ganze Zeit einen Glaskasten von innen anstreichen, erinnert dieser unverfälschte Raum an manchen Stellen der Performance an einen White Cube, aber manchmal sieht er auch völlig trashy aus. Hier wird eine sehr einfache Installation mit einer sehr einfachen Tätigkeit verknüpft, doch zusammengenommen, als Statement, wird das Ganze ziemlich komplex. Es werden gleichzeitig verschiedene Situationen geschaffen: Die Künstler sind in ihrem eigenen Werk gefangen – eingefasst von einer Glasfassade. Diese Fassade trennt sie vom Publikum, doch zugleich spiegelt sich das Publikum im Glas, wie auch der Raum (der White Cube), in dem es sich befindet. Das Publikum ist zwischen einem sich ständig wandelnden, reflektierenden Raum und dem vertrauten, sich anpassenden Ausstellungsraum gefangen. In erster Linie stellt die Performance – auf verschiedenen Ebenen – die Vorstellung von der Neutralität des White Cube in Frage. Doch sie lässt auch andere Lesarten zu. Bill Arning hat die post-pollocksche Theorie des malerischen Farbspritzers als Äquivalent zur männlichen Ejakulation dahingehend erweitert, dass er diese Performance als Allegorie einer schwulen Jack-off-Party aufgefasst hat. Wir hoffen, in der Weise zu einer Neudefinition einer schwulen Ästhetik beitragen zu können, dass wir einen Weg des Übergangs anbieten, Veränderungsmöglichkeiten zeigen. Wir suchen nach Strategien, die die Menschen nicht festnageln und die deutlich machen, dass jede Ästhetik potenziell schwul sein kann.

C.F.: In einigen Arbeiten greift ihr auf das Vokabular typischer Frauenarbeit zurück (das heißt der Hausarbeit), eine Taktik, die in den siebziger Jahren von vielen feministischen Künstlerinnen angewandt wurde. Auch die repetitiven gestischen Strategien der Body Art aus jener Zeit tauchen bei euch wieder auf, mit einem offensichtlichen gesellschaftlichen Inhalt. Was zieht euch an diesen Strategien an?

I.D.: Die in der Anfangszeit des Feminismus angewandte Strategie, die Hausarbeit und Arbeiten, die traditionell als weiblich gelten, auf den Altar der Kunst zu bringen, hat etwas sehr Faszinierendes. Sie haben etwas mit Wert aufgeladen, was als zweitrangige Arbeit galt, Tätigkeiten und Dinge, die man als sinnlos und wertlos ansah. In gewisser Hinsicht haben diese Künstlerinnen bestimmten Dingen erlaubt stattzufinden, Raum einzunehmen – »to take place« –, was auch als Verweis auf den Titel dieses Buches und unserer Ausstellung in der Kunsthalle Zürich gemeint ist. Auf eine ähnliche subversive Weise wurde der Körper mit dem Aufkommen der Body Art als ein im Ganzen nutzbares Material anerkannt, als eine Sprache, ein Medium, mit dem man seine Ideen künstlerisch ausdrücken kann. Es ist dieser Akt der Verwandlung von »Wertlosem« in etwas, das innerhalb eines Systems »wertvoll« ist, der für uns wichtig war.

C.F.: Inwiefern hat sich bei der Weiterentwicklung der

Minimalists such as Carl Andre. And doesn't the assumption that the fact of their being house painters would necessarily negate the aesthetic dimension of their painting seem a bit elitist? It is after all possible to judge the "quality" of house painting—and some professionals do it quite artfully. Many more house painters in the US at least are actually artists who make a living painting houses.

M.E.: We are certainly aware of the existing quality parameters in house painting. When somebody at one point asked one of the painters whether he didn't get bored by repeatedly painting the walls white, he gave a very professional reply: "You see this room has got four layers of white paint, and you notice the bluish tone in this space? The other room there has only got three layers, and if you look carefully enough you'll discover it has a slightly more greenish nuance." It's a bit ignorant to presume that artists per definition abuse what you might label as "ordinary" people—people in general have their own agendas, their own reasons for taking part in art events. I hate when artists do not show respect towards those they involve in their projects, whether it be other artists or anybody else. We all know that some are doing superficial projects in a field of mimicking the tradition of what has been called "social plastique"—artists who fly in for a couple of hours to make a tableau vivant with human beings exposed "as symptoms" and who don't even know the names of the participants or have the slightest interest in who those people are. It demands that you, I think, have a natural interest in other human beings, if you do projects involving others. The whole process must be much slower and sensitive than usual. We do these performative projects which involve a third party also because we are curious about what these will bring in terms of feedback from the participants—we simply want to learn something from those we involve. In Leipzig we got to know a lot about the former

GDR and the living conditions there and about painting—quite relevant to us as we aren't the most skilled ones when it comes to that. Sometimes a collaboration with someone from outside can even result in a permanent friendship, like it did after we had done a project in connection with the Manifesta 3 *exhibition.*

I.D.: Between Other Events *was conceived for the specific context of the Galerie für Zeitgenössische Kunst in Leipzig. While Leipzig's city center was totally renovated and pretty posh looking, the city has pretty grim unemployment statistics, and salaries were far less than in western Germany. Thousands of flats just stood empty. Our project commented very much on this situation. By using our production budget for the exhibition to employ two unemployed painters, a small change was created for a limited amount of time. We were also commenting on how our artistic product is a part of a particular art system. The useless, overdone renovation of the space took on a poetic, meditative character that sharply contrasted with the increasingly popular art spectacles happening all over the world. The exhibition halls got a break. In another project, for the European biennial* Manifesta 3 *in Ljubljana, we worked with a performative aspect in a completely different way. Here we erected a white cube space with one transparent glass wall in that city's Museum of Modern Art. There are no commercial galleries for young contemporary artists in Ljubljana, so three women from the local art scene volunteered to start up their own commercial gallery in our space. They got together a program of artists and organized five different solo shows for the duration of Manifesta. The whole exhibition situation with all the gallery routines was suddenly on display—the activity seemed to be staged or choreographed when you as a spectator watched what was going on through this glass wall.*

Performance *Twelve Hours of White Paint* zu *Zwischen anderen Ereignissen / Between Other Events* die Arbeit dadurch verändert, dass ihr die Performance von Leipzigern Arbeitern habt ausführen lassen? Zu dieser Aktion habe ich in einem Aufsatz geschrieben, dass die Tatsache, dass ihr so etwas in Leipzig macht, eure Arbeit um eine gesellschaftskritische Dimension erweitert, als Kommentar zu der dortigen Arbeitssituation und zur Rolle globaler Kunstveranstaltungen, die in ökonomisch schwachen Regionen ein Bild des Wohlstands und des Überflusses präsentieren. Was meint ihr selbst dazu?

I.D.: Bei *Zwischen anderen Ereignissen* wollten wir jeden Bezug zu dem Diskurs über den Künstler-als-Subjekt und die Präsenz des Körpers des Künstlers in der Arbeit vermeiden. Bei *Twelve Hours of White Paint* waren wir als wir selbst in der Arbeit präsent, als zwei Künstler und als schwules Paar. Diese Live-Installation und die mit ihr verwandte Arbeit *Powerless Structures, Fig. 44*, in der wir einen Glaskasten ununterbrochen von innen weiß angestrichen und die Farbe dann wieder abgewaschen haben, sind seitdem im Rahmen von Malerei-Ausstellungen gezeigt worden. Wir haben die Ausführung dieses Prozesses, bei dem ein Raum wieder und wieder gestrichen wird, zwei arbeitslosen professionellen Malern überlassen, sodass der tatsächliche Akt des Malens auf keinen Fall als etwas verstanden werden konnte, was in den Bereich der Malerei als einer Form des künstlerischen Ausdrucks fällt.

C.F.: Aber macht man nicht damit, dass man Arbeiter in einer Galerie zur Schau stellt, sie und ihre Tätigkeit als Maler zu einem ästhetischen Schauspiel? Zweifellos gibt es ja eine Geschichte der Ästhetisierung körperlicher Arbeit in der Kunst, die von deren Glorifizierung im Sozialistischen Realismus bis zur Nachahmung der Figur des Arbeiters durch Minimalisten wie Carl Andre reicht. Und ist es nicht ein

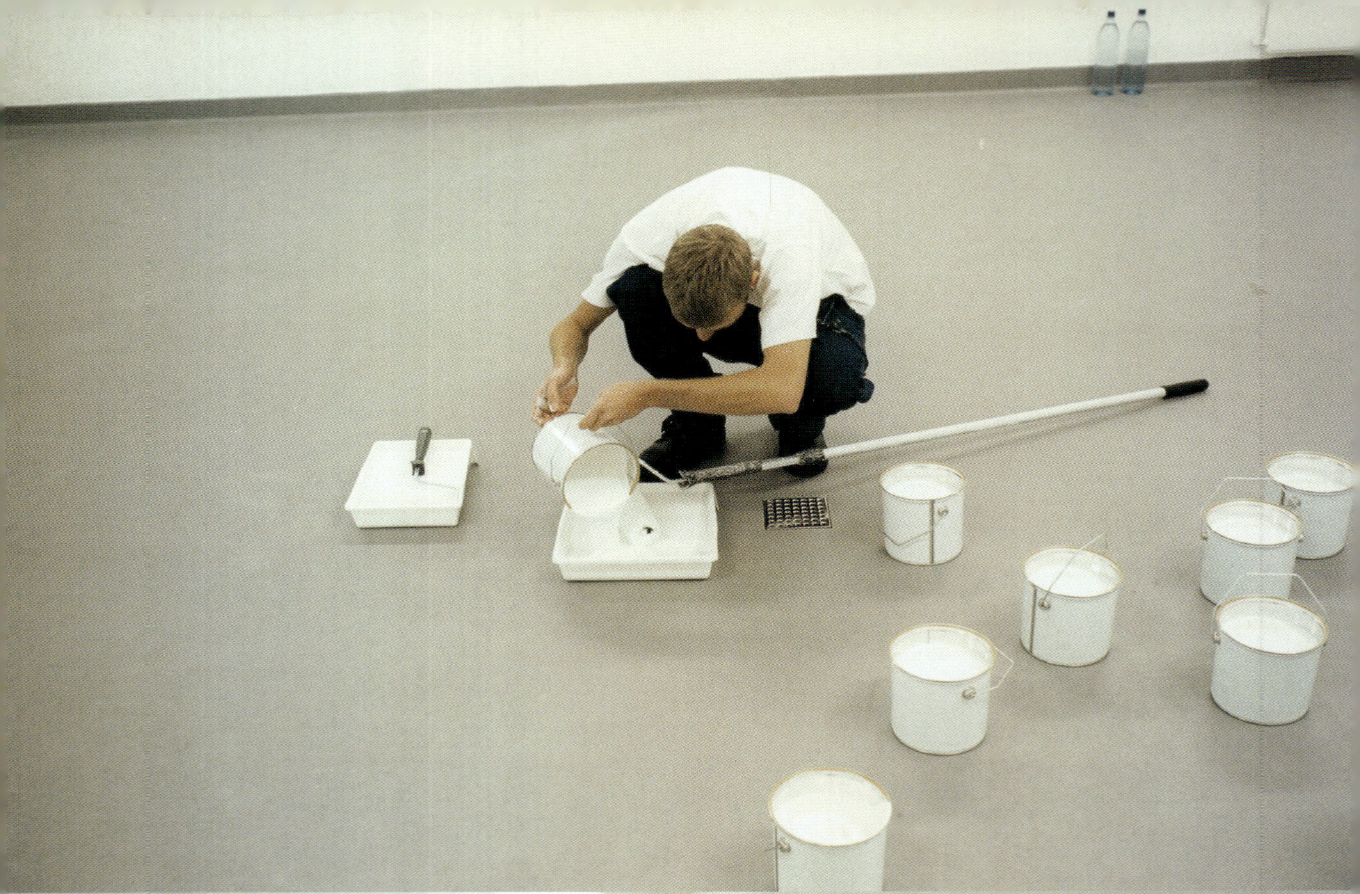

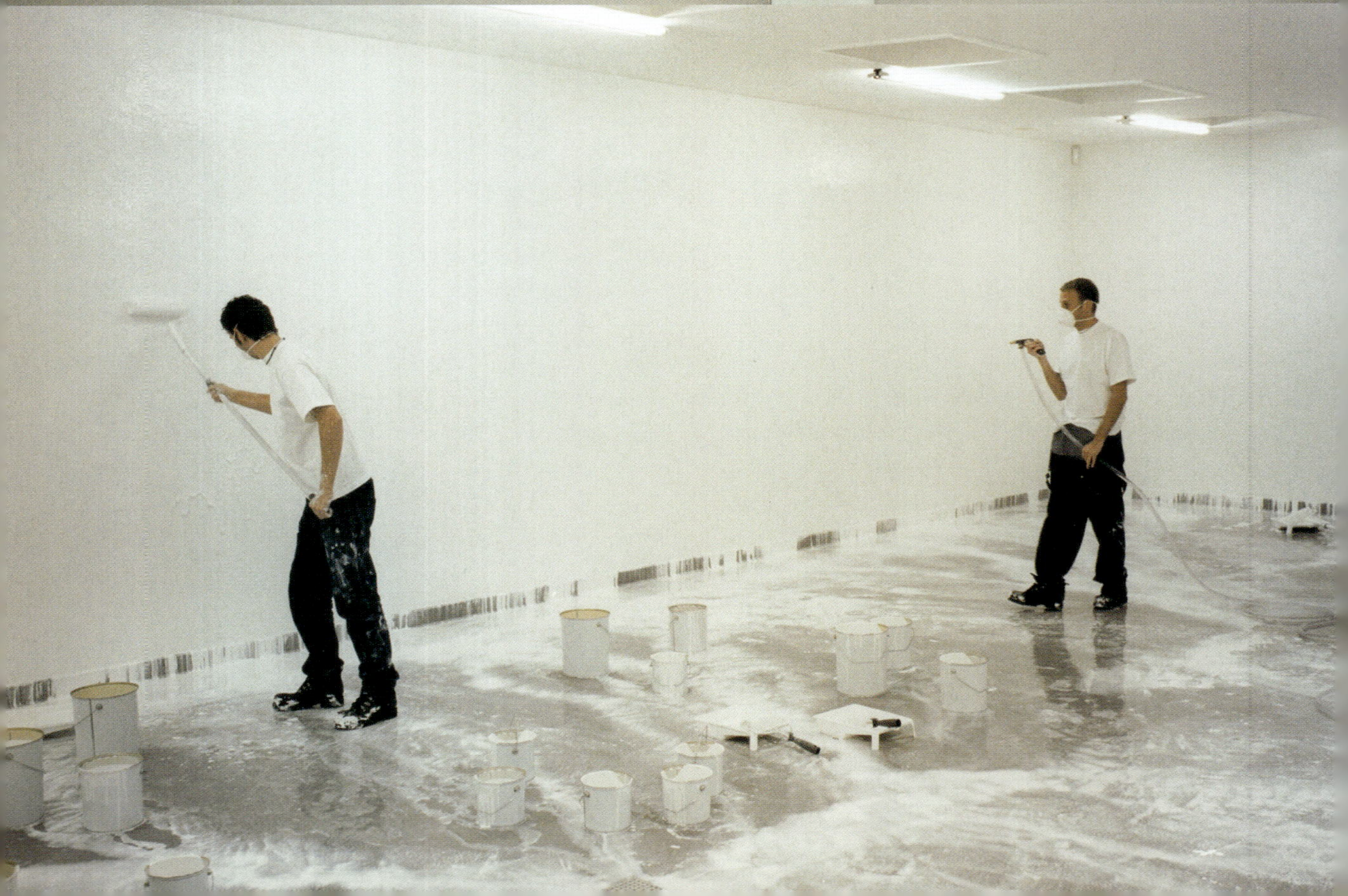

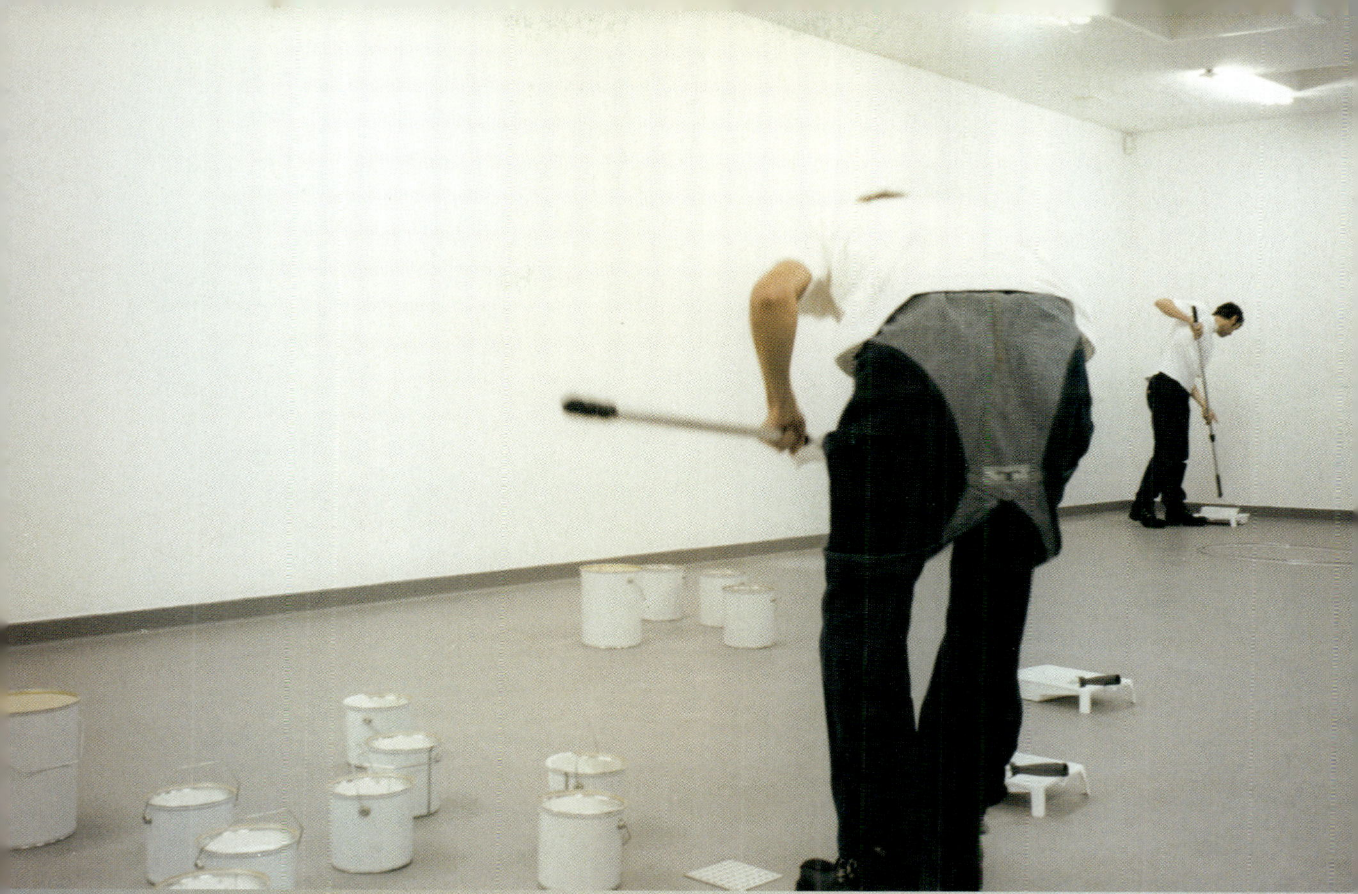

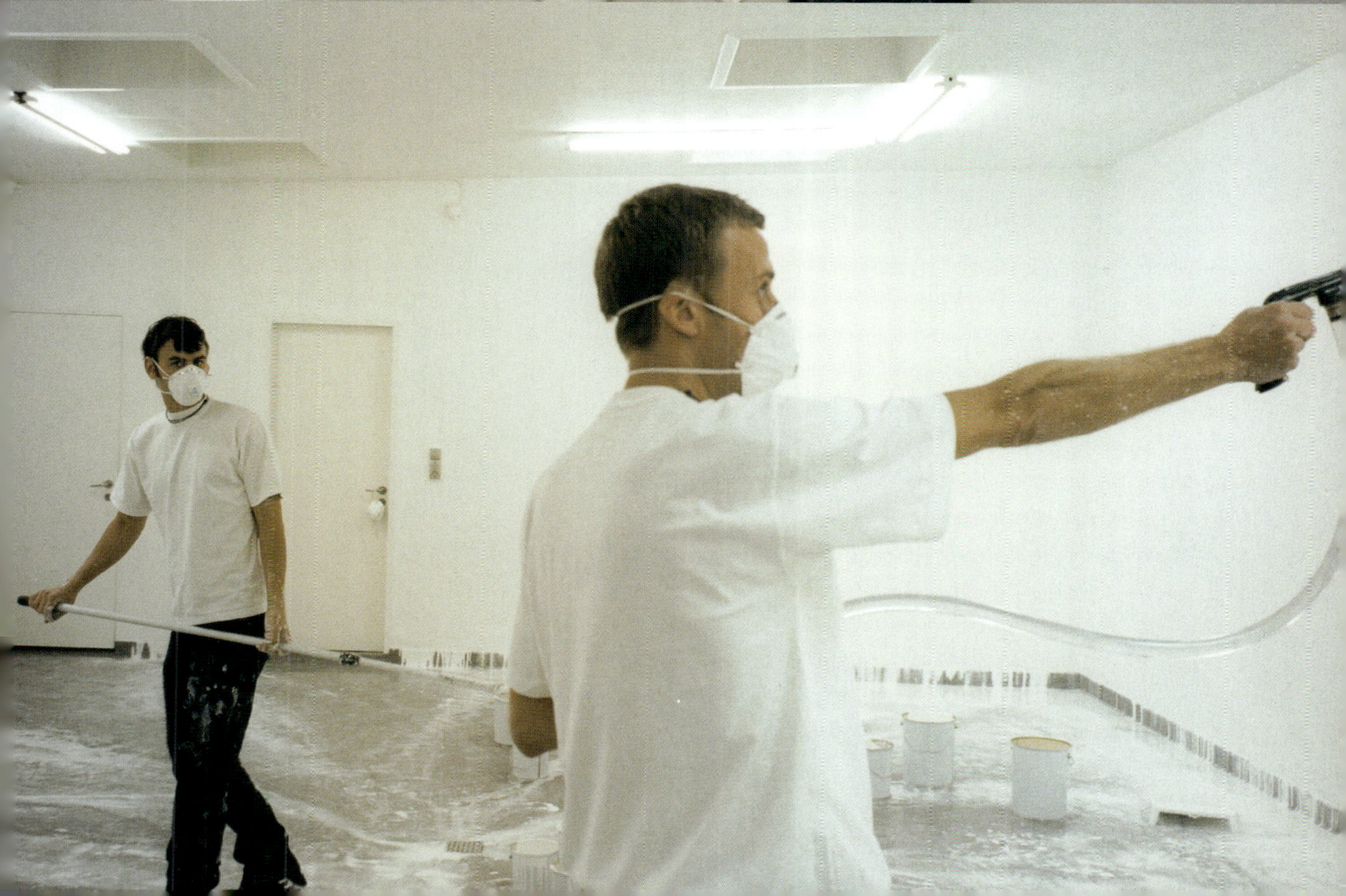

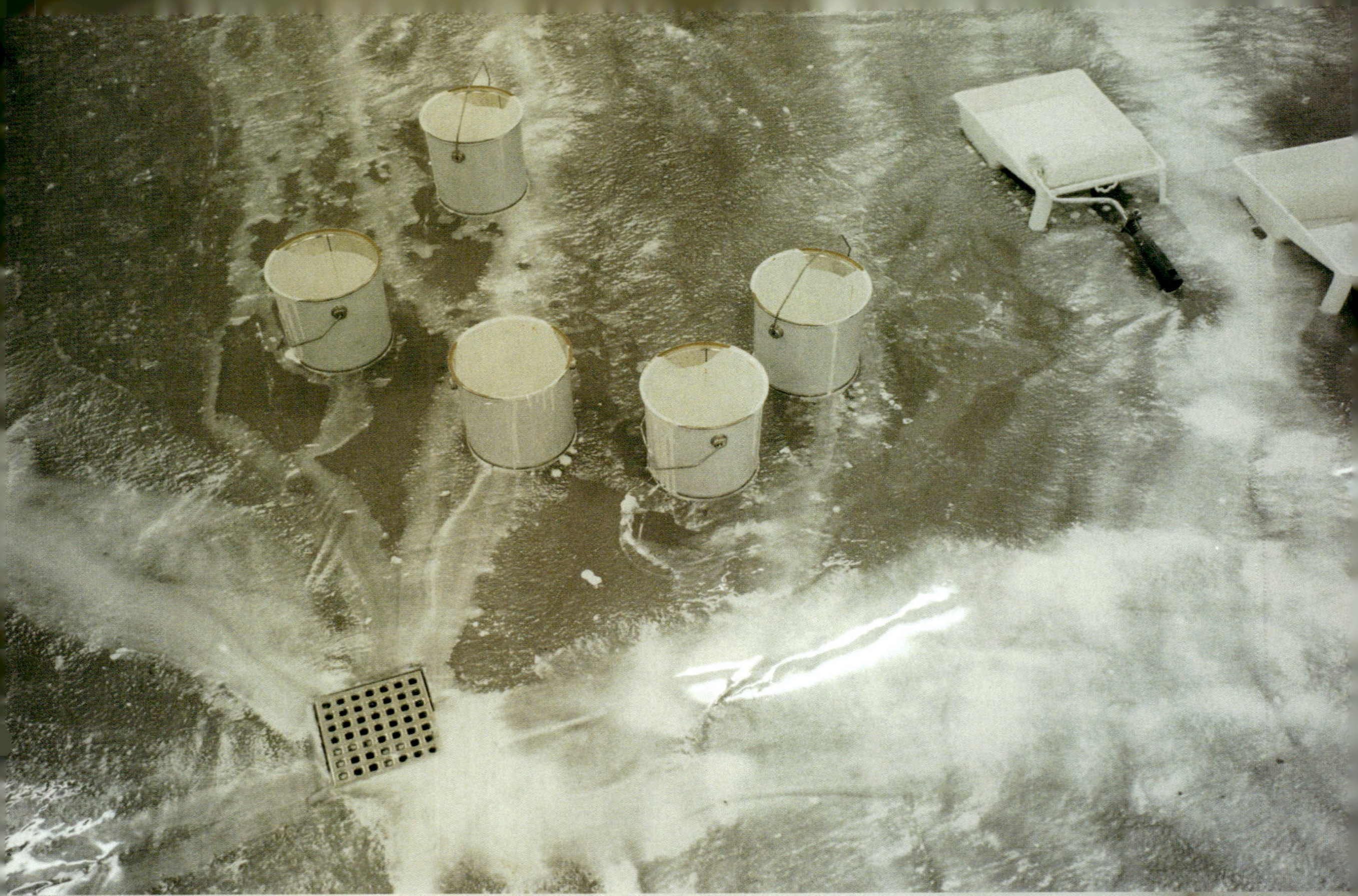

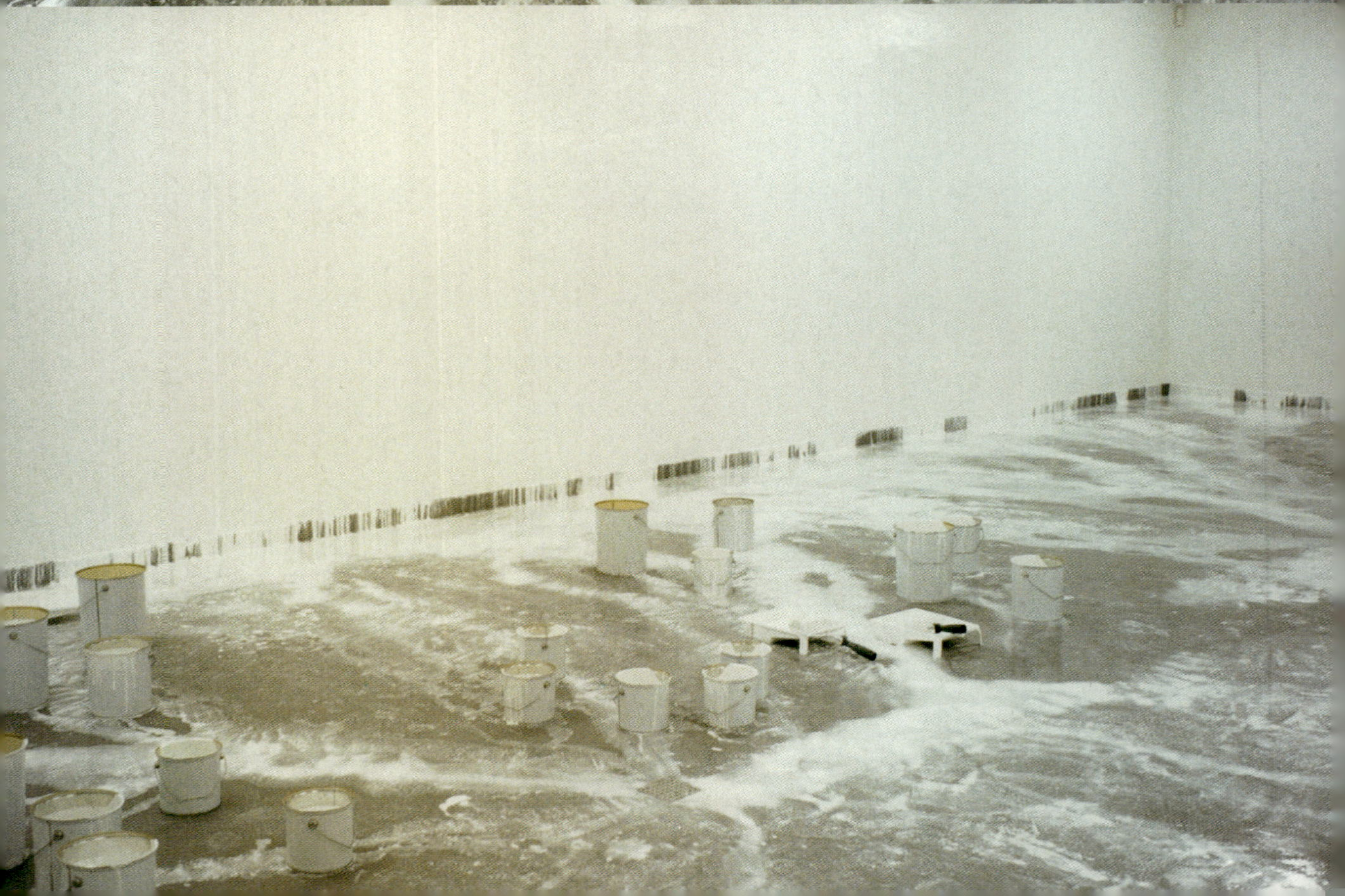

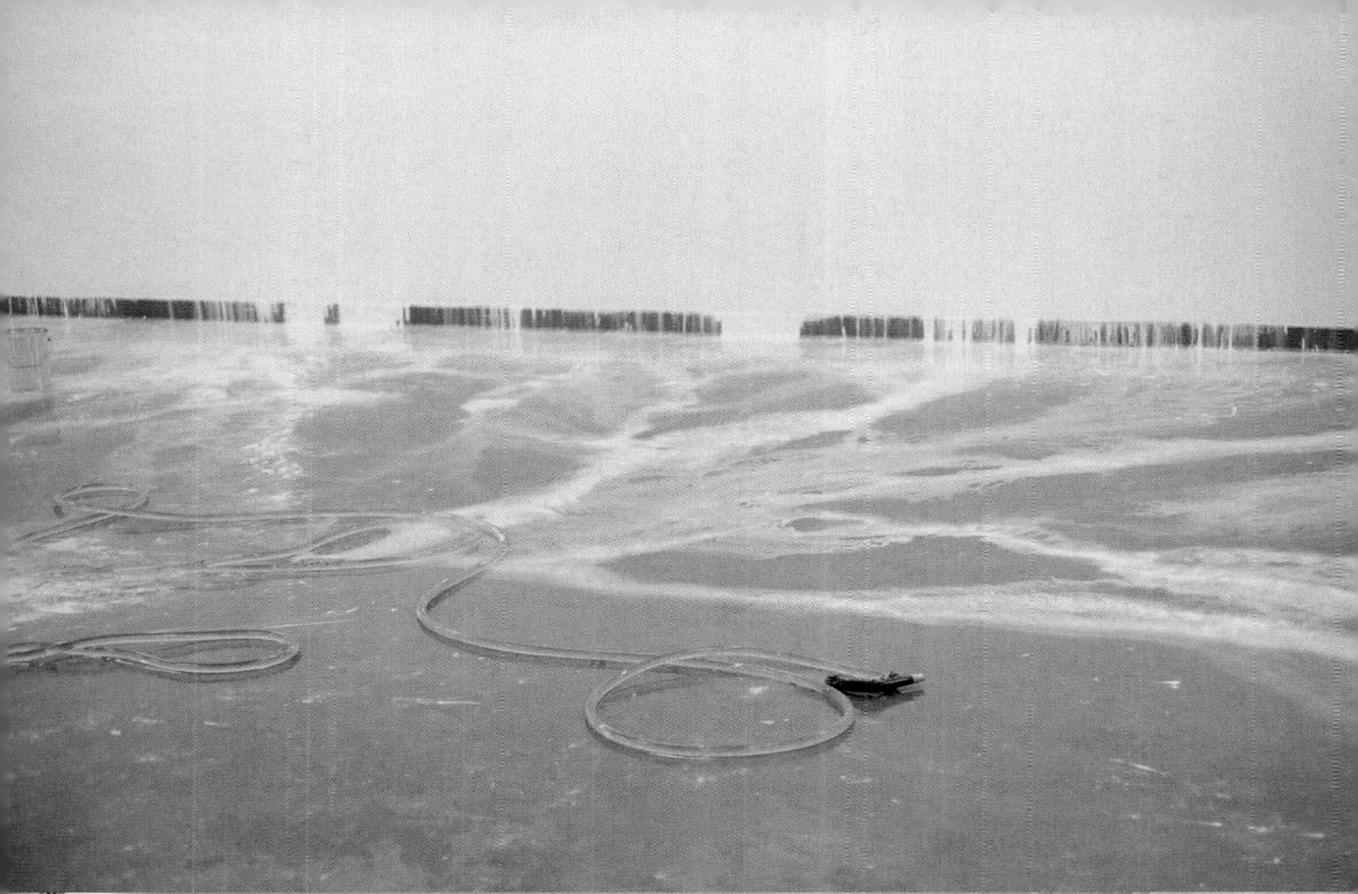

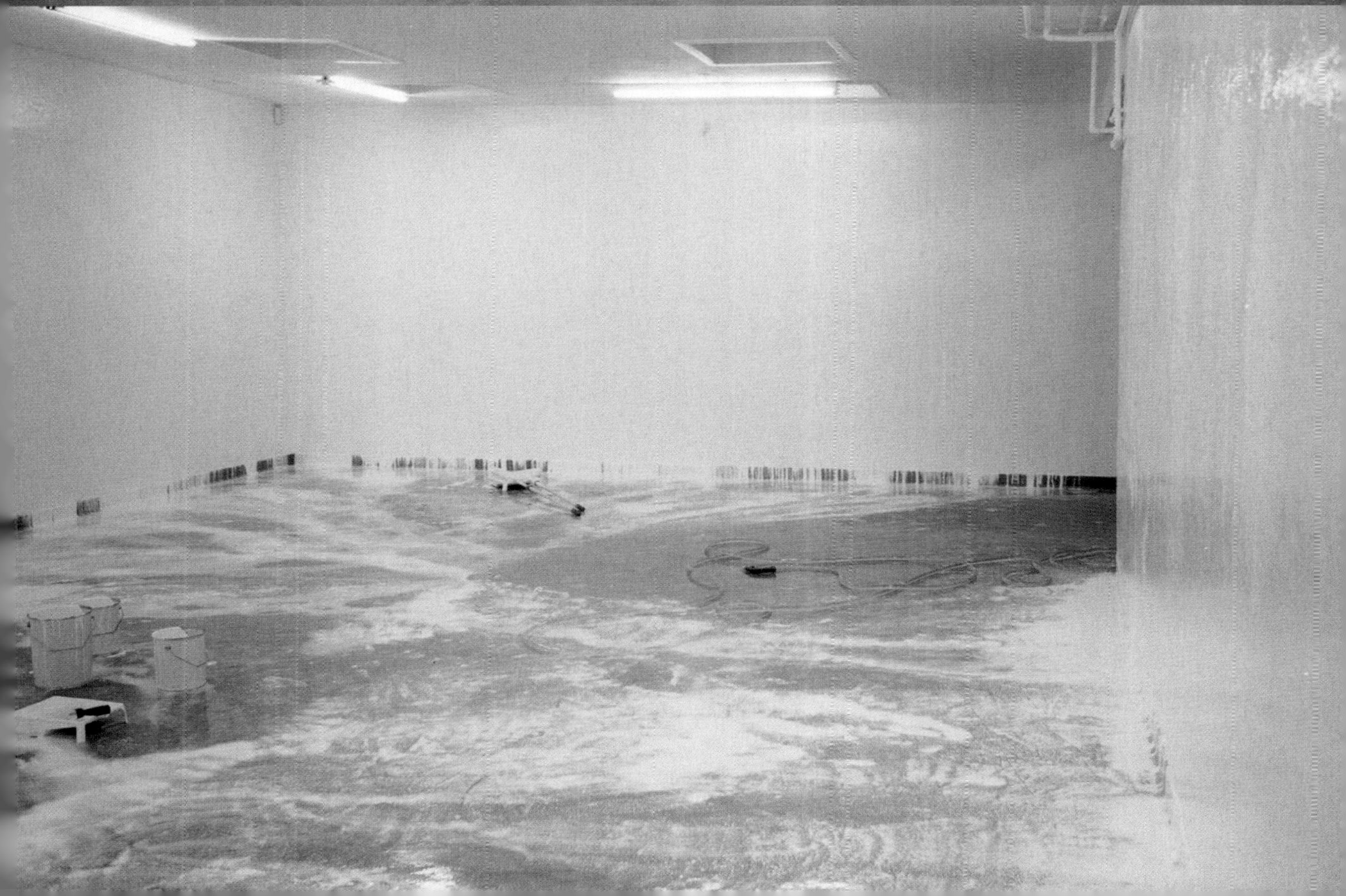

bisschen elitär zu glauben, dass die Tatsache, dass sie Handwerker sind, die ästhetische Dimension ihres Malens notwendigerweise negiert? Schließlich kann man die »Qualität« solcher Malerarbeiten beurteilen – und manche Profis führen sie ziemlich kunstvoll aus. Zumindest sind viele Anstreicher in den USA in Wirklichkeit Künstler, die sich mit dem Häuserstreichen ihr Brot verdienen.
M.E.: Uns ist durchaus bewusst, dass es im Hinblick auf Malerarbeiten bestimmte Qualitätsmaßstäbe gibt. Als einer der Maler irgendwann gefragt wurde, ob es ihm nicht langweilig werde, die Wände immer wieder weiß zu streichen, gab er die sehr professionelle Antwort: »Dieser Raum ist jetzt viermal gestrichen, und sehen Sie diesen bläulichen Ton? Der Raum da drüben ist nur dreimal gestrichen, und wenn Sie ganz genau hinsehen, werden Sie feststellen, dass er eher einen leichten Stich ins Grüne hat.« Es greift ein wenig zu kurz, anzunehmen, dass Künstler Leute, die man als gewöhnliche Menschen bezeichnen könnte, per definitionem missbrauchen – die Leute haben meist ihre eigenen Vorstellungen, ihre eigenen Gründe, die sie veranlassen, an einer Kunstveranstaltung teilzunehmen. Ich hasse es, wenn Künstler keinen Respekt vor den Leuten haben, die sie für ihre Projekte heranziehen, seien es nun andere Künstler oder irgendjemand sonst. Wir alle wissen, dass sich manche Künstler mit oberflächlichen Projekten beschäftigen, in denen sie die Tradition der so genannten sozialen Plastik imitieren – Künstler, die für ein paar Stunden an einen Ort fliegen und dort ein Tableau vivant mit Menschen aufbauen, die »als Symptome« hingestellt werden, wobei die Künstler nicht einmal die Namen der Teilnehmer kennen oder nicht das geringste Interesse daran haben, herauszufinden, wer diese Leute sind. Wenn man Projekte macht, an denen andere Leute beteiligt sind, ist es meiner Ansicht nach nötig, dass man ein natürliches Interesse an anderen Menschen hat. Das Ganze muss viel langsamer und sensibler ablaufen als

C.F.: You often mention that your installations and sculptures are designed to generate reflection on how social spaces define the parameters of social behavior, which is to say that they shape our performative selves. You also refer to how gay people have been compelled in a heterosexist society to reconfigure expected relations between space and performed selves. To make this point you rely on a basic element of Minimalism—which is theatricalized reception. In the case of your work, you use this element to trigger awareness of parallels with spaces outside the aesthetic domain. What I mean here is: what is the social significance of your drawing out this relationship between social codes in non-art spaces and social codes implied by your installations? What kind of social comment do you want to make?
I.D.: One intention is to try to sketch out, to improve on a small scale, in this almost model-like way, that changes are possible—and by challenging what might seem to be very authoritarian and static structures, we want to underline these structures' actual fragility—within both the cityscape and the art institutional system.
C.F.: I am curious about the possible heroic or triumphalist reading of this gesture because other critics have borrowed the wildly popular Deleuzian notion of the nomadic and deterritorialized self to describe your work. In other words, it has been argued that the potential for transformation that your spaces offer points to an anti-essentialist notion of being-in-process, of transitional modes of becoming. But are you suggesting that art can show us how to perform differently and thus change our relation to space? Or are you suggesting that social space is a kind of trap or game with clearly defined limits that we may struggle to transform, but can't? No one actually jumps off your diving board that pierces a window, for example, and your painters paint the same walls over and over without visibly "progressing." Your suspended and underground rooms are visible

but inaccessible, causing us to imagine action we cannot complete.

M.E.: The Danish art critic Lars Bang Larsen once wrote that our works are fucking up space because space is fucked up. So far nothing really indicates that anything or anybody will be able to provide the citizens of urban metropolises with more flexible public and private spaces than what we have now, or environments which are more suitable for the individual human needs and dreams. Within the urban landscape, man-made structures are unfortunately not becoming less restrictive. Public space is getting more and more limited, and profit interests are shaping our patterns of movements the minute we leave home. But we do have another kind of space, the imaginary space of our dreams and visions, and this mental space can be in constant transition, and to that we can appeal for progression and for expansion. However, we have succeeded in creating a few real architectural set-ups which have proved their ability, at least temporarily, to function differently than they would in their usual contexts. We made a pavilion in a Danish forest to host gay men's cruising activity. We made a small private gallery space inside a public art institution in Ljubljana. We made a transformable white cube, which was used as a platform for projects by the art students at the Städelschule in Frankfurt. I'm quite convinced that visual art is not the most suitable medium for actual political change in a broader sense, but art projects can catalyze some smaller changes or alter a few conditions for a group of people. A performance can add a new significance to a space that was meant for something else. You mention that the two painters from Leipzig make no difference, but painting the walls over and over again without anything happening—that is exactly what I think of as a pretty radical change in the spatial conditions of that place. The exhibition space emptied of all art objects. It got a break in a busy exhibition program. The rooms become

sonst. Wir machen diese performativen Projekte, an denen Dritte beteiligt sind, unter anderem auch deshalb, weil wir neugierig auf das Feedback von den Beteiligten sind – wir möchten ganz einfach etwas lernen von denen, die wir für unsere Arbeit heranziehen. In Leipzig haben wir viel über die frühere DDR und die Lebensbedingungen dort erfahren und auch über das Streichen – was für uns ziemlich wichtig ist, da wir in dieser Hinsicht nicht besonders geschickt sind. Manchmal kann die Zusammenarbeit mit jemandem, der von außen kommt, sogar zu einer bleibenden Freundschaft führen, wie es etwa bei unserem Projekt im Rahmen der *Manifesta 3* der Fall war.

I.D.: *Zwischen anderen Ereignissen* wurde speziell für den Kontext der Galerie für Zeitgenössische Kunst in Leipzig ausgearbeitet. Während das Stadtzentrum von Leipzig komplett restauriert worden ist und ziemlich schick aussieht, zeigt sich die Arbeitslosenstatistik der Stadt ziemlich finster, und die Gehälter liegen weit unter denen in Westdeutschland. Tausende von Wohnungen stehen einfach leer. Unser Projekt war in vielerlei Hinsicht ein Kommentar zu dieser Situation. Dadurch, dass wir unser Budget für die Ausstellung dazu verwendet haben, zwei arbeitslose Maler anzustellen, ist für einen begrenzten Zeitraum eine kleine Veränderung eingetreten. Zugleich war das Projekt ein Kommentar dazu, dass unser künstlerisches Produkt Teil eines bestimmten Kunstsystems ist. Die sinnlose, übertriebene Renovierung des Raumes nahm einen poetischen, meditativen Charakter an, der in einem scharfen Gegensatz zu den immer populärer werdenden Kunstspektakeln stand, die überall auf der Welt stattfinden. Die Ausstellungsräume durften eine Zeit lang pausieren. Bei einem anderen Projekt – für die europäische Biennale *Manifesta 3* in Ljubljana – haben wir in einer ganz anderen Weise mit einem performativen Aspekt gearbeitet. Dort haben wir im Museum of Modern Art einen White Cube mit einer durchsichtigen Glaswand errichtet. Es gibt in Ljubljana keine kommerziellen Galerien für junge zeitgenössische Künstler, und so haben sich drei Frauen aus der dortigen Kunstszene bereit erklärt, in unserem Raum ihre eigene kommerzielle Galerie aufzuziehen. Sie haben ein Programm mit verschiedenen Künstlern zusammengestellt und während der Dauer der *Manifesta* fünf Einzelausstellungen organisiert. Auf einmal wurde die ganze Ausstellungssituation mit der Alltagsroutine in einer Galerie selbst ausgestellt – wenn man sich als Zuschauer ansah, was dort hinter der Glaswand vor sich ging, hatte man den Eindruck, diese Tätigkeiten wären inszeniert oder folgten einer bestimmten Choreografie.

C.F.: Ihr habt oft erklärt, dass eure Installationen und Skulpturen zur Reflexion darüber anregen sollen, wie gesellschaftliche Räume die Parameter unseres sozialen Verhaltens bestimmen, das heißt, wie sie unser performatives Ich prägen. Außerdem habt ihr darauf hingewiesen, dass Schwule in einer heterosexistischen Gesellschaft gezwungen werden, die gewohnten Verhältnisse zwischen dem Raum und dem performativen Ich neu zu gestalten. Um das deutlich zu machen, stützt ihr euch auf ein Grundelement des Minimalismus: die theatralisierte Rezeption. In euren Arbeiten benutzt ihr dieses Element, um ein Bewusstsein für die Parallelen zu Räumen außerhalb des ästhetischen Bereichs zu erzeugen. Was ich sagen will, ist: Welche gesellschaftliche Bedeutung hat euer Herausarbeiten dieser Beziehung zwischen sozialen Codes in Räumen, die nichts mit Kunst zu tun haben, und den sozialen Codes in euren Installationen? Was wollt ihr damit im Hinblick auf die Gesellschaft sagen?

I.D.: Unser Ziel ist es, andeutungsweise, in verkleinertem Maßstab – sozusagen am Modell – zu zeigen, dass Veränderungen möglich sind. Und indem wir Strukturen angreifen, die sehr autoritär und sehr statisch zu sein scheinen, möchten wir unterstreichen, dass diese Strukturen in

something more than discrete art containers. The painting was like an endless ritual, a process severed from the efficiency one would normally associate with this kind of labor.

Space has become so functional and standardized in its design and city planning has become so uniform that it is no longer meant for anyone. Political authorities freak out these days if a Turkish family is barbecuing in the Tiergarten, one of the few green areas in Berlin. Kids get sent to prison if they are caught writing graffiti. Gay men are harassed if they are jerking off together behind some bushes in a park. The social construction of space and the control of social activity in public space is a primary source of alienation among urban populations. In both our performances and in our installations, we hope to specify and humanize various overly rigid environments just a bit.

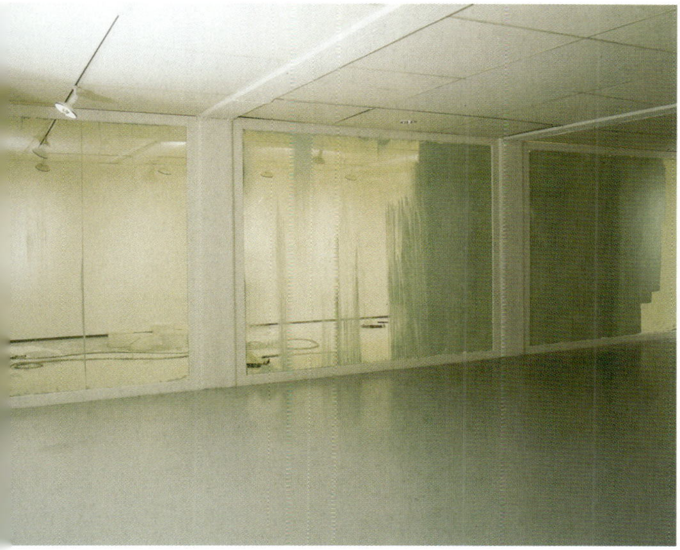

Wirklichkeit sehr fragil sind – sowohl im städtischen Raum als auch innerhalb des institutionellen Systems der Kunst.
C.F.: Mich interessiert die mögliche heroische oder triumphalische Deutung dieser Geste, denn andere Kritiker haben, um eure Kunst zu beschreiben, auf Deleuzes äußerst populäre Vorstellung des nomadischen und des deterritorialisierten Ichs zurückgegriffen. Mit anderen Worten, es ist behauptet worden, dass das Transformationspotenzial, das eure Räume enthalten, auf eine anti-essenzialistische Vorstellung von einem Im-Prozess-Sein, von Übergangsformen des Werdens verweist. Aber meint ihr, die Kunst kann uns zeigen, wie wir uns anders verhalten und dadurch unser Verhältnis zum Raum verändern können? Oder wollt ihr damit sagen, dass der soziale Raum eine Art Falle ist oder ein Spiel mit klar definierten Grenzen, an dem wir, sosehr wir es auch versuchen, nichts ändern können? So springt zum Beispiel niemand wirklich von eurem Sprungbrett, das durch ein Fenster hindurchgeht, und eure Maler streichen dieselben Wände wieder und wieder, ohne einen sichtbaren »Fortschritt«. Eure aufgehängten und eingegrabenen Räume sind zwar sichtbar, aber nicht zugänglich und wecken in uns die Vorstellung einer Handlung, die wir nicht ausführen können.
M.E.: Der dänische Kunstkritiker Lars Bang Larsen hat einmal geschrieben, unsere Arbeiten würden den Raum kaputtmachen, weil der Raum kaputt sei. Bis jetzt deutet nichts darauf hin, dass irgendetwas oder irgendjemand in der Lage sein wird, den Bewohnern von Großstädten öffentliche und private Räume zur Verfügung zu stellen, die flexibler sind als die, die wir haben, oder eine Umgebung, die den individuellen Bedürfnissen und Träumen der Menschen eher entspricht. Was den städtischen Raum betrifft, werden die von Menschen geschaffenen Strukturen leider keineswegs weniger restriktiv. Der öffentliche Raum wird immer begrenzter, und sobald wir das Haus verlassen, werden unsere

Bewegungsmuster von wirtschaftlichen Interessen bestimmt. Doch es gibt noch einen anderen Raum, den imaginären Raum unserer Träume und Visionen, und dieser geistige Raum kann sich beständig verändern, und auf diesen können wir unsere Forderung nach Fortschritt und Erweiterung beziehen. Aber wie dem auch sei, wir haben doch einige reale architektonische Bauten errichten können, die sich zumindest vorübergehend als fähig erwiesen haben, anders zu funktionieren, als sie es in ihrem gewohnten Kontext täten. So haben wir in Dänemark in einem Wald einen Pavillon aufgebaut, der eine Cruising Area für Schwule ist. In Ljubljana haben wir in einer öffentlichen Kunstinstitution eine kleine private Galerie installiert. Wir haben einen verwandelbaren White Cube geschaffen, der von Kunststudenten der Städelschule in Frankfurt als Plattform für ihre Projekte benutzt wurde. Ich bin mir ziemlich sicher, dass Kunst nicht das beste Medium ist, um auf breiterer Ebene wirkliche politische Veränderungen zu erreichen, aber Kunstprojekte können der Auslöser für kleinere Veränderungen sein oder die Lebensbedingungen einer bestimmten Gruppe von Menschen in begrenztem Maße verändern. Eine Performance kann einen Raum, der zu etwas anderem bestimmt war, um eine neue Bedeutungsdimension erweitern. Du sagst, die beiden Leipziger Maler würden keinen Unterschied machen, sondern nur wieder und wieder die Wände streichen, ohne dass etwas passiert – genau das halte ich für eine ziemlich radikale Veränderung hinsichtlich der räumlichen Bedingungen jenes Ortes. Ausstellungsräume ohne irgendein Kunstwerk darin. Es war wie eine Pause in einem dichten Ausstellungsprogramm. Die Räume wurden plötzlich zu etwas mehr als nur diskrete Behältnisse für Kunst. Das Streichen war wie ein endloses Ritual, ein Prozess, der losgelöst war von der Effizienz, die man normalerweise mit dieser Art von Arbeit

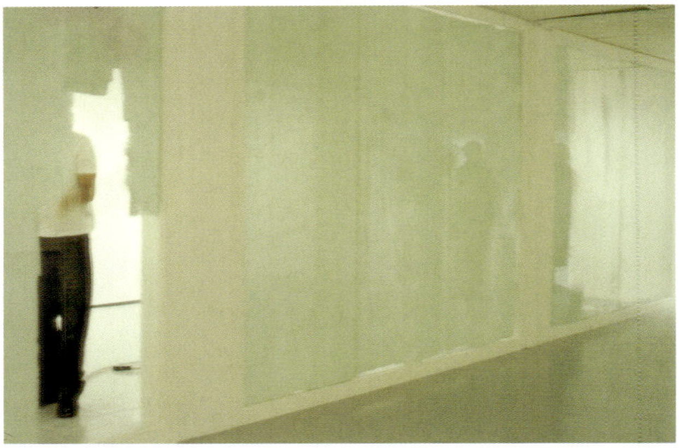

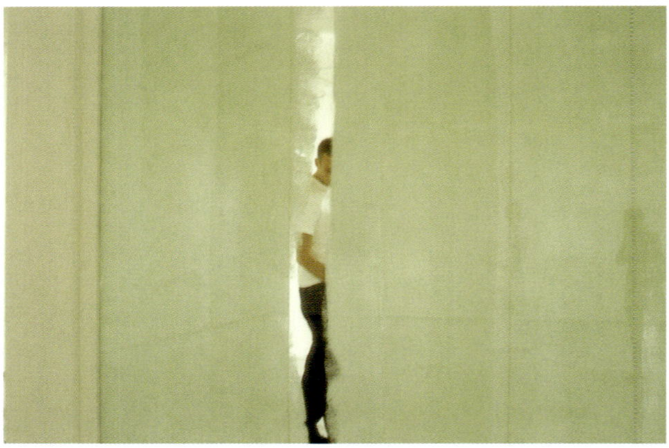

verbindet. Der Raum ist so sehr funktionalisiert und von der Gestaltung her so sehr standardisiert worden, und die Stadtplanung ist so einförmig geworden, dass er für niemanden mehr bestimmt ist. Heutzutage drehen die Behörden durch, wenn eine türkische Familie im Tiergarten grillt – eine der wenigen Grünzonen in Berlin. Jugendliche werden ins Gefängnis gesteckt, wenn sie beim Graffiti-Sprühen erwischt werden. Schwule werden schikaniert, wenn sie sich in einem Park hinter den Büschen gemeinsam einen runterholen. Die gesellschaftliche Gestaltung des Raumes und die Kontrolle der sozialen Aktivität im öffentlichen Raum sind ein Hauptgrund der Entfremdung innerhalb der städtischen Einwohnerschaft. Sowohl mit unseren Performances als auch mit unseren Installationen hoffen wir, verschiedene allzu festgeschriebene Räume zu benennen und ein klein wenig menschlicher zu machen.

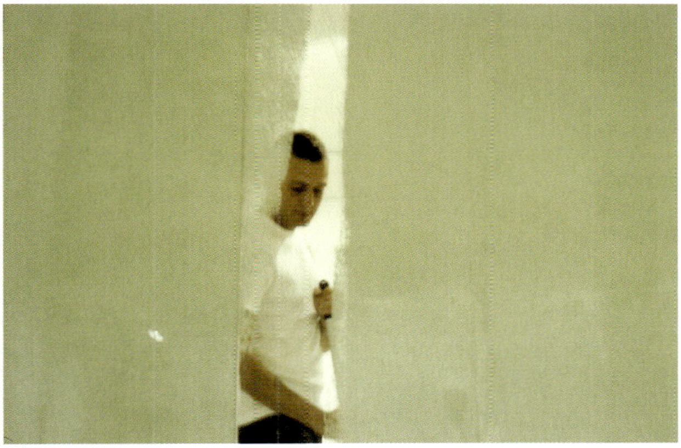

seite | page 39–42

Powerless Structures, Fig. 44, 1998

Glas, Stahl, Farbe, Malerwerkzeug /
Glass, steel, paint, painting tools
230 x 500 x 500 cm
Performance, Kunstnernes Hus, Oslo, 1999
Photo: Martine Castoriano
Courtesy Tanya Bonakdar Gallery, New York;
Klosterfelde, Berlin; Galleri Nicolai Wallner,
København

seite | page 46–47, 49–51

Powerless Structures, Fig. 44, 1998

Glas, Stahl, Farbe, Malerwerkzeug /
Glass, steel, paint, painting tools
230 x 600 x 600 cm
Performance, Wiener Secession, Wien
Photo: Pez Hejduk
Courtesy Tanya Bonakdar Gallery, New York;
Klosterfelde, Berlin; Galleri Nicolai Wallner,
København

seite | page 54–57

Zwischen anderen Ereignissen / Between Other Events, 2000

Ortsbezogenes Projekt / Site-specific project,
Galerie für Zeitgenössische Kunst, Leipzig
Photo: PUNCTUM / H.-Ch. Schink
Photo: Carla Åhlander
Courtesy Tanya Bonakdar Gallery, New York;
Klosterfelde, Berlin; Galleri Nicolai Wallner,
København

seite | page 62–65

Twelve Hours of White Paint/ Powerless Structures, Fig. 15, 1997

160 Liter Farbe, Malerwerkzeug, Wasserschlauch /
160 liters of paint, painting tools, water hose
Performance, Galleri Tommy Lund, Odense
Photo: Leif Hansen
Courtesy: Elmgreen & Dragset

seite | page 69–71

Powerless Structures, Fig 144, 2000

Glas, Stahl, weiße Farbe, Malerwerkzeug /
Glass, steel, white paint, painting tools
250 x 750 cm
Performance, Rooseum, Malmö
Photo: Jan Engsmar
Photo: Petra Bauer
Courtesy Tanya Bonakdar Gallery, New York;
Klosterfelde, Berlin; Galleri Nicolai Wallner,
København

Arbeit am White Cube
Work on the White Cube

Die *Powerless Structures* des Künstlerpaares Michael Elmgreen & Ingar Dragset – die ins Paradoxe perpetuierte Ausmalung eines Ausstellungsraumes, die Umfunktionierung eines Galeriebetriebes in einen Barbetrieb, der Einbau eines Galerieraumes in einen Museumsraum – stehen nicht voraussetzungslos im aktuellen Kunstbetrieb, sondern reihen sich ein in die Tradition der theoretischen und künstlerischen Auseinandersetzung mit einem Phänomen des 20. Jahrhunderts, das lange unbeachtet blieb, jedoch die Entfaltung der Modernen Kunst erst ermöglichte: mit dem weißen Galerieraum – besser bekannt unter dem Namen White Cube[1].

Schauplatz Leipzig, Galerie für zeitgenössische Kunst am 6. Februar im Jahre 2000: Zwei arbeitslose Anstreicher mit Namen Richter und Rothe beginnen im Auftrag der beiden Künstler die weißen Ausstellungshallen mit weißer Farbe auszumalen: Decken, Wände und Fensterleibungen. Verdutzte Vernissagegäste fragen sich, ob sie sich im Datum auf der Einladungskarte verguckt haben. Ist die Ausstellung noch nicht fertig, ja sind die Kunstwerke noch nicht da? Beherzt wendet sich ein Besucher an einen Arbeiter auf dem Gerüst, was er denn da mache. »Wir malen«, war die lapidare Antwort. »Aber soll das etwa Kunst sein?«, »Ja sicher, wir malen ja.« Die Episode fasst anschaulich die drei Grundprinzipen des dänisch-norwegischen Künstlerpaares zusammen: Arbeit am White Cube, die Sichtbarmachung dieser Arbeit als künstlerische Performance und die widersprüchliche Verknüpfung der Funktionen von Inhalt und Rahmen, Text und Kontext. Im Laufe der siebenwöchigen Ausstellung werden die Oberflächen des Galerieraumes noch 35 mal weiß gestrichen mit dem paradoxen Ergebnis, dass am Ende die Räume für die nächste Ausstellung renoviert werden müssen. »Durch Pflege zerstört«, könnte man mit Lucius Burckhardt diese Aktion kommentieren. Was von dieser gewitzten Unternehmung übrig bleibt, ist ein kritisches

The Powerless Structures *of the artist duo Michael Elmgreen & Ingar Dragset—their repetitious painting of an exhibition room culminating in paradox, their conversion of a gallery space into a bar setting, the construction of a gallery room inside a museum room—are not without precedent in contemporary art. Indeed, they are part of a tradition of theoretical and practical artistic concern with a 20th-century phenomenon which, though long neglected, was nonetheless a prerequisite for the development of modern art: the white gallery space—better known as the White Cube.[1]*
February 6, 2000: The scene is the Galerie für zeitgenössische Kunst in Leipzig. Two unemployed house painters named Richter and Rothe begin coating the white exhibition rooms with white paint as requested by the two artists—ceilings, walls, and window bays. Puzzled guests at the opening wonder whether they have misread the date on their invitations. Isn't the exhibition ready? Haven't the works of art arrived yet? One visitor turns to a worker standing on the scaffolding and asks what he is doing. "We're painting," he answers laconically. "But is that supposed to be art?" "Well, of course. We're painting, aren't we?" This episode vividly illustrates the three fundamental principles of the Danish-Norwegian artist duo: work on the White Cube, the visualization of that work as artistic performance, and the contradictory linking of the functions of content and framework, text and context. In the course of the seven-week exhibition, the surfaces of the gallery room were given thirty-five more coats of white paint, the paradoxical outcome being that it then had to be renovated. One might say that it had been "destroyed by care," to quote Lucius Burkhardt. What remains of this witty undertaking is a critical reflection on the conventions governing the making, exhibiting, and viewing of art, conventions for which the 20th-century art business "invented" the seemingly so neutral box known as the White Cube, whose supposed innocence has been the object of considerable

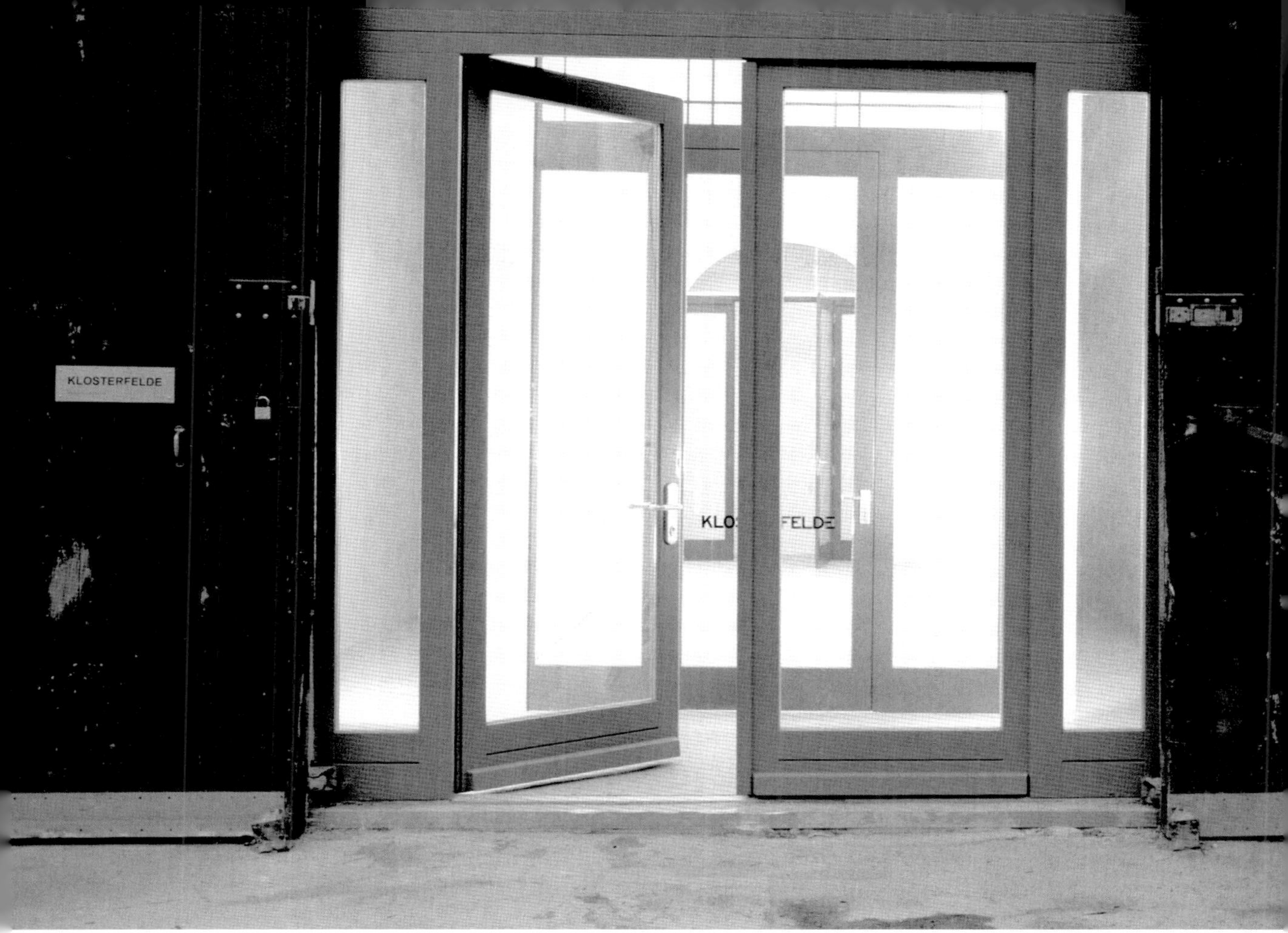
KLOSTERFELDE

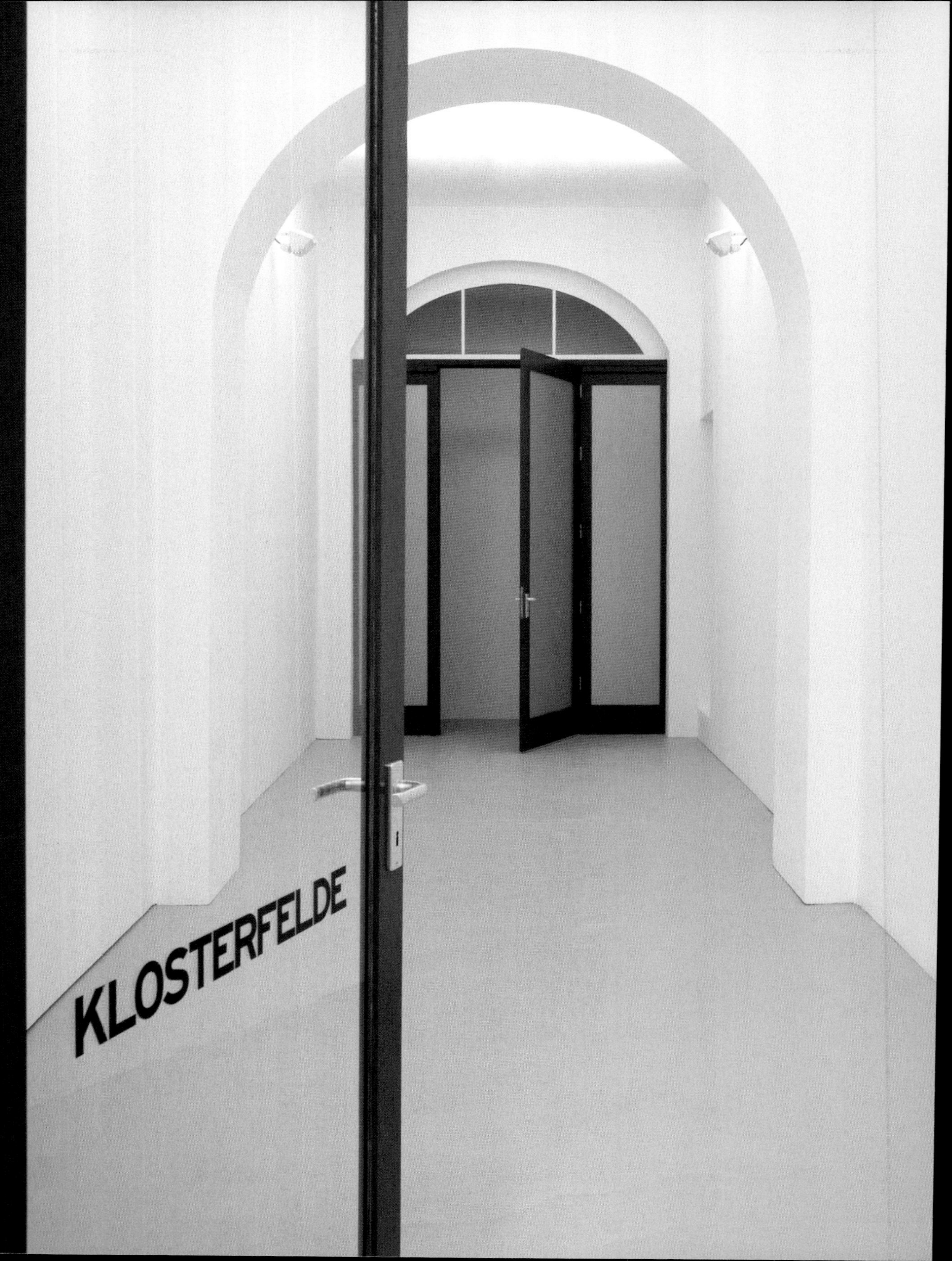
KLOSTERFELDE

sociological, economic, and aesthetic study since the sixties. Michael Elmgreen & Ingar Dragset find themselves in the third generation of this research tradition, which not only seeks to investigate and describe symptoms but also views "work on the White Cube" as an attempt to revise or even transform it. In order to understand what is current and new about their contribution, we should take a glance at the previous work of other artists and theorists.

Late Modernist Critique of the White Cube

We mark the beginning of this phase with an observation by a New York Times *critic in 1963. His name is Brian O'Doherty, and his remark appeared in a letter to art historian Wolfgang Kemp: "I noted in a review that the art gallery had become so transformative that you could take virtually anything into it and it would look like art; back outside it would resume its banal identity."* [2] *Although Duchamp had anticipated this situation with his Readymades some sixty-five years earlier, O'Doherty's statement still sounds today like a heretical attack upon all too fondly regarded certainties. It is not the intrinsic determinants of a work that define it as an object of art, but the surrounding space—the White Cube as its context.*

It was this same art critic, an artist himself who began producing "site-specific installations" under the pseudonym "Patrick Ireland" in 1972, who published the three-part essay "Inside the White Cube" in 1976 and followed it with "Gallery as Gesture" in 1981. The White Cube, "a convention as strong as its predecessor counterpart," [3] *the 19th-century art gallery luxuriously furnished in plush and velvet, has since become an exhibition object in its own right—"art in potential." We encounter the White Cube again and again at exhibitions, as the walk-in box installed in gallery space, as the model of fictitious or real exhibition spaces into which viewers gaze from above, or simply as the sculptural cube, much like the one Elmgreen & Dragset erected at the Vienna Secession in 1998*

Nachdenken über die Konventionen des Machens, Ausstellens und Betrachtens von Kunst, für das der moderne Kunstbetrieb eben jene scheinbar so neutrale Kiste White Cube »erfunden« hat, deren vorgebliche Unschuld seit den sechziger Jahren aber zum Gegenstand soziologischer, ökonomischer und ästhetischer Untersuchungen geworden ist. Michael Elmgreen & Ingar Dragset stehen gleichsam in der dritten Generation dieser Forschertradition, die aber nicht nur ermitteln und Symptombeschreibung betreiben will, sondern die die »Arbeit am White Cube« als eine Revision, ja Transformation der »weißen Zelle« versteht. Um zu begreifen, was sie an Aktuellem und Neuem einbringen, werfen wir einen Blick auf die bisher von anderen Künstlern und Theoretikern geleistete Arbeit.

Die spätmoderne Kritik am White Cube

Am Anfang stand 1963 die Beobachtung eines *New York Times*-Kritikers. Brian O'Doherty war sein Name, und er berichtete in einem Brief an den Kunsthistoriker Wolfgang Kemp: »I noted in a review that the art gallery had become so transformative that you could take virtually anything into it and it would look like art; back outside it would resume its banal identity.« [2] Obwohl Duchamp dieses Faktum rund 65 Jahre zuvor mit seinen Ready-Mades praktisch vorexerzierte, klingt O'Dohertys Feststellung auch heute noch wie ein häretischer Ausfall gegen allzu lieb gewordene Gewissheiten. Nicht die inneren Bestimmungen eines Werkes definieren ein Objekt als Kunst, sondern der Umraum, der White Cube als Kontext.

Eben dieser Kunstkritiker, der 1972 unter dem Pseudonym »Patrick Ireland« anfing, selbst »site-specific installations« herzustellen, publizierte 1976 in der renommierten Kunstzeitschrift *Artforum* die dreiteilige Essayfolge »Inside the White Cube« mit einem Nachschlag 1981: »Gallery as a Gesture«. Der White Cube, »eine Konvention so stark wie

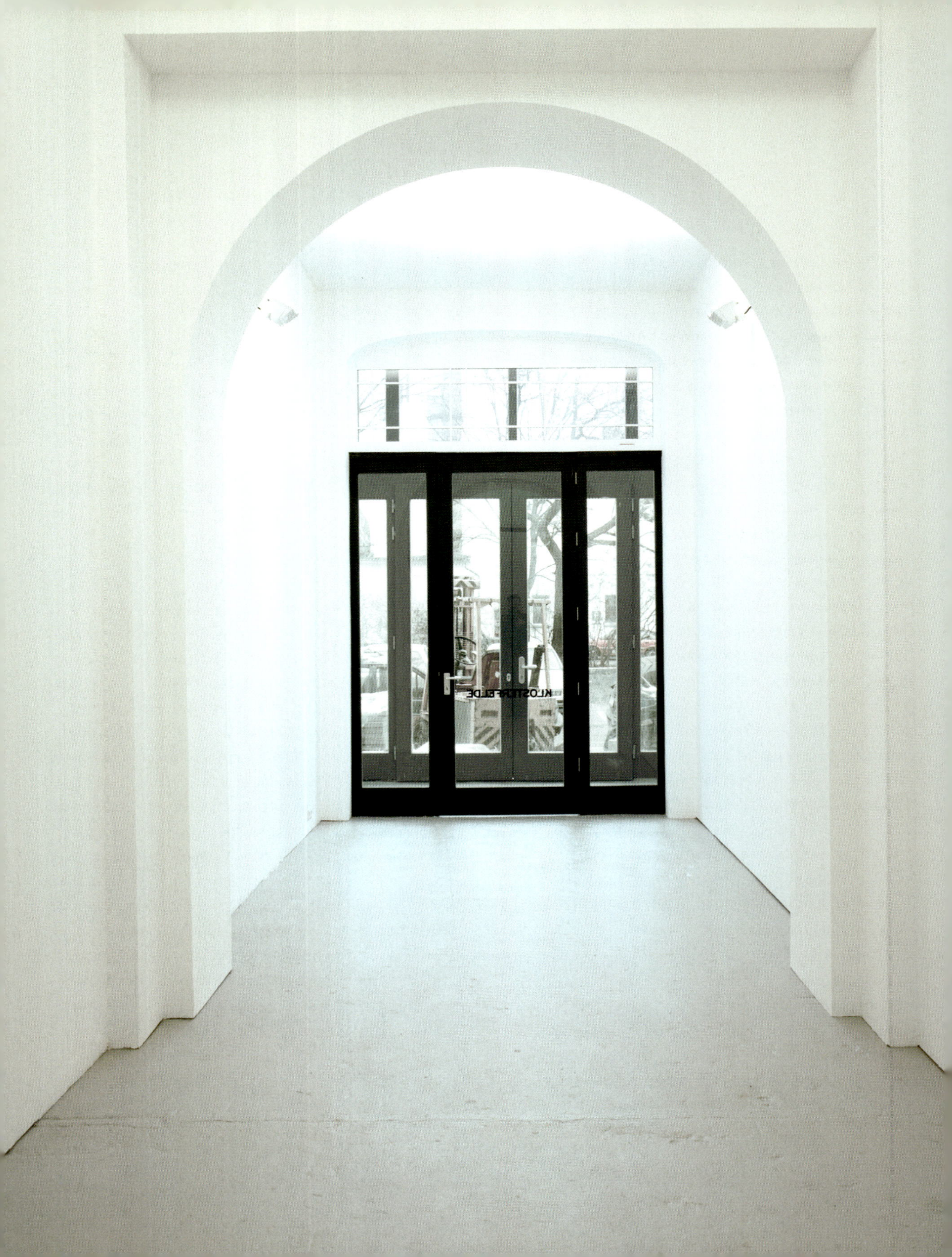
KLOSTERFELDE

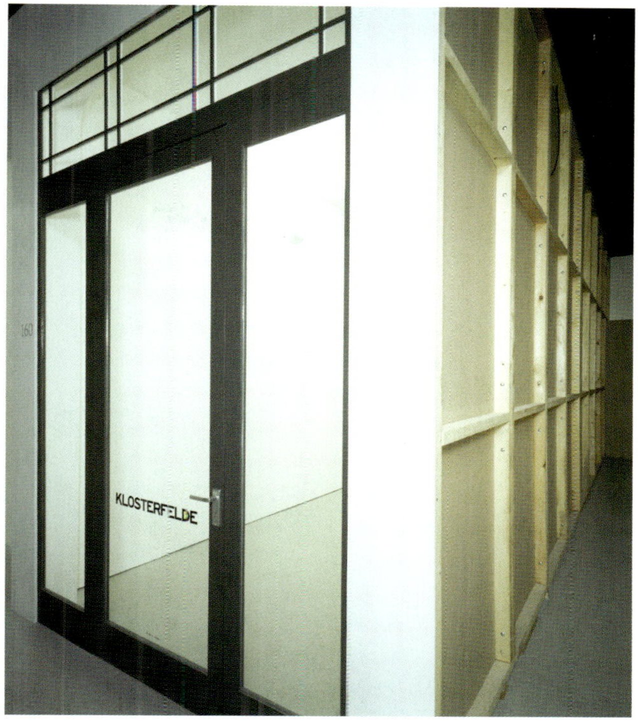

and repeatedly painted and washed clean (pp. 46–47, 49–51). In his essay series O'Doherty was still concerned with the art environment of his time. In 1968, Lawrence Weiner, exhibiting at the legendary Bern show When Attitudes Become Form, *removed a section of white plaster measuring thirty-six by thirty-six inches from the wall of the Kunsthalle and presented the exposed red brick wall behind it as a picture. That same year, Daniel Buren sealed the Galleria Apollinaire in Milan with green-and-white-striped fabric and thus compelled visitors to view the exhibition site as an art product from the outside. In 1974, Michael Asher removed an entire wall at the Claire Copley Gallery and joined the exhibition room with the office. The presentation space became an expanded office, and the administrative area became an exhibition object. In 1976, the year* Inside the White Cube *was published, Germano Celant invited thirteen artists to the Venice Biennial to realize installations in thirteen separate exhibition rooms under the title* Ambiente Arte. *Dan Graham divided his cell into two compartments separated by a sound-absorbing thermopane glass panel, adding a box fitted with a mirrored wall. Public Space, as the work was entitled, generated a confusing reception context which called attention to the behavior of viewers inside the Minimalist sculpture enlarged to form a spatial cell.*

At this point, we could easily make the transition to the works Elevated Gallery/Powerless Structure, Fig. 146*, 2001 (pp. 84–86) and* Dug Down Gallery/Powerless Structure, Fig. 45*, 1998 (pp. 88–91) by Elmgreen & Dragset. This fall, the two artists hung a freely suspended gallery room from the ceiling of an exhibition space at the Statens Museum in Copenhagen. Three years before that, they buried a similarly designed gallery room in the garden of the Reykjavik Art Museum. The floating cube had neither floor nor ceiling and thus could not be used but was viewable as a sculpture. Nor did the below-ground gallery cell have an entrance. Viewers could only*

sein Gegenbild und Vorgänger«,[3] die mit Plüsch und Samt luxuriös ausgekleidete Kunstgalerie des 19. Jahrhunderts, ist seither selbst zum Exponat, zur »Kunst in Potenz«, avanciert. Immer wieder trifft man in Ausstellungen auf den weißen Würfel, sei es die in den Raum gebaute und real betretbare Kiste, sei es als von oben einsehbares Modell von fiktiven oder konkreten Ausstellungsräumen oder sei es einfach auch der skulpturale Würfel, wie etwa jener, den Elmgreen & Dragset 1998 in die Wiener Secession gestellt und immer wieder weiß angestrichen und abgewaschen haben (Abb. Seite 46/47, 49–51). O'Dohertys Essayfolge fokussierte noch auf das künstlerische Umfeld seiner Zeit. 1968 schälte Lawrence Weiner in der legendären Berner Ausstellung *When Attitudes Become Form* ein 36" x 36" großes Stück weißen Putzes von der Kunsthallenwand und legte die darunter liegende rote Backsteinmauer als Bild frei. Im gleichen Jahr versiegelte Daniel Buren die Galleria Apollinaire in Mailand mit weiß-grünen Stoffstreifen und zwang damit das Publikum, das Kunst-institut von außen als Kunstprodukt wahrzunehmen. 1974 entfernte Michael Asher in der Claire Copley Gallery

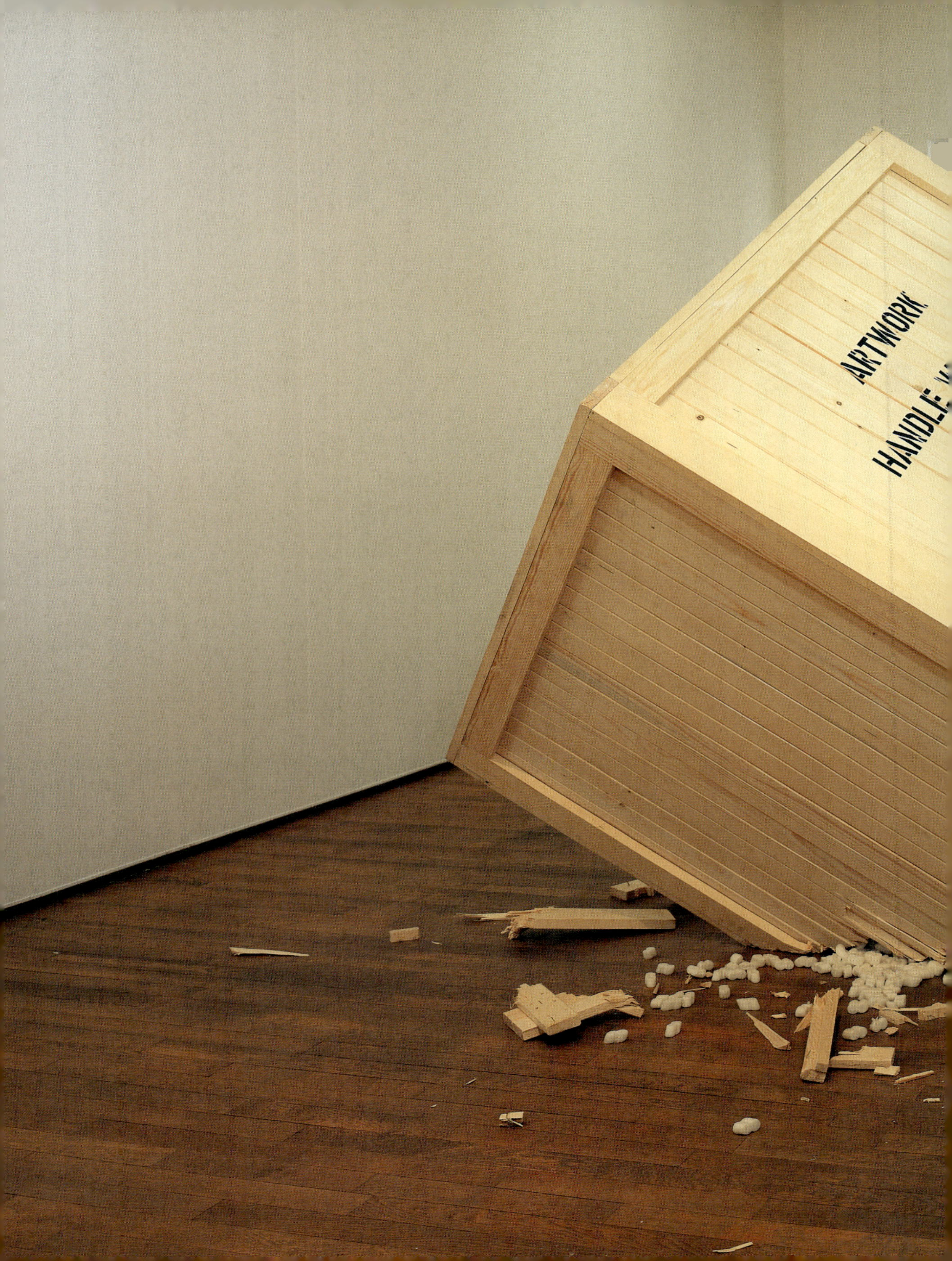
ARTWORK
HANDLE

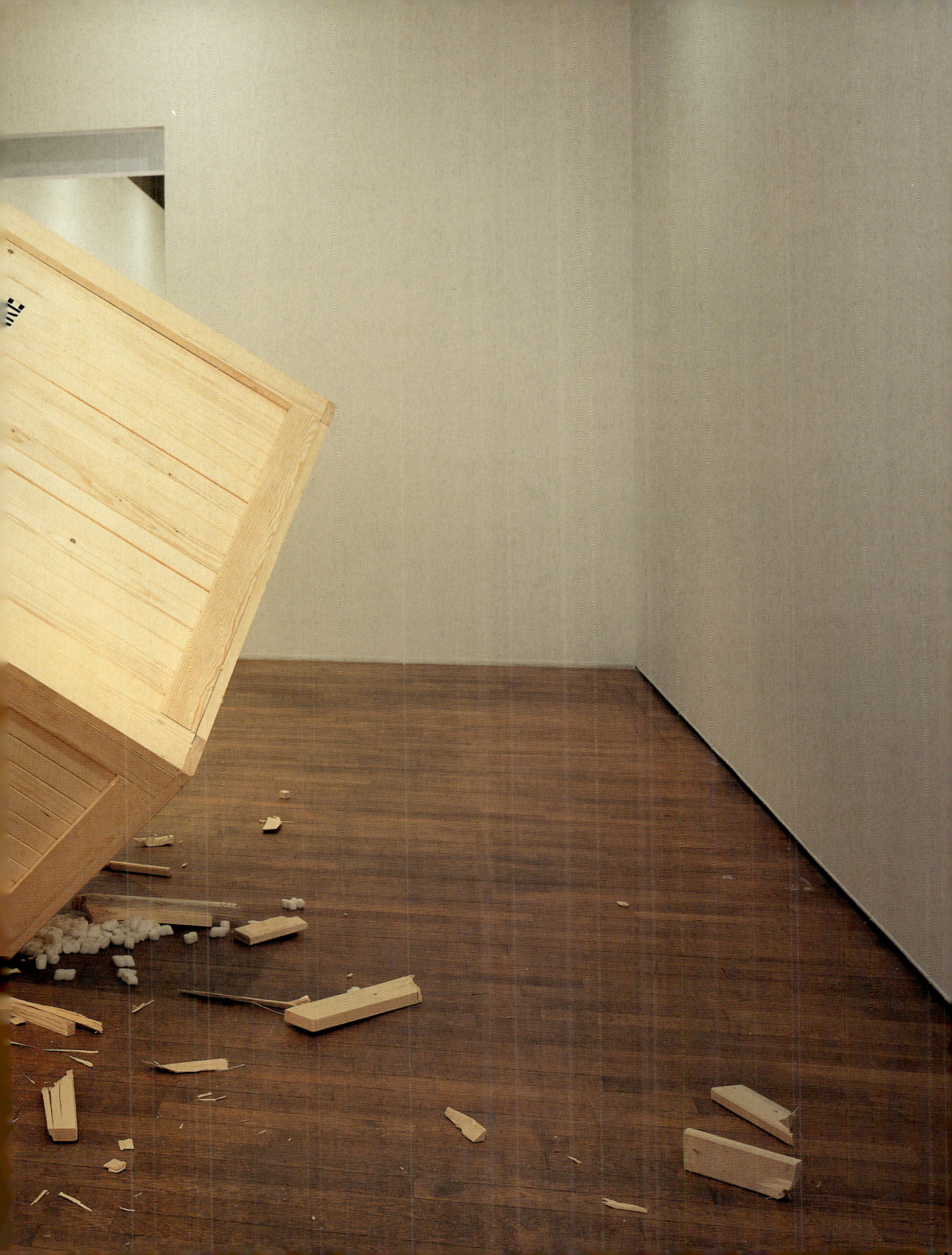

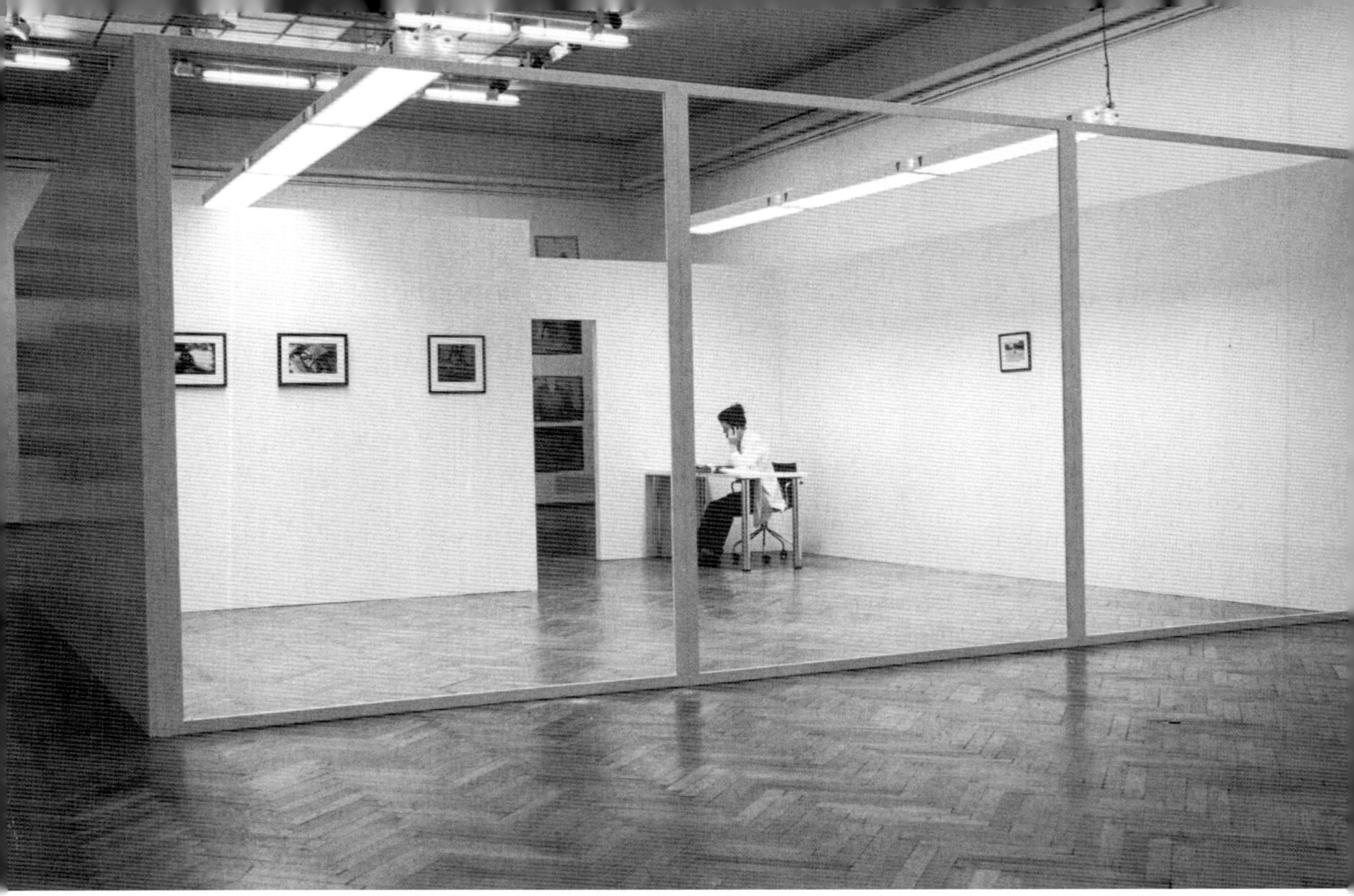

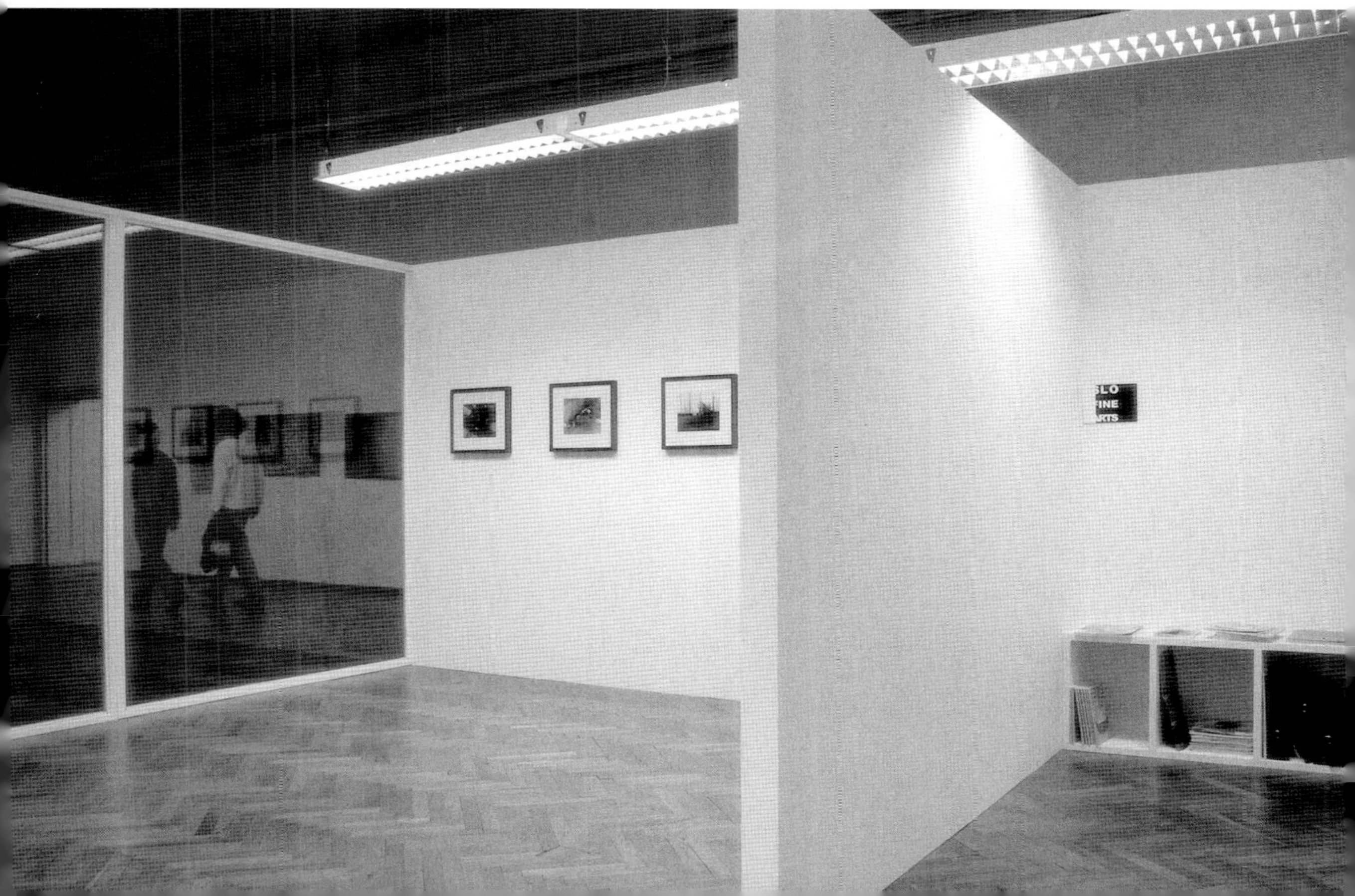
SLO
FINE
RTS

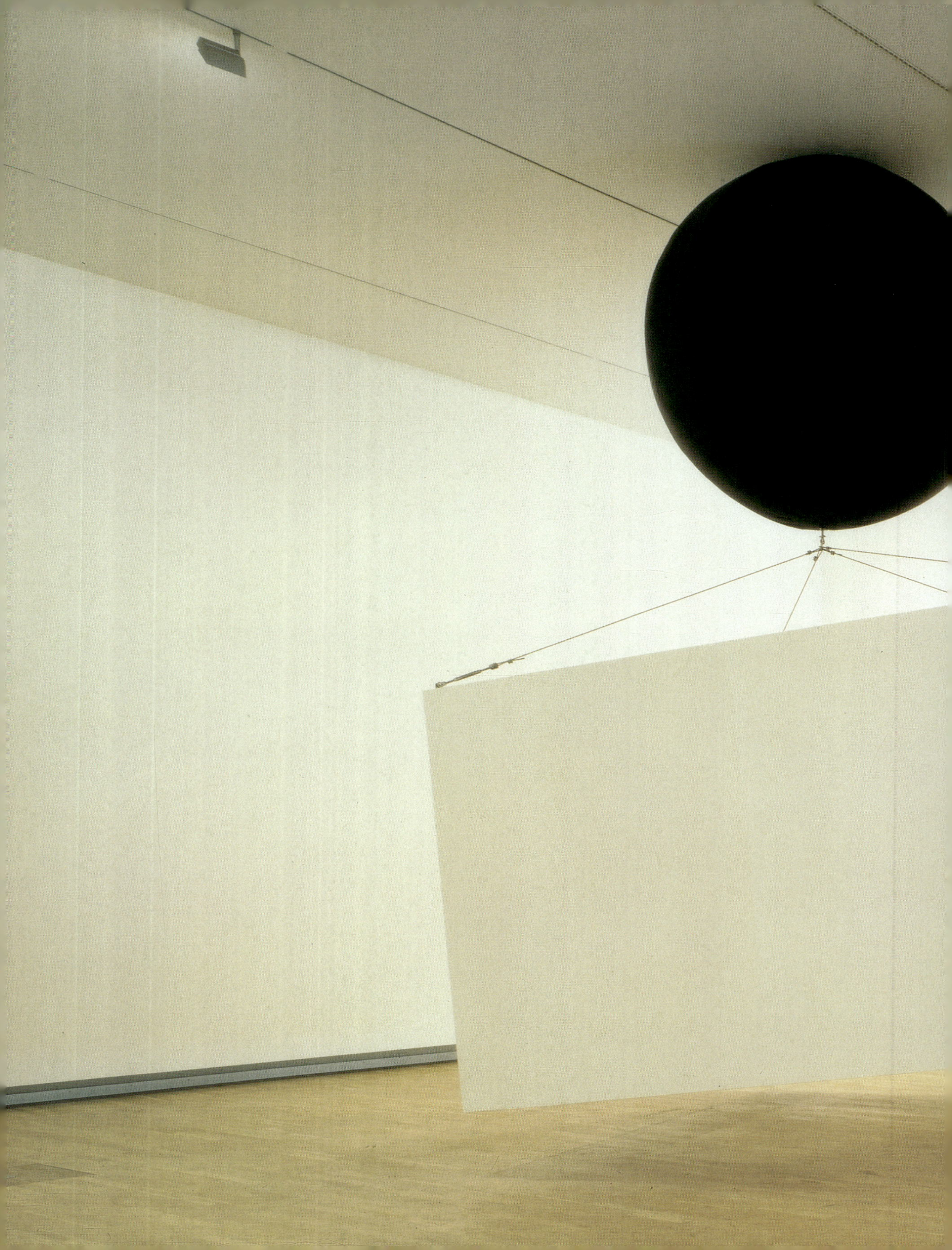

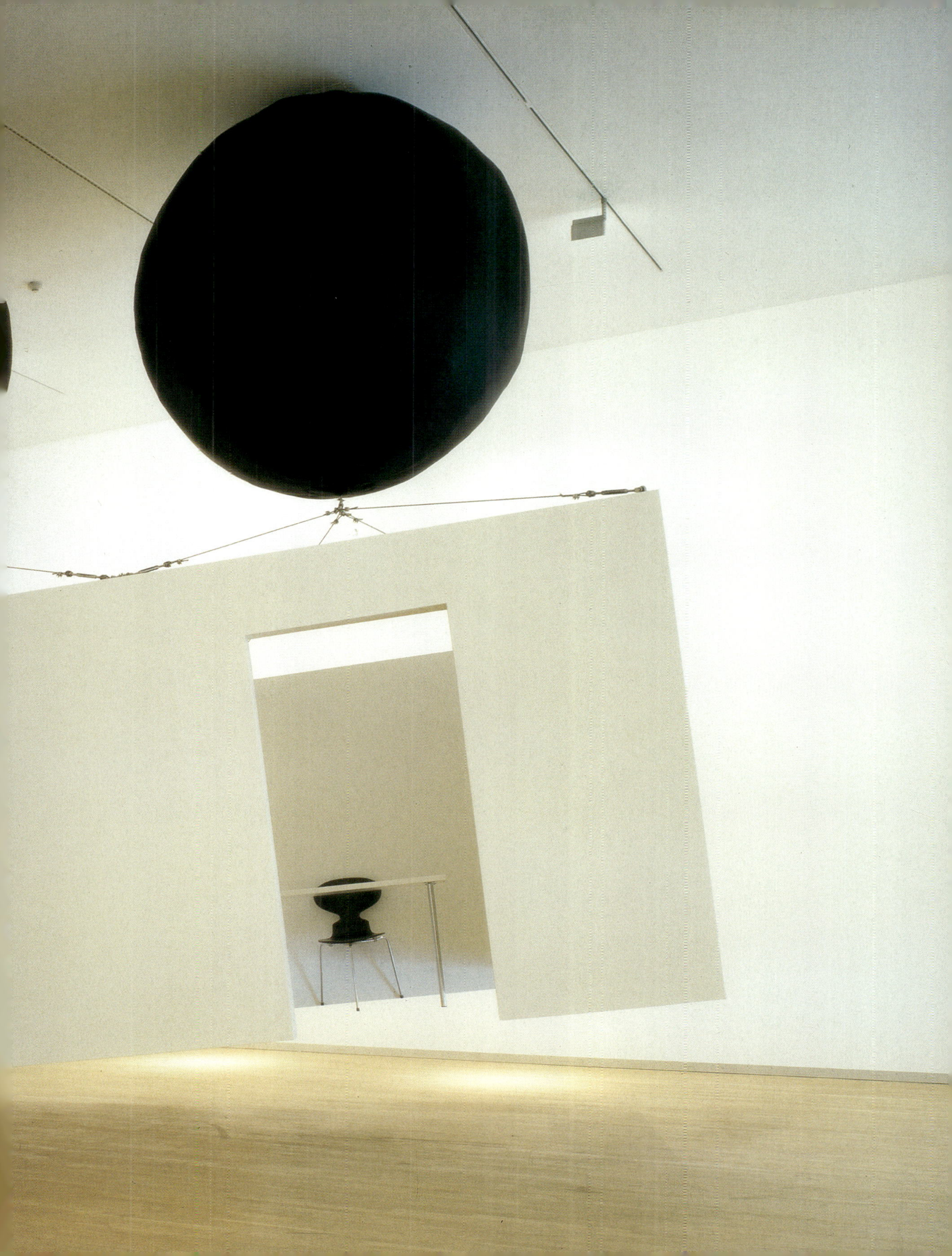

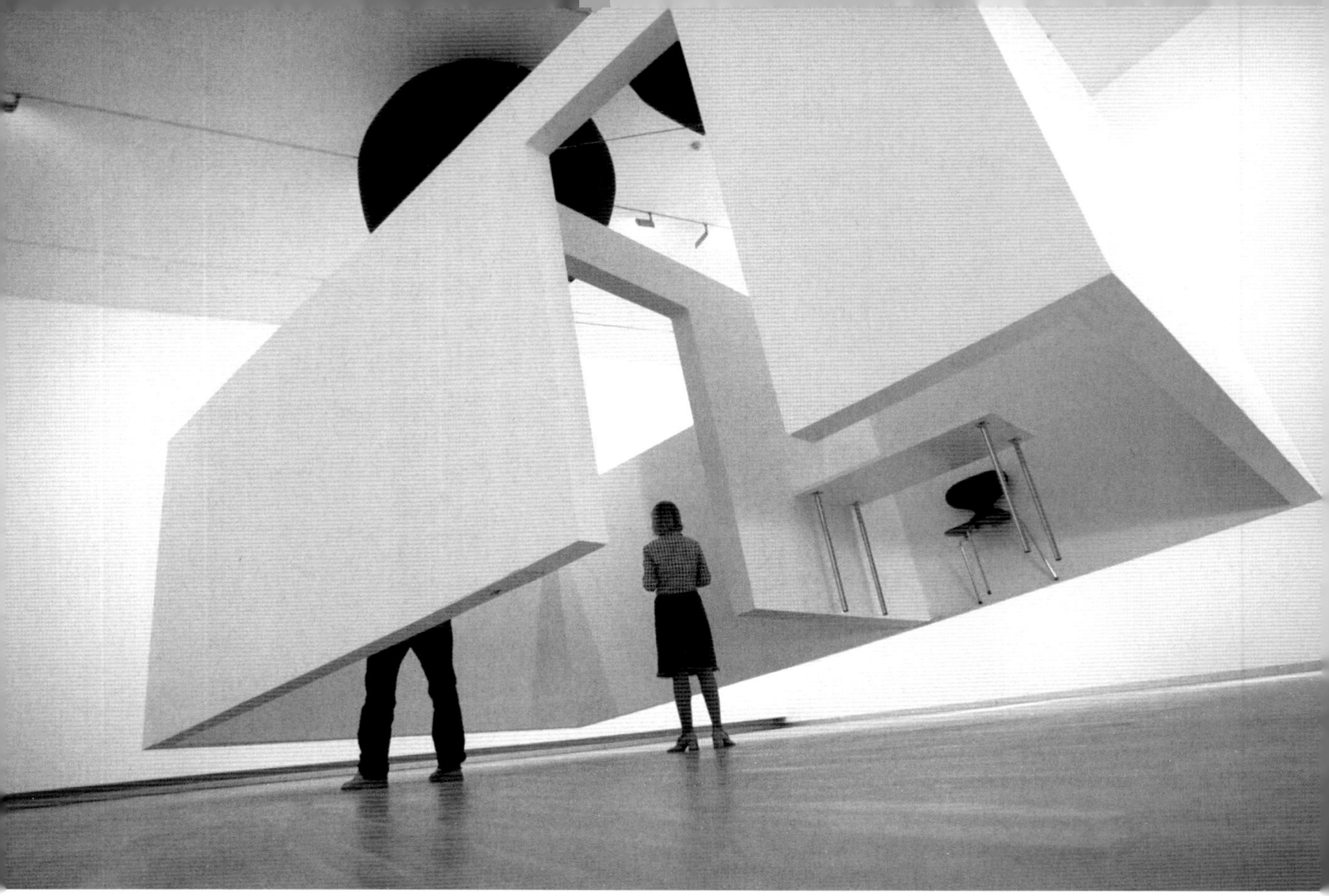

look into it from above, much like an architectural model. But another entire generation lies between the pioneers of late modern Conceptual Art and these Neo-Modernist transformers of the White Cube—and with it the Postmodern shudder of the White Cube.

The Postmodern Shudder of the White Cube

"With postmodernism," Brian O'Doherty contends, " the gallery space is no longer 'neutral.' The wall becomes a membrane through which esthetic and commercial values osmotically exchange. As this molecular shudder in the white walls becomes perceptible, there is a further inversion of context. The walls assimilate; the art discharges. How much can the art do without? This calibrates the degree of the gallery's mythification. How much of the object's eliminated content can the white wall replace? Context provides a large part of late modern and postmodern art's content. That is … art's main issue, as well as its strength and weakness." [4]

The author recognized this transformation in the increasing permeability of walls. Walls of containers become membranes, and a process of osmosis takes place between the inside and the outside. In establishing this, the author himself did away with one of the most stubborn preconceptions about the White Cube—that of its isolation, which was persistently equated with the transcendent quality of religious spaces. On the other hand, however, the claim of autonomy is increasingly justified by system theory, which has become a major supplier of theories for contemporary art. It confirms the significance and productivity of the autonomy of so-called "autopoietic" functional systems within the larger system of "society." Thus since the demise of the avant-garde, the White Cube occupies this field of tension between autonomy and osmosis, between isolation and metabolic exchange. And in this highly charged atmosphere, it repeatedly takes shape as reified context.

gleich eine ganze Galeriewand und schloss den Ausstellungsraum mit dem Büroraum kurz. Der Präsentationsraum wurde zum erweiterten Office, und umgekehrt verwandelte sich die Administration zum Ausstellungsgegenstand. 1976, dem Erscheinungsjahr von Inside the White Cube, lud Germano Celant 13 Künstler zur Biennale nach Venedig ein, um unter dem Titel Ambiente Arte in je einem eigenen Raum raumfüllende Installationen vorzunehmen. Dan Graham teilte seine Zelle in zwei Kompartimente, die durch eine schallschluckende Thermopanelglasscheibe voneinander getrennt waren. Eine Box besaß zusätzlich eine verspiegelte Wand. Public Space, so der Titel, erzeugte verwirrende Rezeptionssituationen, die das Verhalten des Betrachters in der zur Raumzelle vergrößerten Minimal-Skulptur untersuchten.
An dieser Stelle könnten wir nahtlos auf die beiden Arbeiten *Elevated Gallery/Powerless Structure, Fig. 146,* 2001 (Abb. Seite 84–86) und *Dug Down Gallery/Powerless Structure, Fig. 45,* 1998 (Abb. Seite 88–91) von Elmgreen & Dragset verweisen. In diesem Herbst hingen die beiden einen frei schwebenden Galerieraum schräg an die Decke des Ausstellungsraumes im Statens Museum in Kopenhagen und drei Jahre zuvor vergruben sie einen ähnlich gestalteten Galerieraum im Garten des Reykjavik Art Museum. Dem schwebenden Kubus fehlten Decke und Boden. Er war daher unbenutzbar, aber als Skulptur betrachtbar. Auch zur eingegrabenen Galeriezelle gab es keinen Zugang. Sie war lediglich von oben einsehbar, wie bei einem Architekturmodell. Doch zwischen den Pionieren der spät-modernen Konzeptkunst und dieser neu-modernen Transformatoren des White Cube liegt noch eine ganze Generation – liegt noch die postmoderne Erschütterung des White Cube.

Die postmoderne Erschütterung des White Cube.

»Mit dem Anbruch der Postmoderne«, räsoniert Brian O'Doherty, »ist der Galerieraum nicht mehr ›neutral‹. Die

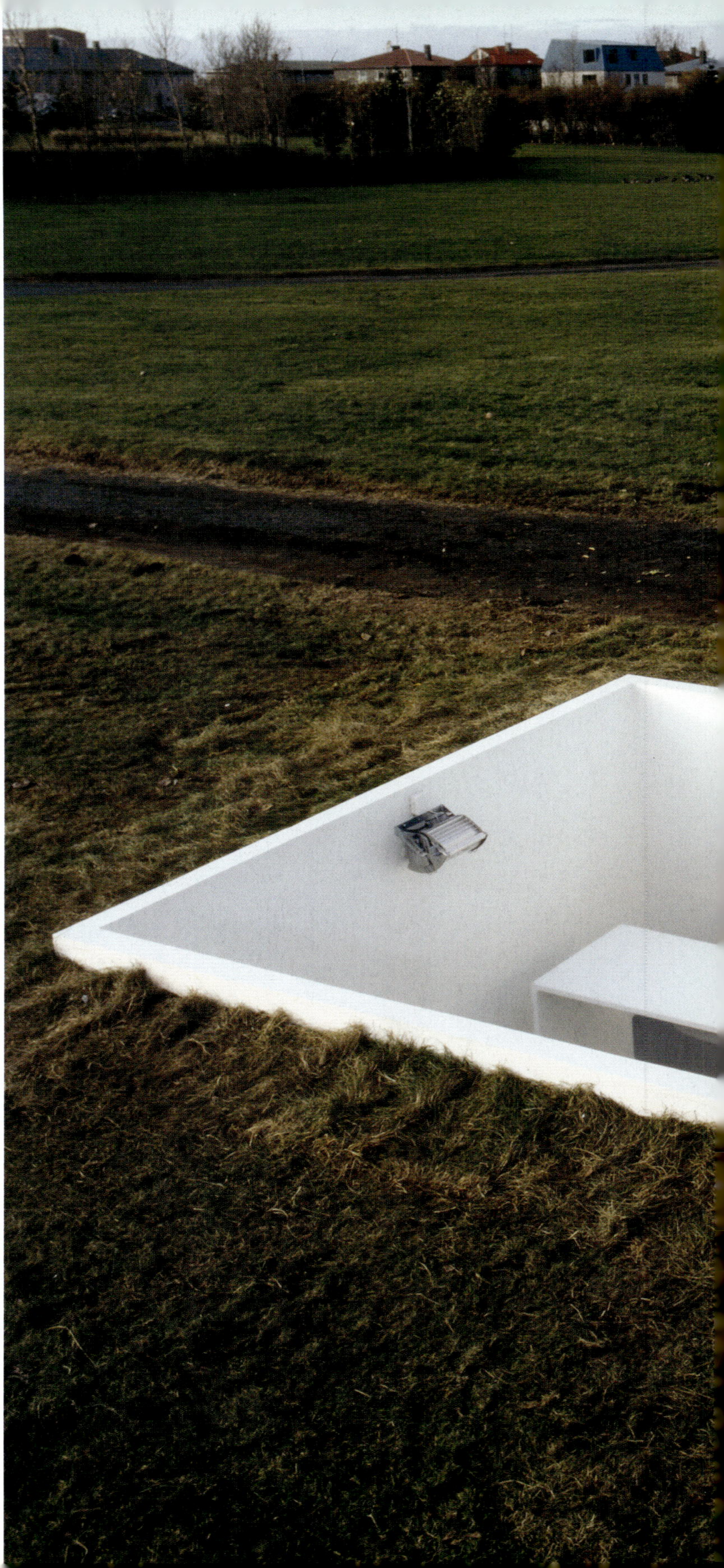

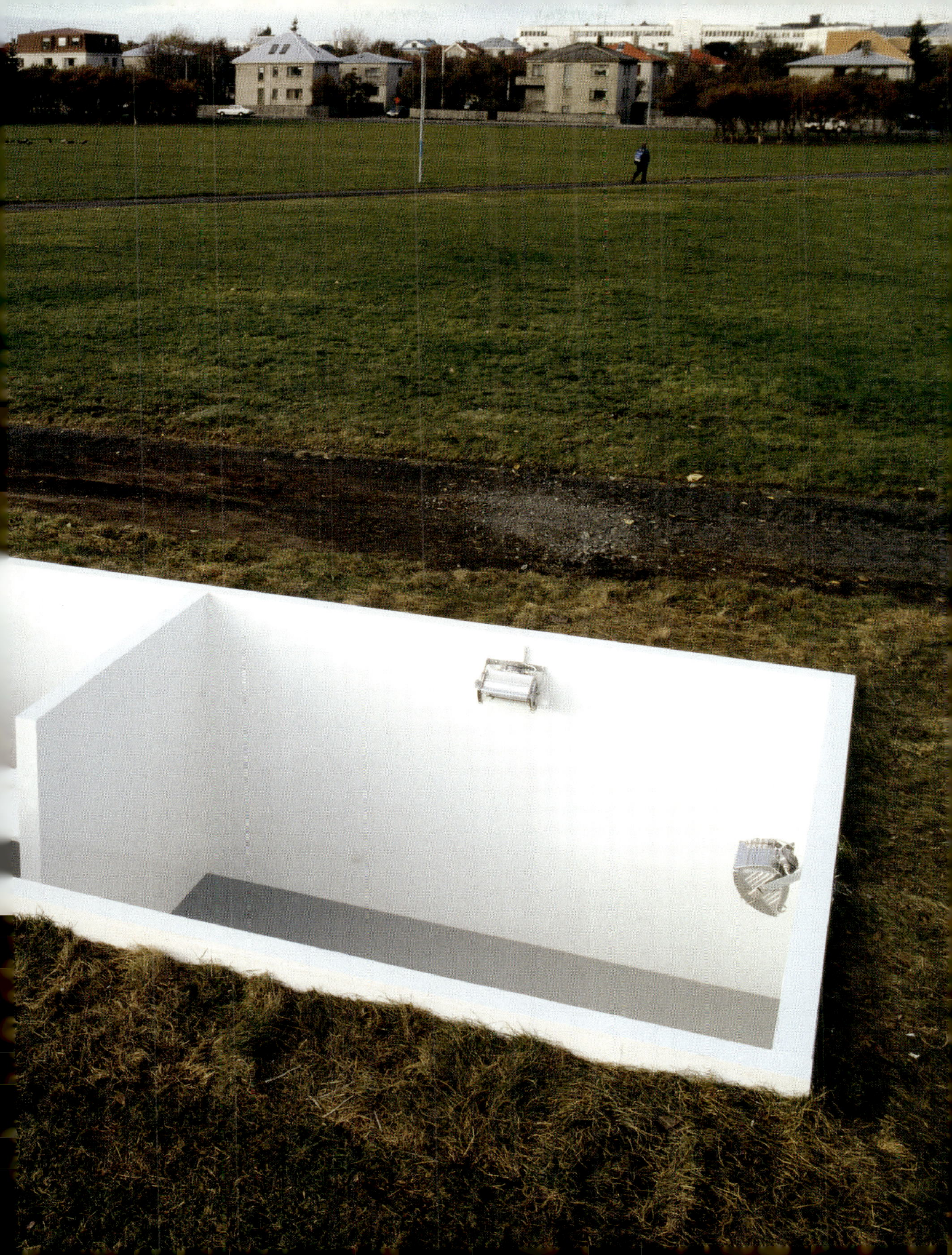

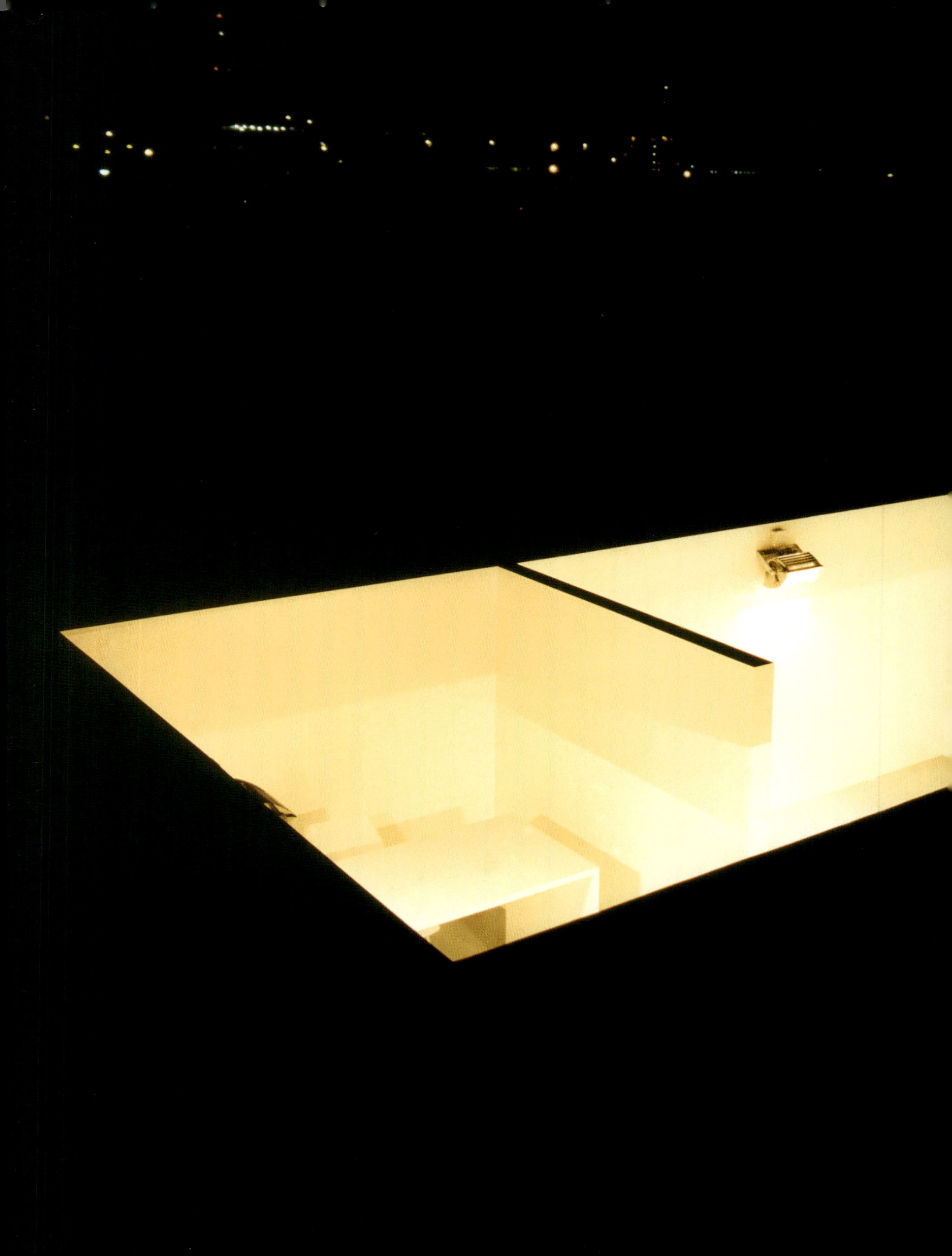

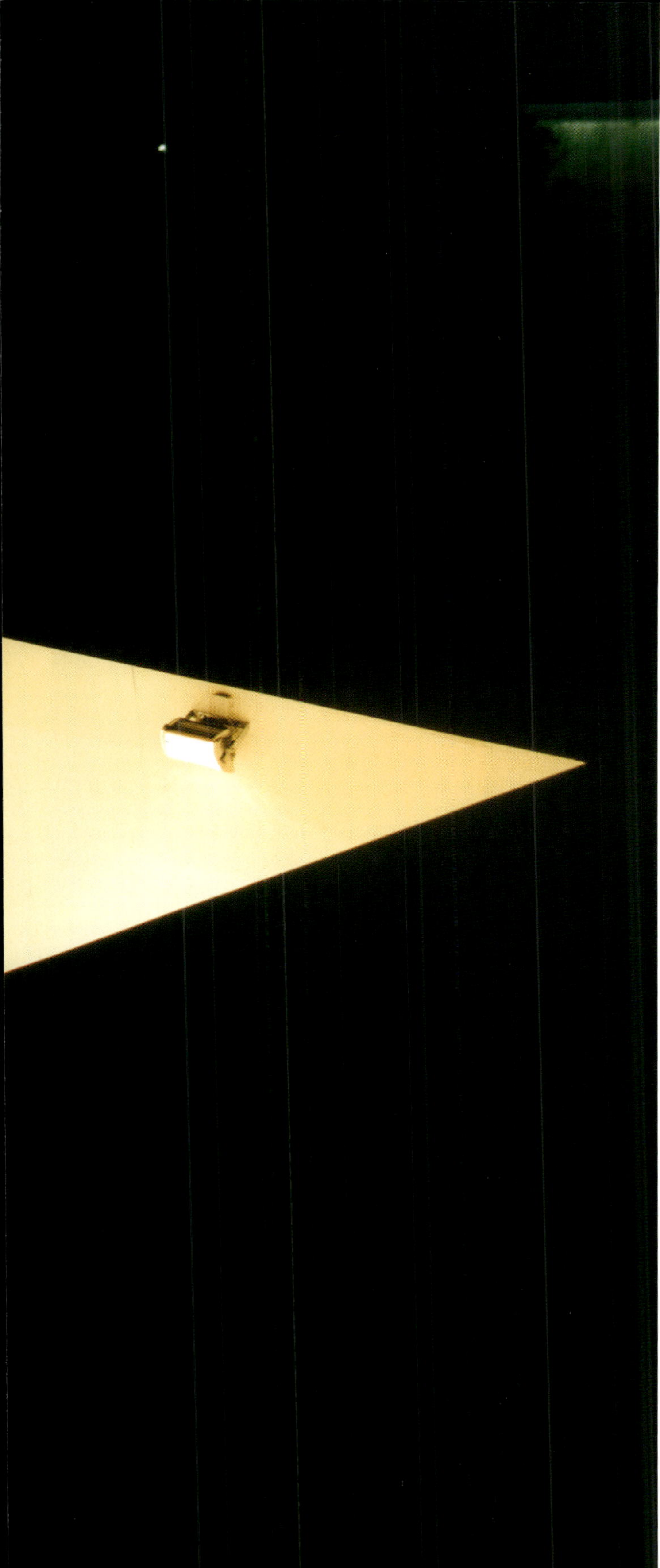

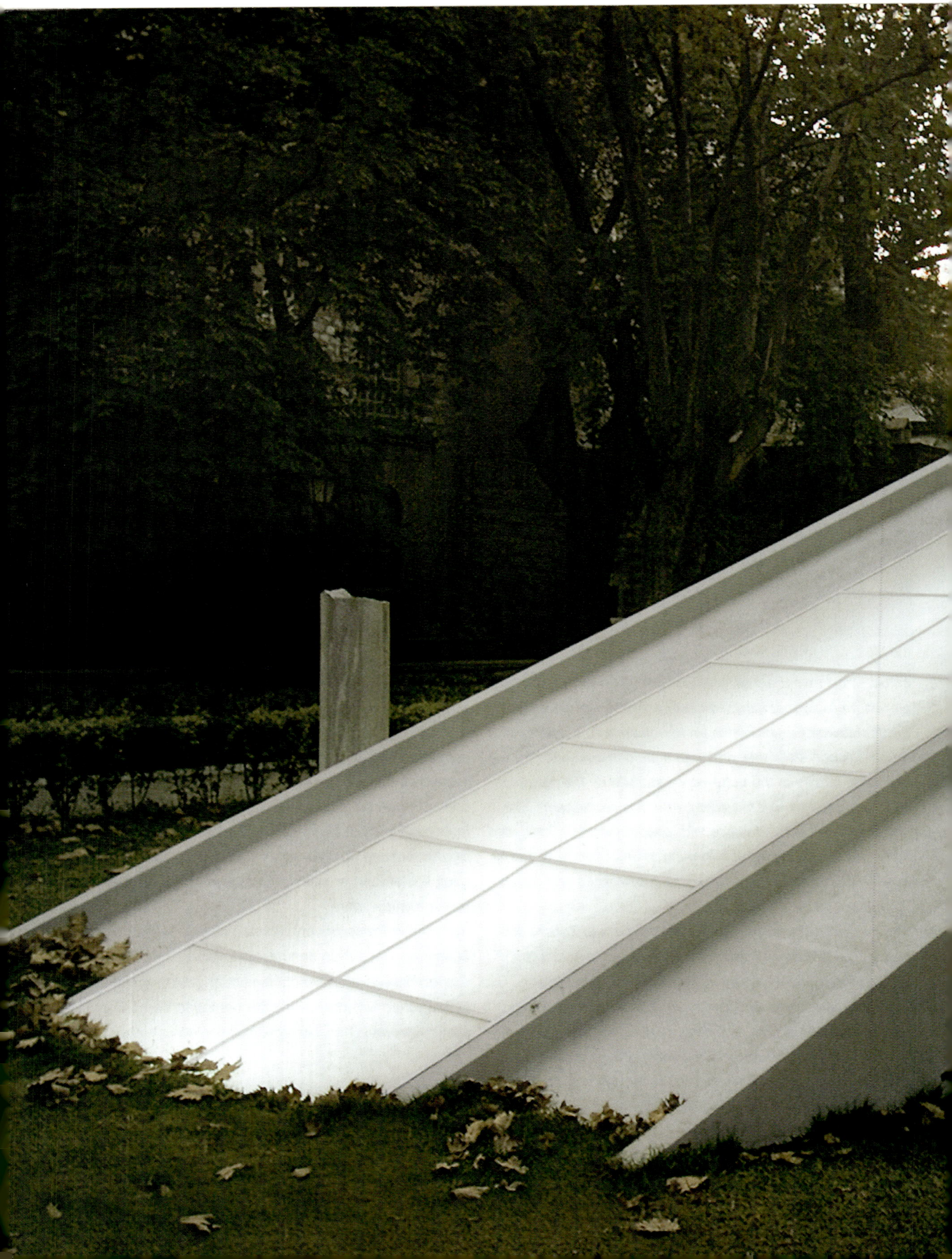

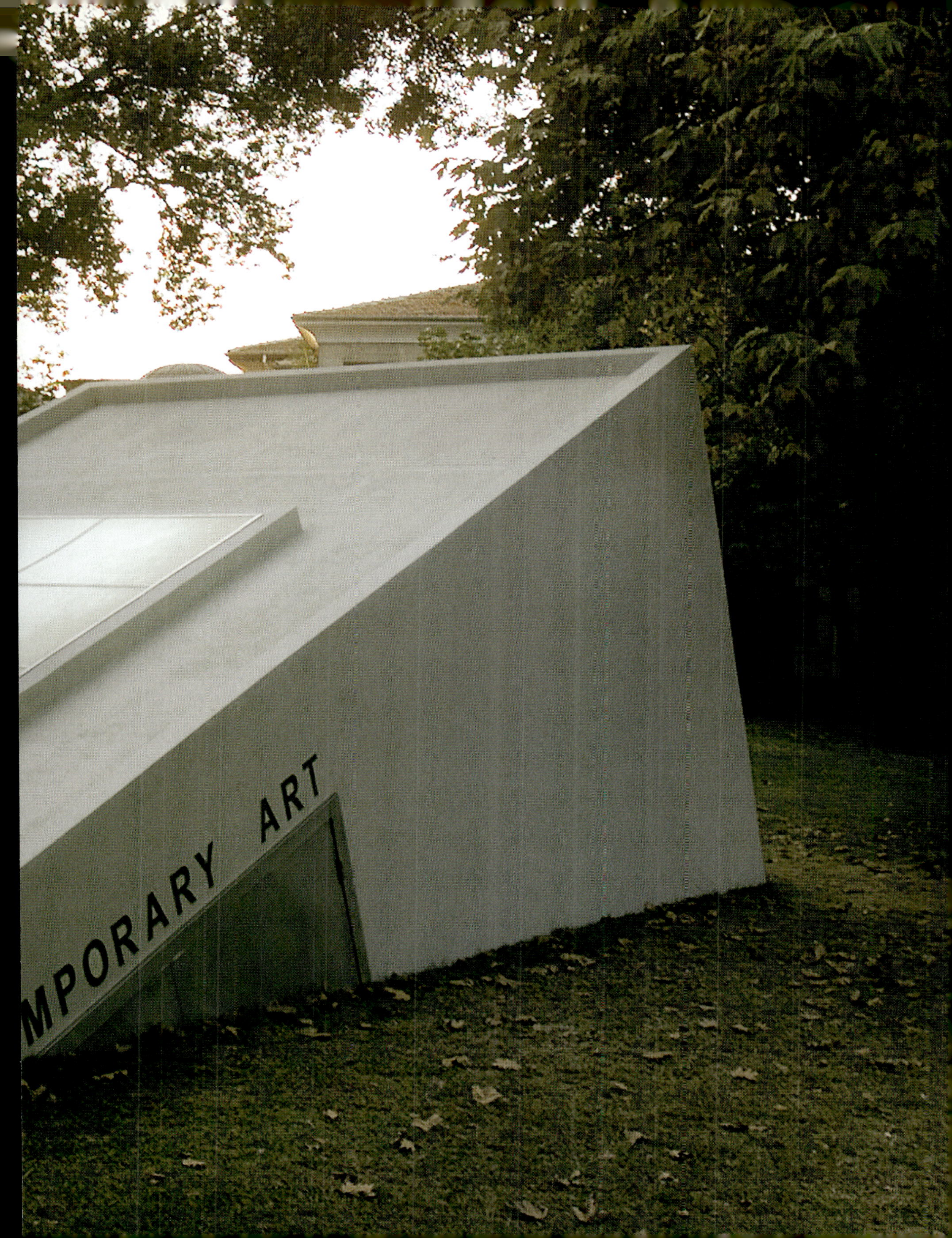
MPORARY ART

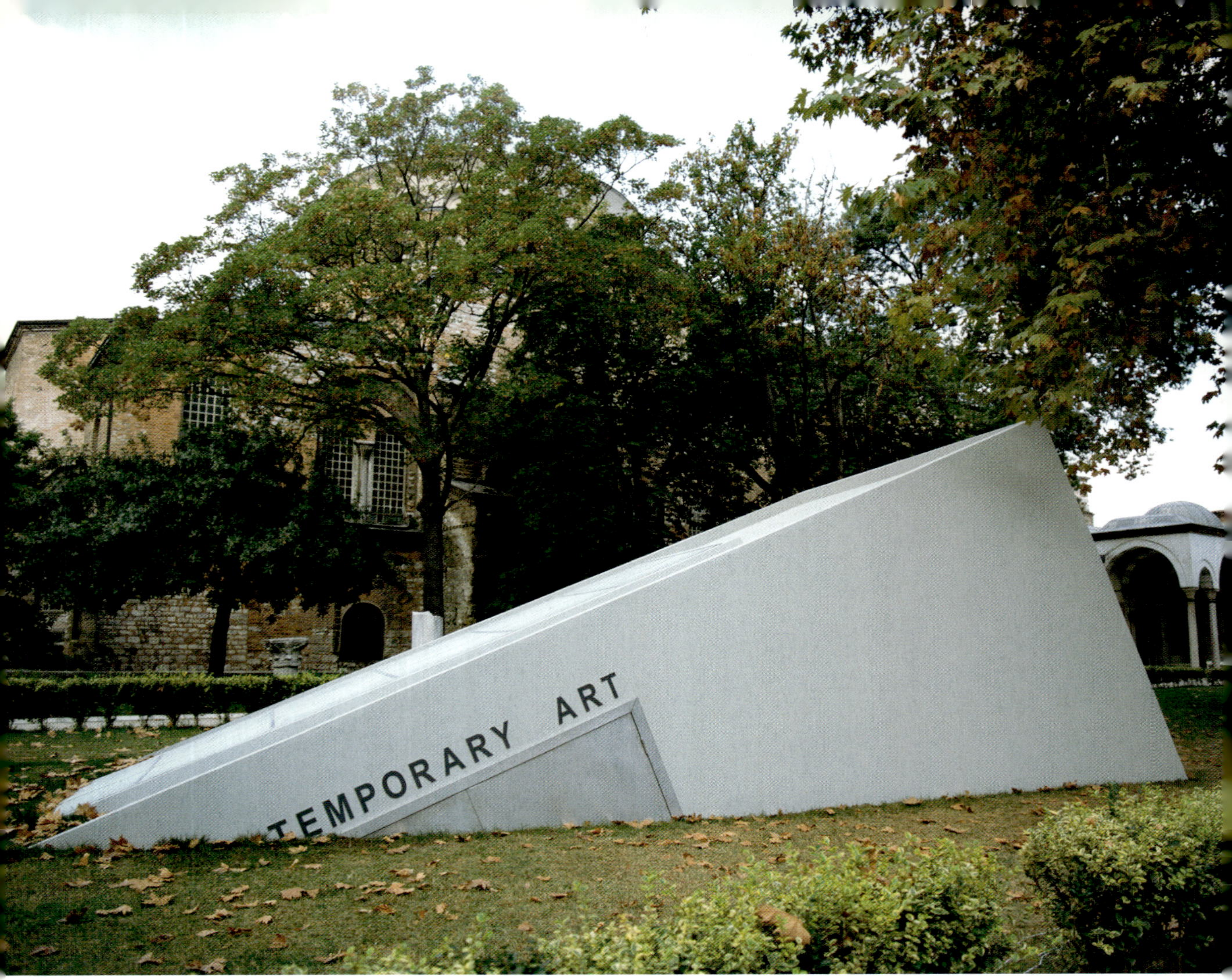
TEMPORARY ART

had begun to turn the conditions governing its manifestation into art itself: the box had become the contents. While Zobernig drags the White Cube onto the stage, as a kind of zero form rendered by its own laconic self-consciousness, Rockenschaub sets the viewer in motion and prompts him to explore the aesthetic and institutional limits of the White Cube by looking into it and outward from it.

A telephone conversation on November 5, 2001, 5:10 p.m.: I hear loud hammering and sawing noises in the background, preparations for the exhibition Taking Place*, which is to open the following Friday. The Kunsthalle Zürich is a construction site! Ingar Dragset tells me on the phone what they have in mind with their exhibition and with the institution: an infrastructural improvement of the existing exhibition display. The enfilade of exhibition compartments is to be made more exciting, the office and library are to be turned into an open reception area from which visitors have a view of the backstage spaces. Over the course of the show, the architectural and institutional utility of the Kunsthalle Zürich becomes the real theme of the exhibition. And the process of redesign and reconstruction itself is addressed. Once it is over, Dragset presumes, nothing of the planning and renovation process thus transformed into art is to remain immediately perceptible, in order to avoid disturbing normal operations devoted to future projects—except for one relic, a "blind door" in the office. But that is not certain yet.*

The most prominent features of third-generation "work on the White Cube" are its process- and action-oriented (performative) character and the aspect of functional revitalization. In concluding, I would cite to add two additional elements that relate specifically to the work of Elmgreen & Dragset: the sexualization of the White Cube and the process of delocation or, as Deleuze/Guattari express it, "deterritorialization."

Kunstwerdung des weißen Würfels im Rahmen der Kontextkunst der neunziger Jahre bis schließlich zur performativen Refunktionalisierung bei Michael Elmgreen & Ingar Dragset. Im Zusammenhang mit der Refunktionalisierung möchte ich zwei Realisationen in Erinnerung rufen, die beide auf dem Kunstplatz Zürich stattfanden, daher ein sinniges Vergleichsmoment zum Ereignis in der Kunsthalle Zürich darstellen und den Übergang von der zweiten zur dritten Generation der »Arbeit am White Cube« demonstrieren.

Der Weisse Würfel wird Kunst

Mit Anbruch der neunziger Jahre wird der weiße Würfel zum betracht- und begehbaren Kunstobjekt. 1991 stellte Heimo Zobernig in das für Kunst schwer bespielbare, rau verputzte Zürcher Architektur Forum am Neumarkt eine provisorische Ausstellungskiste, die leer blieb. Die Idealität wurde aber durch den feuerpolizeilich vorgeschriebenen Notausgang gestört. Die Skulptur, die den »Raum mit Raum füllte« (Moritz Küng), war gleichzeitig zur rahmenden Architektur geworden, die die institutionellen Bedingungen zu berücksichtigen und als Kunst mitzureflektieren hatte.

Schauplatz Galerie Walcheturm in Zürich, ein Jahr zuvor: Gerwald Rockenschaub spannte drei leere Wände in den Raum, der durch sein frontfüllendes Fenster eher einem Schaufenster als einem Ausstellungsraum gleicht. Der Künstler hatte mit diesem einfachen Eingriff den ehemaligen Kinosaal in eine betretbare Mogelkiste verwandelt, in dem sich der verdutzte Betrachter langsam vorantasten musste, um zu entdecken, dass die Kunst nicht verschwunden, sondern darangegangen ist, die Rahmenbedingungen ihres Erscheinens selbst zur Kunst zu machen: Die Schachtel ist Inhalt geworden. Während Zobernig die »weiße Kiste« durch ihre lakonische Selbstbezogenheit gleichsam als Nullform auf die

Bühne schiebt, setzt Rockenschaub den Betrachter in Bewegung und lässt ihn durch Ausblicke und Einblicke die ästhetischen wie auch institutionellen Grenzen des White Cube erforschen.

Telefontermin am 5. November 2001, 17:10 Uhr: Im Hintergrund ist lautes Hämmern und Sägen hörbar, Vorbereitungen zur Ausstellung *Taking Place*, die am kommenden Freitag eröffnet werden soll. Die Kunsthalle Zürich: eine Baustelle! Ingar Dragset teilt mir durchs Kabel mit, was sie mit ihrer Ausstellung, mit dieser Institution vorhaben: eine infrastrukturelle Verbesserung des bestehenden Ausstellungsdisplays. Die Enfilade der Kojen soll spannender gestaltet werden, das Office mit der Bibliothek soll zum offenen Empfangsraum werden, von dem der eintretende Besucher Einblick in die Back-Stage-Bereiche bekommt. Die architektonische und institutionelle Brauchbarkeit der Kunsthalle Zürich entfaltet sich während der Zeit der Ausstellung zum eigentlichen Thema der Ausstellung. Und auch der Vorgang des Umbaues selbst wird thematisiert. Danach soll von diesem kunstgewordenen Planungs- und Umbauprozess nichts unmittelbar spürbar bleiben, um den Normalbetrieb der künftigen Projekte nicht zu stören – außer das Relikt einer »blinden Tür« im Büro – vermutet Dragset. Sicher ist das noch nicht.
Der prozess- und handlungsbezogene (performative) Charakter und auch die zweckdienliche Revitalisierung sind Hauptmerkmale der »Arbeit am White Cube« in der dritten Generation. Ich möchte abschließend noch zwei weitere Elemente, die speziell die Arbeit von Elmgreen & Dragset betreffen, anfügen: die Sexualisierung des White Cube und die Delokation oder mit Deleuze/Guattari gesprochen, die »De-Territorialisierung«.

Die Delokation des White Cube

Mit *Dug Down Gallery/Powerless Structure, Fig. 45* (Abb. Seite 88–91) von 1998 exportierten die beiden Künstler das

The Delocation of the White Cube

In their Dug Down Gallery/Powerless Structure, Fig. 45 *(pp. 88–91) of 1998, the artists exported the ideal model of a gallery space from the protective zone of the museum into the wilderness of public space, where they lowered it into a pit dug in the lawn outside the building. Whereas the cell of the White Cube transformed everything placed inside it into art, the banished White Cube was compelled to assert itself as an object of art on hostile ground, not as an enclosed cube but as an open container that exposed its insides defenselessly under the open sky. Hurrying passers-by cast brief glances (and probably other things) into the pristine white of the cell, with its reception table and the empty showroom stand. One can easily imagine what this container looked like after four weeks of exposure to the whims of pedestrians and the rugged climate of Iceland!*
As a logical sequel to this exportation of the White Cube into the everyday context, Elmgreen & Dragset brought an aspect of the everyday into the museum. In Queer Bar/ Powerless Structures, Fig. 21 *(pp. 116–117) the cube-shaped form of a bar in a gay club was transferred into the exhibition space. In a direct reference to the White Cube, the artists turned everything inside out, placing the beer taps outside and and the bar stools for guests in the inaccessible interior. This paradoxical negation of the utilitarian function of a place of communication had its correlative in a social phenomenon specific to Nordic countries. Liberal legislatures there were among the first to recognize gay marriages, but in doing so, they devastated the bar scene. By granting them middle-class legitimacy, they turned outsiders in the communicative context into self-enclosed small families who preferred to spend their evenings at home. The association of this process of desocialization with the isolation of the white gallery space could be an allusion to the avant-garde which experienced a similar fate in the White Cube. After all, the neutralization of the exhibition wall resulted in a very similar*

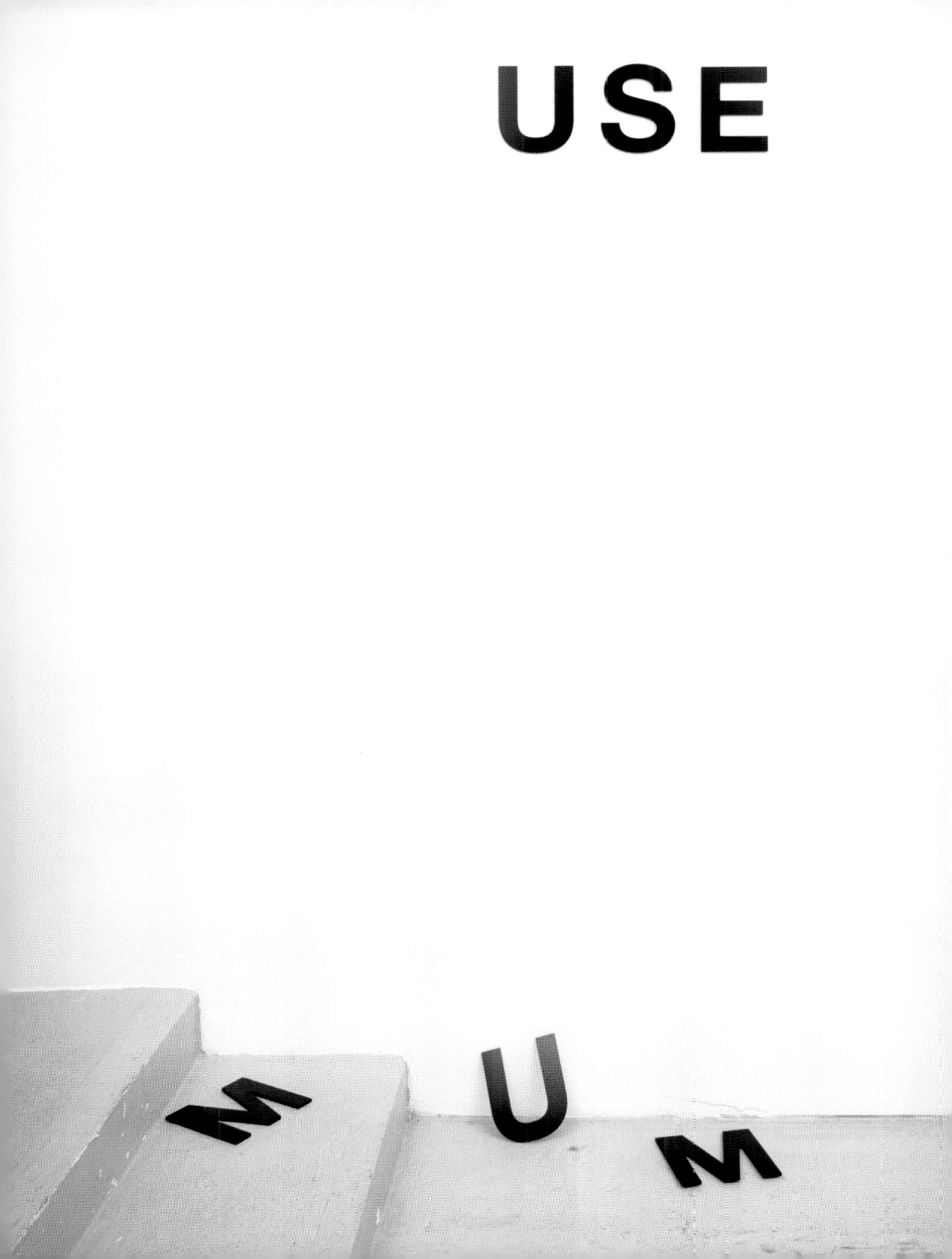
USE
M
U
M

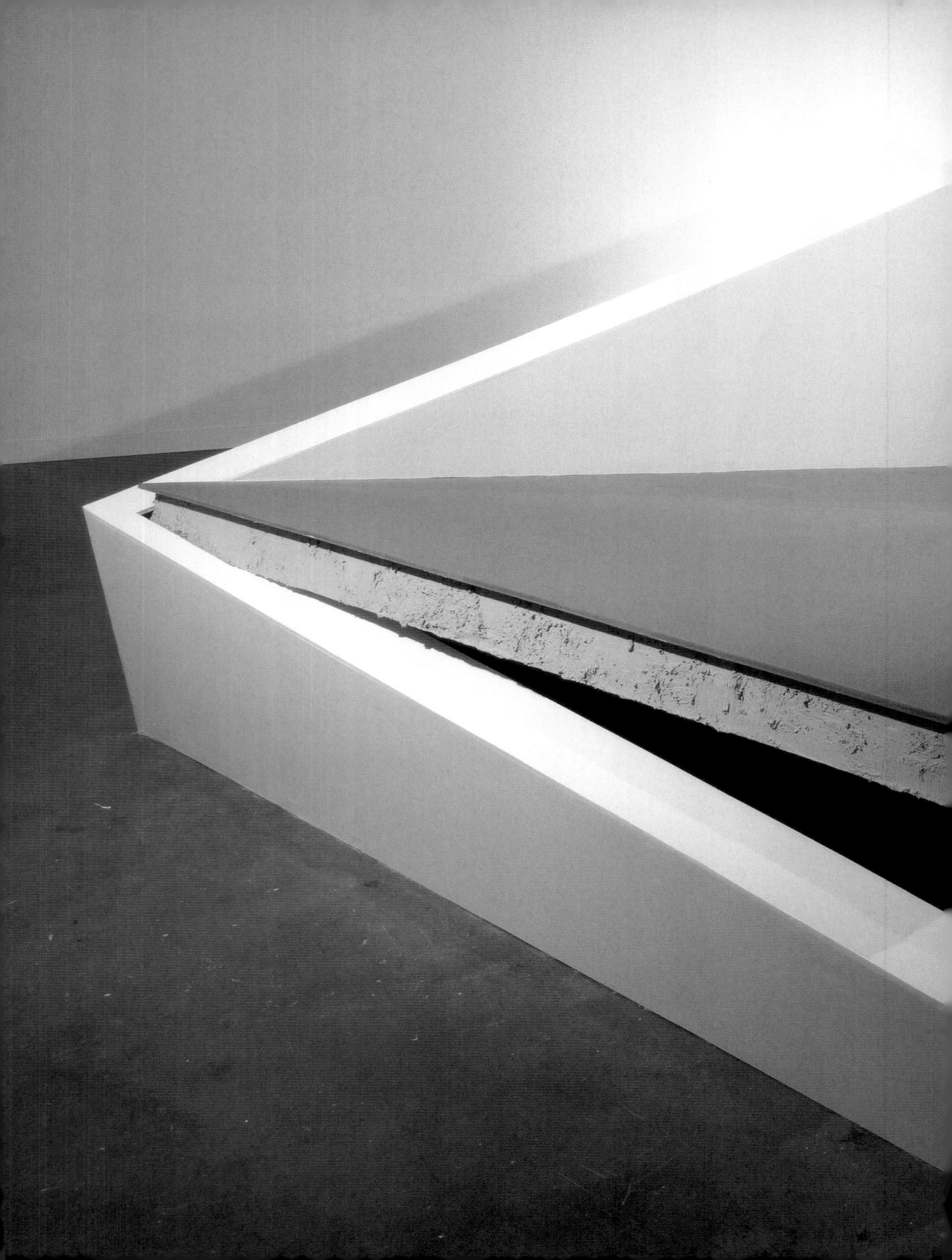

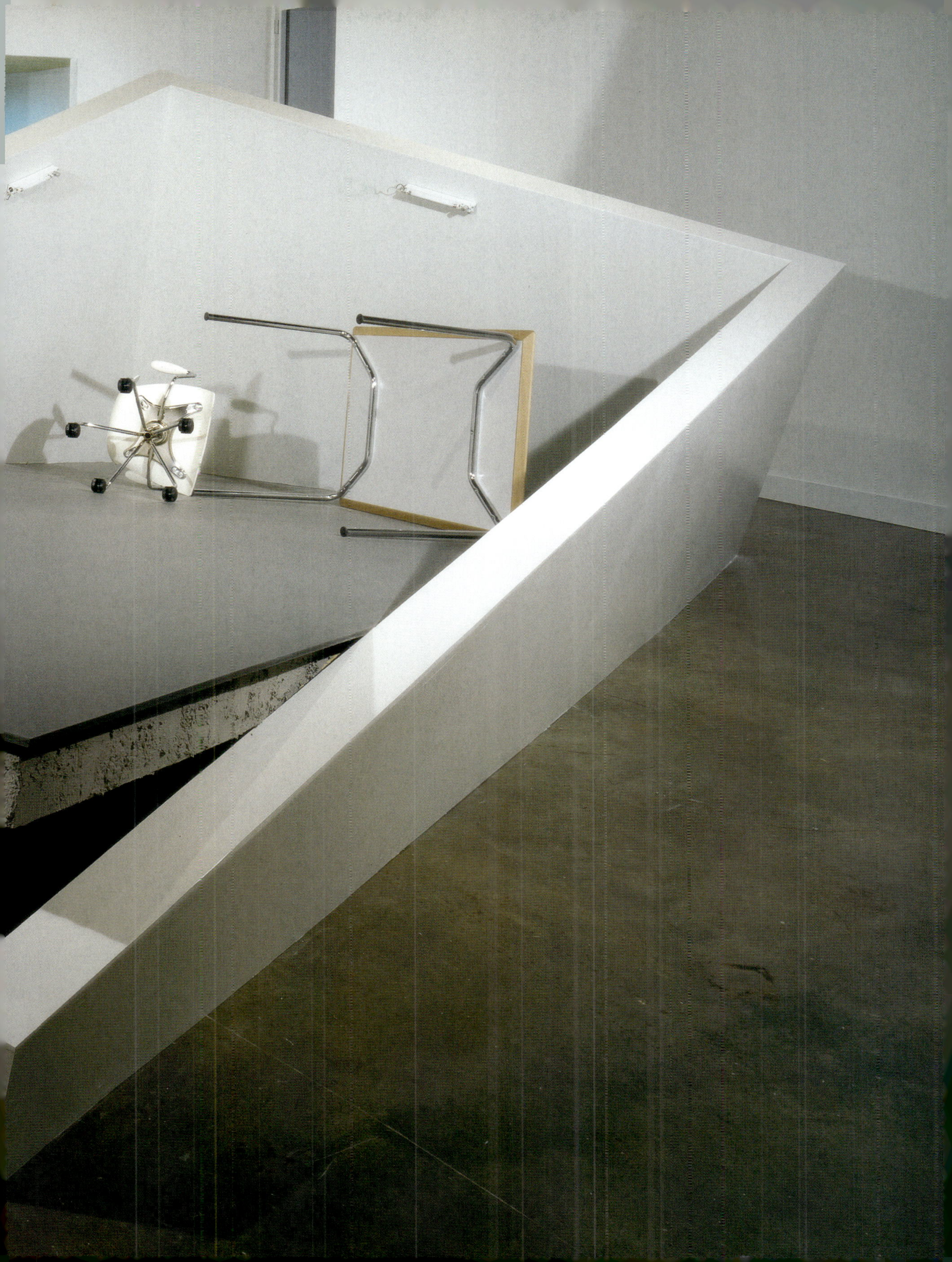

Idealmodell eines Galerieraumes aus der Schutzzone des Museums in die Wildnis des öffentlichen Raumes und versenkten es ebenerdig in der Wiese vor dem Gebäude. Verwandelte die Zelle des White Cube alles, was in sie hineingestellt wurde, in Kunst, so musste der verbannte White Cube sich auf feindlichem Territorium als Kunstobjekt behaupten, und zwar nicht als abgeschlossener Würfel, sondern als offenes Gefäß, das sein Innerstes schutzlos unter freiem Himmel entblößte. Die vorbeieilenden Passanten warfen kurz von oben einen Blick (und wohl noch andere Dinge) in die makellos ausgemalte Zelle mit dem Empfangstisch und der leeren Ausstellungskoje. Man kann sich vorstellen, wie dieser Behälter an dem frequentierten Spazierweg und in dem rauen Klima von Island nach vier Wochen ausgesehen hat!
Folgerichtig zu diesem Export des White Cube in den Alltag praktizieren Elmgreen & Dragset auch den Import von Alltäglichem ins Museum: In *Queer Bar/Powerless Structure, Fig. 21* (Abb. Seite 116–117) wurde aus einem Gay-Lokal die kubische Konstruktion des Bar-Tresens in den Ausstellungsraum transferiert. In Angleichung an den White Cube verkehrten die Künstler Innen und Außen, sodass die Bier-Zapfhähne außen und die Barhocker für die Gäste im unzugänglichen Inneren zu stehen kamen. Die paradoxe Aufhebung der Gebrauchsfähigkeit eines Ortes der Kommunikation korrespondierte mit einem sozialen Phänomen in nordischen Ländern. Die liberalen Gesetze erlaubten dort schon früh die Heirat unter Homosexuellen und förderten damit die Verödung der Bar-Szene. Die Verbürgerlichung machte aus den kommunikativen Außenseitern abgeschlossene Kleinfamilien, die abends lieber zu Hause blieben. Die Verknüpfung dieser De-Sozialisierung mit der Abkapselung des weißen Galerieraums könnte andeuten, dass es mit der avantgardistischen Kunst im White Cube ein ähnliches Schicksal nahm. Hatte die Neutralisierung der Ausstellungswand doch eine ähnliche Sterilisierung der Kunst zur Folge. Kritiker haben das auch immer wieder bemängelt. Doch gerade Brian O'Doherty hat

sterilization of art, as critics have consistently pointed out. Yet Brian O'Doherty described the White Cube—as mentioned above—as more than the dilemma of Modernism, which prevented the avant-garde from forging an alliance with life; indeed, as the American art critic writes, "for better or worse it is the single major convention through which art is passed," and "it has incubated ideas that would have abolished [society]." [5]

THE SEXUALIZATION OF THE WHITE CUBE

Nevertheless, a prominent characteristic of third-generation "work on the White Cube" is that it overcomes sterility. O'Doherty recognized the osmotic permeability of white gallery walls even during the transition to Postmodernism. Young women artists in particular have sought to sexualize their asexuality, as it were, by converting the seemingly neutral surfaces of exhibition space into an ultrasensitive, sexual spatial skin. In her mentally and physically exhausting action entitled The Licked Room *(2000), Ene-Liis Semper licked the entire exhibition room with her tongue. The Latvian artist thus carried Modernism's neurotic obsession with purity to the point of absurdity, while intensifying at the same time the physical sensations of the visitors who entered the room after watching the action in the empty, "licked" room on a video monitor. At the 2001 Venice Biennial, Priscilla Monge covered the inside—floor, walls, ceiling, and door—of an exhibition room measuring approximately four by four by four meters with sanitary napkins. The immaculate and "unlicked" (translation of a highly evocative German word used to describe something perfectly clean) white gallery wall suddenly became a projection screen for psychic isolation, for the cultural stigmatization of a specifically female bodily function, and for violence.*
Michael Elmgreen & Ingar Dragset's approach to the sexualization of the White Cube is closely related to the processes of deterritorialization and reterritorialization described

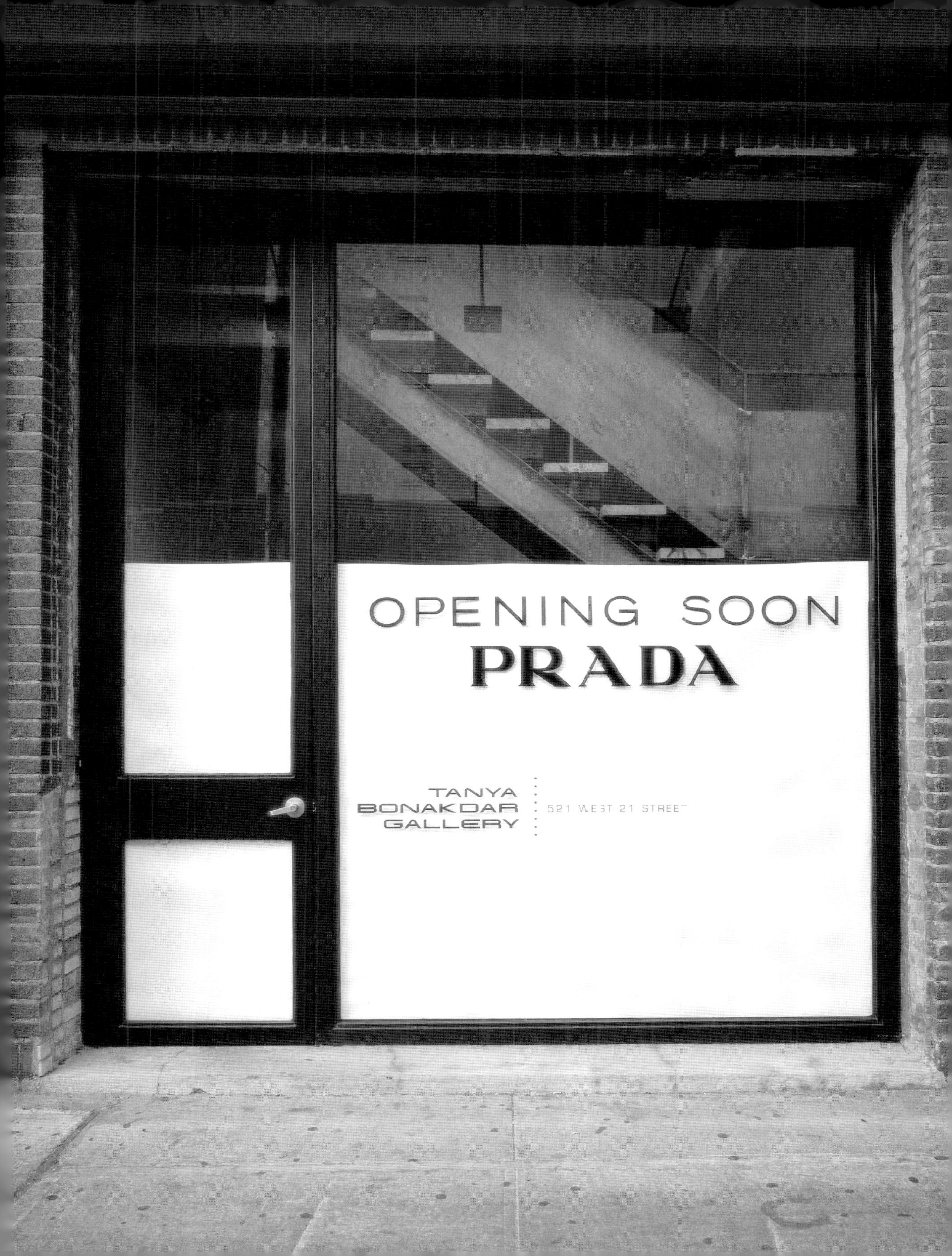
OPENING SOON
PRADA
TANYA
BONAKDAR
GALLERY
521 WEST 21 STREET

den White Cube – wie oben schon erwähnt – nicht nur als das Dilemma der Moderne, der die Avantgarde hinderte, sich mit dem Leben zu verbinden, beschrieben. Er sei, so der amerikanische Kunstkritiker, »im Guten wie im Schlechten die einzige bedeutende Konvention des Kunstlebens«, und er hat »Ideen ausgebrütet, die dieser Gesellschaft den Garaus gemacht hätten.«[5]

Die Sexualisierung des White Cube

Nichtsdestotrotz kennzeichnet die Überwindung der Sterilität die »Arbeit am White Cube« in der dritten Generation. O'Doherty ortete schon beim Übergang zur Postmoderne eine osmotische Durchlässigkeit der weißen Galeriewände. Vor allem junge Künstlerinnen versuchen die Geschlechtslosigkeit nun gleichsam zu sexualisieren, indem sie die scheinbar neutrale Oberfläche des Raumes in eine hochsensible geschlechtliche Raum-Haut umpolen. Ene-Liis Semper leckte in ihrer physisch und psychisch bis zur Erschöpfung reichenden Aktion *The Licked Room*, 2000, mit ihrer eigenen Zunge den gesamten Ausstellungsraum aus. Die lettische Künstlerin führte damit das neurotische Reinheitsdiktat der Moderne ad absurdum und verschärfte gleichzeitig das Körperempfinden der anschließend eintretenden Besucher, die die Aktion in der leeren, »ausgeleckten« Zelle am Video nachvollziehen konnten. Priscilla Monge kleidete an der diesjährigen Biennale in Venedig eine zirka 4 x 4 x 4 Meter große Ausstellungskiste innen mit schneeweißen »sanitary napkins« (Damenbinden) aus – Boden, Wände, Decke und Tür! Die unbefleckte und – im Deutschen gibt es ein schönes Wort:– »unbeleckte« weiße Galeriewand wurde plötzlich zur Projektionsfläche für psychische Isolation, für die kulturelle Stigmatisierung einer spezifisch weiblichen Körperfunktion und für Gewalt.

Michael Elmgreens & Ingar Dragsets Sexualisierung des White Cube steht in engem Zusammenhang mit der oben schon ausgeführten De- und Reterritorialisierung. Für ein

above. In a project commissioned by the Danish city of Århus, they exported a White Cube into a public park, the infamous Mindeparken, and designated the structure as a meeting point for gays (Pavilion/Powerless Structures, Fig. 55, pp. 124–129). The interior and exterior were interconnected in a labyrinthine configuration, and benches were placed inside. There were holes in the walls, allusions to the "glory holes" of gay vernacular—openings to be penetrated or looked through.

It is true that this third generation is engaged in highly diverse transformations of the White Cube—social, economic, institutional, religious, sexual, psychological, et cetera. Yet it is obvious that artists continually revert to the "ghetto" of white gallery space as a viable system of meaning and differentiation precisely because of its attributes of isolation and neutralization, revitalizing it—to quote from O'Doherty's (admittedly skeptical) concluding essay—as an "unchallenged arena of discourse."[6]

Markus Brüderlin

1 *See also Markus Brüderlin, "Die Transformation des White Cube—Wirkung und künstlerisches Umfeld der Essayfolge 'Inside the White Cube' von Brian O'Doherty", in Brian O'Doherty,* Die weiße Zelle/Inside the White Cube, *ed. Wolfgang Kemp, Berlin 1996, pp. 139–166*

2 *Brüderlin 1996, p. 141.*

3 *Wolfgang Kemp, "Vorwort," in O'Doherty 1996 (see note 1), p. 5.*

4 *Brian O'Doherty,* Inside the White Cube. The Ideology of the Gallery, *Santa Monica and San Francisco 1986, p. 79.*

5 . *O'Doherty 1986, pp. 80–81*

6 *O'Doherty 1986, p. 91*

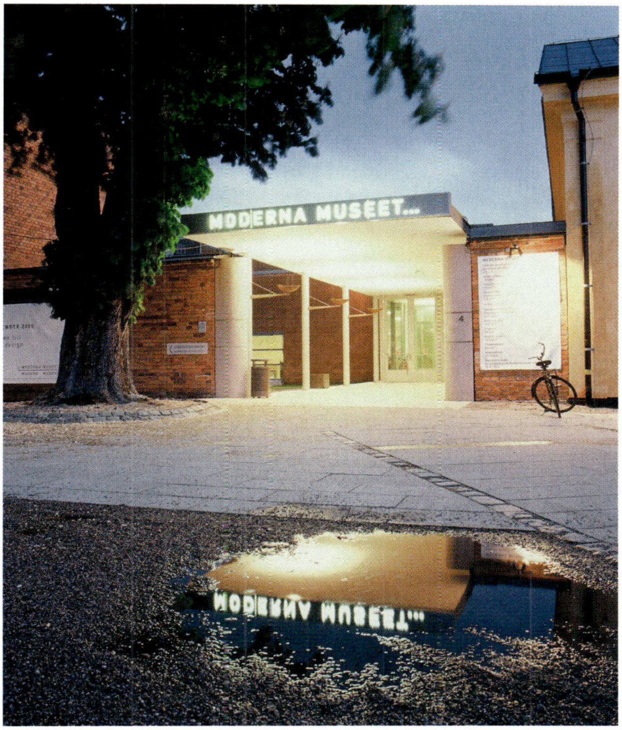

Projekt der dänischen Stadt Århus exportierten sie einen White Cube in einen öffentlichen Park, dem berüchtigten Mindeparken, und erklärten diese Konstruktion zum Schwulen-Treff *(Pavilion/Powerless Structures, Fig. 55;* Abb. Seite 124–129). Innen und Außen waren in einem labyrinthischen Spiegelverhältnis miteinander verbunden. Innen standen Bänke. In den Wänden gab es Löcher, in der Schwulensprache so genannte »gloryholes« – Öffnungen zum Penetrieren oder Durchschauen.
In der Tat: Diese dritte Generation arbeitet an den vielfältigsten Umnutzungen des White Cube: soziale, ökonomische, institutionelle, sakrale, sexuelle, psychologisierende usw. Auffällig ist aber, dass der als Getto kritisierte weiße Galerieraum gerade wegen seiner Qualitäten der Isolation und Neutralität immer wieder als funktionsfähiges System der Bedeutungs- und Differenzbildung herangezogen und – wie es O'Doherty in seinem allerdings skeptischen Nachwort nannte – als »unbestrittenes Forum des Diskurses«[6] revitalisiert wird.

Markus Brüderlin

1 Siehe auch: Markus Brüderlin, »Die Transformation des White Cube – Wirkung und künstlerisches Umfeld der Essayfolge »Inside the White Cube« von Brian O'Doherty, in: Brian O'Doherty, *Die weiße Zelle / Inside the White Cube*, hrsg. von Wolfgang Kemp, Berlin 1996, S. 139–166.
2 Brüderlin, S. 141.
3 Wolfgang Kemp, »Vorwort«, in: O'Doherty, 1996, S. 5.
4 O'Doherty, S. 88.
5 O'Doherty, S. 90.
6 O'Doherty, S. 137

seite | page 75–76, 78–79

Linienstrasse 160, 2001

Sperrholz, Türrahmen, Farbe, Halogenspots, Glas, Text / Plywood, wooden doorframe, paint, halogen spotlights, glass, sign text
400 x 290 x 900 cm
Klosterfelde, Berlin
Photo: Jens Ziehe
Private Collection / Privatsammlung, Athens

seite | page 80–81

Powerless Structures, Fig. 184, 2001

Holz, Styropor, Schablonenschrift / Wood, styrofoam, stenciled lettering
120 x 120 x 120 cm
Casino Luxembourg, Forum d'art contemporain, Luxembourg
Photo: Christian Mosar
Courtesy Klosterfelde, Berlin

seite | page 82–83

Powerless Structures, Fig. 88, 2000

Ortsbezogenes Projekt / Site-specific project
Holz, Farbe, Glas, Stahl, Büroausstattung / Wood, paint, glass, steel, office furniture, office equipment
240 x 600 x 600 cm
Manifesta 3, Ljubljana
Photo: Elmgreen & Dragset
Courtesy Tanya Bonakdar Gallery, New York; Klosterfelde, Berlin; Galleri Nicolai Wallner, København

seite | page 84–85

Elevated Gallery/ Powerless Structures, Fig. 146, 2001

MDF, Holz, Farbe, Kabel, Vinylballons, Büromöbel / MDF, wood, paint, cables, vinyl balloons, office furniture
530 x 575 x 340 cm
Ausstellungsansicht / Installation view, Statens Museum for Kunst, København
Photo: SMK Foto
Courtesy Tanya Bonakdar Gallery, New York; Klosterfelde, Berlin; Galleri Nicolai Wallner, København

seite | page 86

Elevated Gallery/ Powerless Structures, Fig. 146, 2001

Statens Museum for Kunst, København
Photo: Andreas Szlavik

seite | page 88–91

Dug Down Gallery/ Powerless Structures, Fig. 45, 1998

Holz, Farbe, Büromöbel, Halogenspots / Wood, paint, office furniture, halogen spots
220 x 320 x 500 cm
Galleri i8; Reykjavik Art Museum, Reykjavik
Photo: Bórkur Arnarson
Courtesy Tanya Bonakdar Gallery, New York; Klosterfelde, Berlin; Galleri Nicolai Wallner, København

seite | page 92

Powerless Structures, Fig. 107, 2001

Ortsbezogene Installation / Site-specific installation
Vinylschrift auf Plexiglas / Vinyl lettering on Perspex
101.5 x 122 cm
The Armory Show, New York
Courtesy Tanya Bonakdar Gallery, New York

seite | page 94–95

Traces of a Never Existing History/ Powerless Structures, Fig. 222, 2001

Holz, Edelstahl, Aluminium, Plexiglas, Fluoreszenzlicht, Farbe / Wood, stainless steel, aluminum, Perspex, fluorescent lighting, paint
310 x 430 x 780 cm
Ausstellungsansicht / Installation view, The 7th International Istanbul Biennial, Istanbul
Photo: Kim Nielsen
Courtesy Galleria Massimo de Carlo, Milano

seite | page 96

Traces of a Never Existing History/ Powerless Structures, Fig. 222, 2001

The 7th International Istanbul Biennial, Istanbul
Photo: Muammer Yanmaz

seite | page 99

MUSEUM/Powerless Structures, Fig. 118, 2001

Acrylbuchstaben / Acrylic letters
Größe variabel / Dimensions variable
Klosterfelde, Berlin
Photo: Jens Ziehe
Private Collection / Privatsammlung, New York

seite | page 100–101

Descending Gallery/ Powerless Structures, Fig. 145, 2001

MDF, Holz, Farbe, Zement, Büromöbel, Fluoreszenzlicht / MDF, wood, paint, cement, office furniture, fluorescent lights
240 x 300 x 500 cm
Ausstellungsansicht / Installation view, MIT List Visual Arts Center, Cambridge
Photo: Dan Soper Photography
Courtesy Tanya Bonakdar Gallery, New York; Klosterfelde, Berlin; Galleri Nicolai Wallner, København

page | seite 103

Opening Soon/ Powerless Structures, Fig. 242, 2001

Plastikbuchstaben, Papier / Plastic lettering, paper
360 x 208 cm
Ausstellungsansicht / Installation view, Tanya Bonakdar Gallery, New York
Photo: Mark Lutrelle
Courtesy Tanya Bonakdar Gallery, New York

page | seite 105

Powerless Structures, Fig. 120, 2000,

Ortsbezogene Installation / Site-specific installation
Aluminium, Plexiglas, Fluoreszenzlicht / Aluminum, Perspex, fluorescent lighting
40 x 529 x 20 cm
Ausstellungsansicht / Installation view, Moderna Museet, Stockholm
Photo: Anna Kleberg
Sammlung / Collection: Moderna Museet, Stockholm

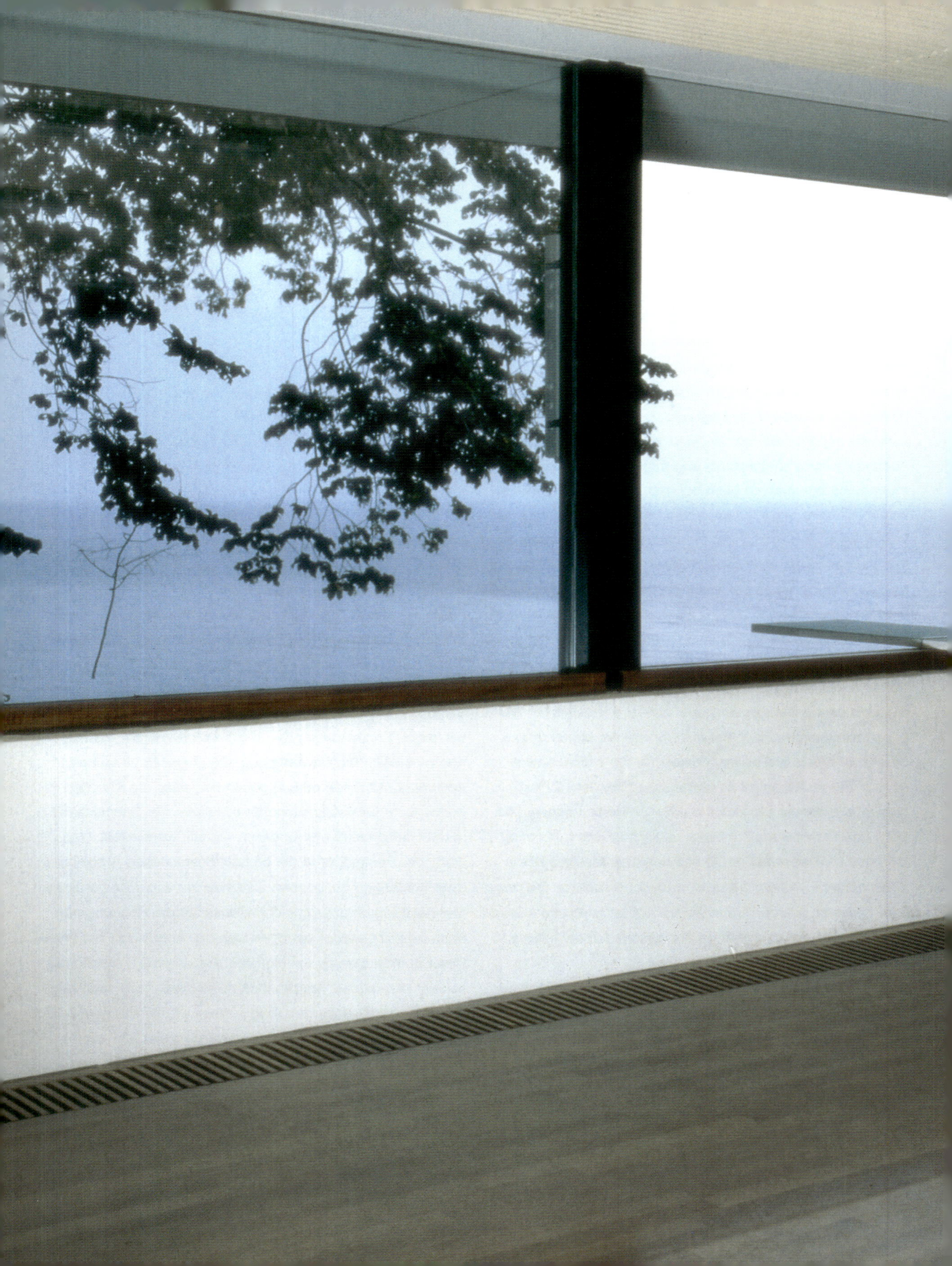

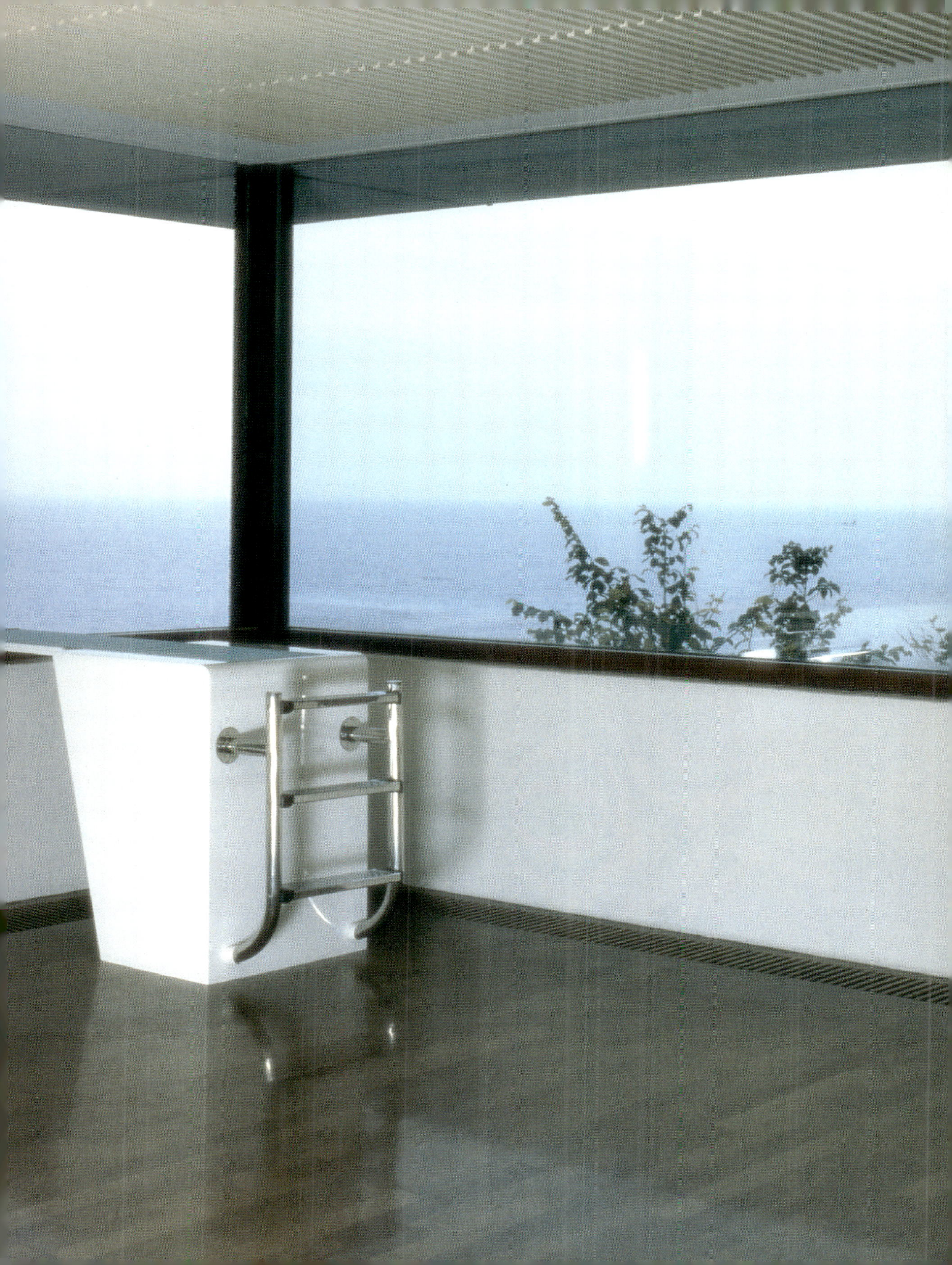

Die Arbeiten des dänisch-norwegischen Künstlerduos Michael Elmgreen und Ingar Dragset stellen in vielerlei Hinsicht einen fortlaufenden visuellen und empirischen Essay über die Frage dar, inwiefern Hoffnung und Enttäuschung weiterhin einen wichtigen Subtext zu unserer Erfahrung der Moderne aus dem Blickwinkel dessen bilden, was vorläufig an ihre Stelle getreten ist. Tief in unserem Innern möchten wir weiter an das Versprechen der Moderne glauben, sosehr wir um ihre Unzulänglichkeiten in Bezug auf die Erfahrungen heute tätiger Künstler wissen. Andererseits erlaubt es uns die Postmoderne nicht, so viel in die mit ihrem Projekt verbundenen Aussichten zu investieren, und so müssen wir diese Bedürfnisse sicher auf Armeslänge von uns halten.

Die meisten Künstler scheinen mehr oder weniger damit zufrieden zu sein, sich auf die eine oder andere Seite dieser Debatte zu stellen, und bemühen sich entweder um eine ironische Monumentalität oder um eine distanzierte Haltung, die ans Klinische grenzt. Elmgreen & Dragset dagegen ziehen es vor, unsere Aufmerksamkeit auf das Paradox zu lenken, das sich im Kern jeder Ablehnung der Väter durch eine Künstlergeneration verbirgt. Fällt nicht nach einer gewissen Zeit auch das Verlangen nach dem künstlerischen Vatermord in die Kategorie der Dinge, die es zu überwinden gilt? Indem sie die Möglichkeit zu begrüßen scheinen, dass sich Formen, die man einst für einander widersprechend hielt, jetzt verbinden lassen, melden Elmgreen & Dragset ebenso sehr Ansprüche auf das weiter geltende Versprechen der kulturellen Macht der Moderne an wie auf ihren letztendlichen Untergang aufgrund ihres eigenen Idealismus.

Als Elmgreen & Dragset die Kategorie der »*Powerless Structures*«, der machtlosen Konstruktionen oder Strukturen, erfanden, taten sie dies aus dem gemeinsamen Wunsch heraus, der im Erbe der Moderne enthaltenen Frustration einen Platz in den funktionalen Prämissen der ortsspezifischen Kunst zuzuweisen. Eine der ersten Arbeiten aus dieser noch nicht abgeschlossenen Serie, *Powerless Structures, Fig. 11,*

believing in the promise of Modernity, even though we know full well its shortcomings as applied to the experience of an artist working today. On the other hand, Postmodernity does not allow us to invest so deeply in the hopefulness of its project, so we are expected to keep those needs safely at arm's reach. Most artists, it seems, are fairly content to accept one or another side of this argument, aspiring either to an ironic monumentality or to a detachment that borders on the clinical. Elmgreen & Dragset, by contrast, prefer to draw our attention to the paradox that lies at the heart of each artistic generation's rejection of its fathers: after a certain length of time, does not the desire to commit artistic patricide itself fall under the category of things to be dispensed with? In an apparent embrace of the possibility that modes which were once thought of as mutually exclusive can now be brought together, Elmgreen & Dragset stake as strong a claim to the continuing promise of Modernism's cultural ascendancy as they do to its eventual downfall by way of its own idealism.

When Elmgreen & Dragset invented the category of "Powerless Structures," they did so as part of a shared desire to locate the frustration implicit in modernism's legacy within the functional premises of site-specific art. One of the earliest works in this open-ended series, Powerless Structures, Fig. 11, created in 1997 for an exhibition at the Louisiana Museum, articulates the intensity of its own compulsion toward modernist perfection with an easily articulated "goal": a diving board that would invite a viewer to propel himself from the inside of the museum's galleries into the chilly embrace of the nearby Baltic Sea. Rather than locate this structure entirely within or outside the gallery's confines, however, they split the difference, placing half of it inside and half outside. Therefore, when the viewer encounters the grounded portion of a diving board leading up to the window, with the other half extending outward into inaccessible

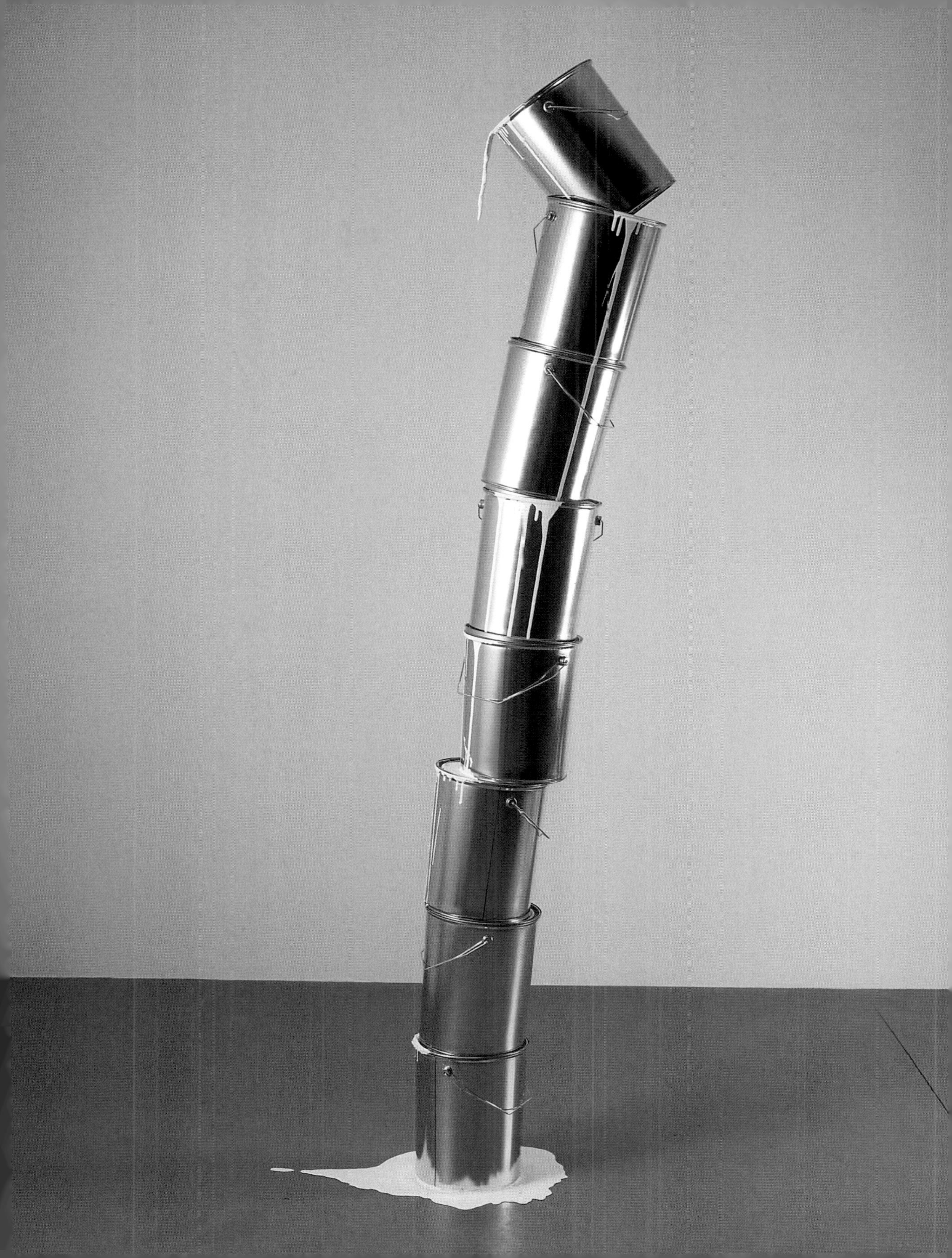

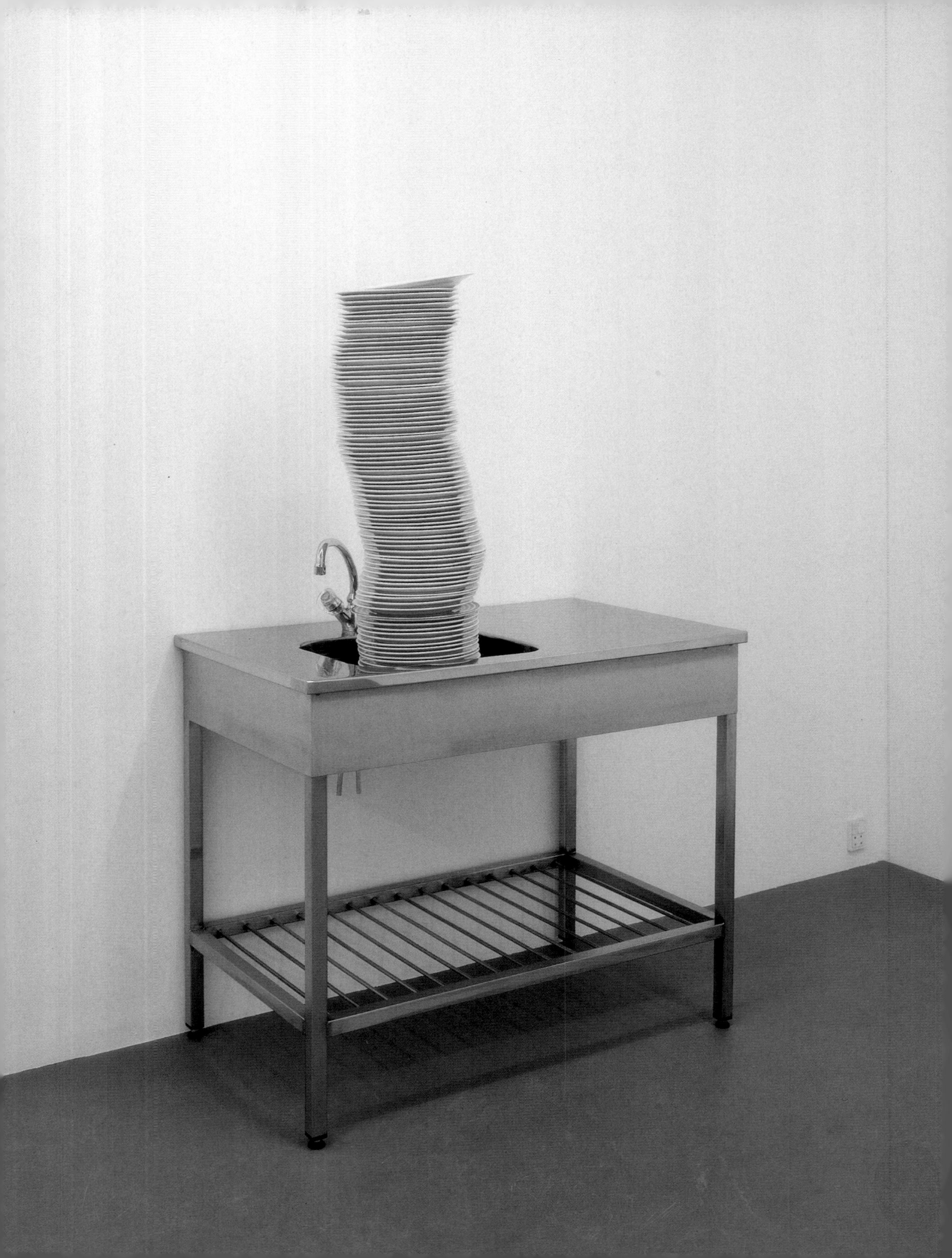

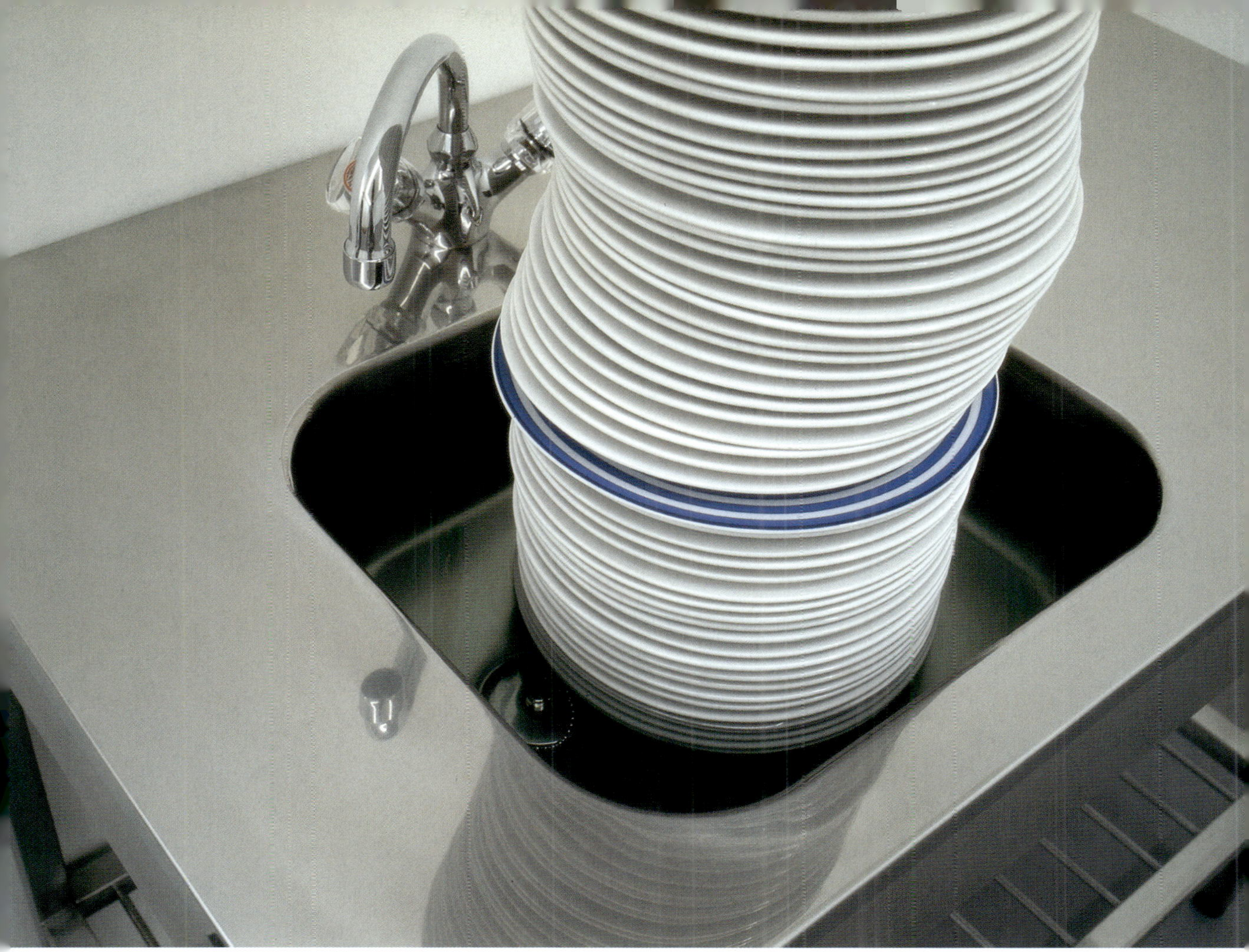

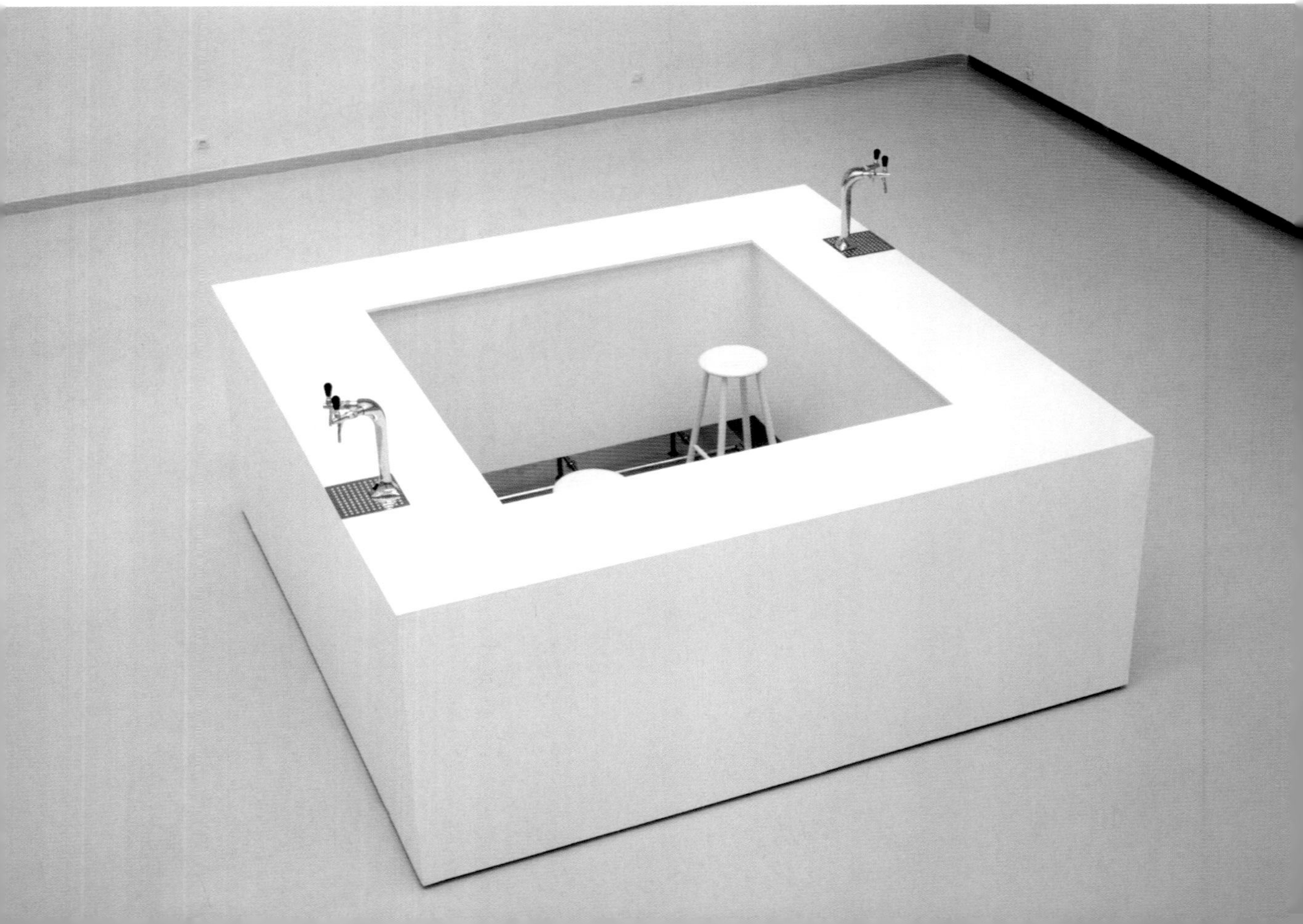

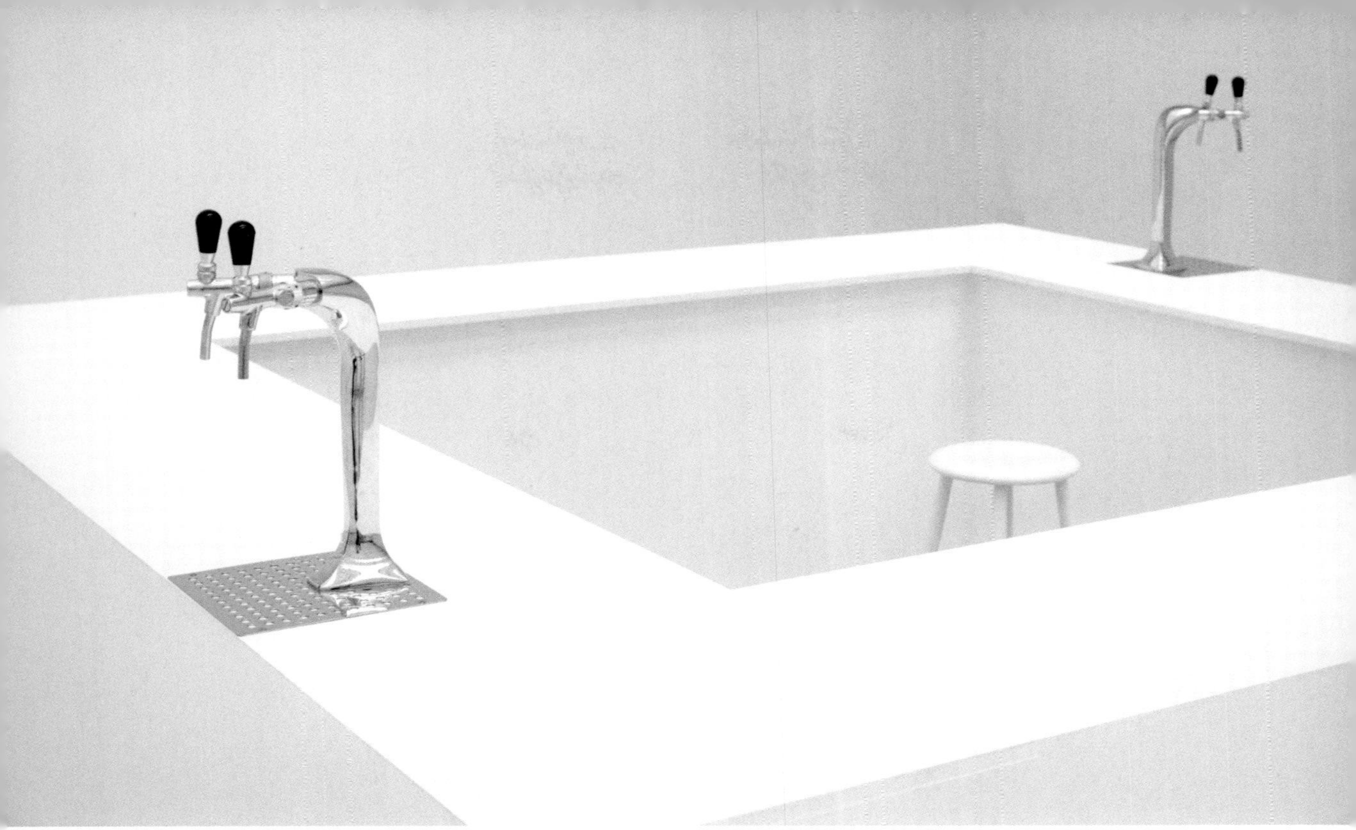

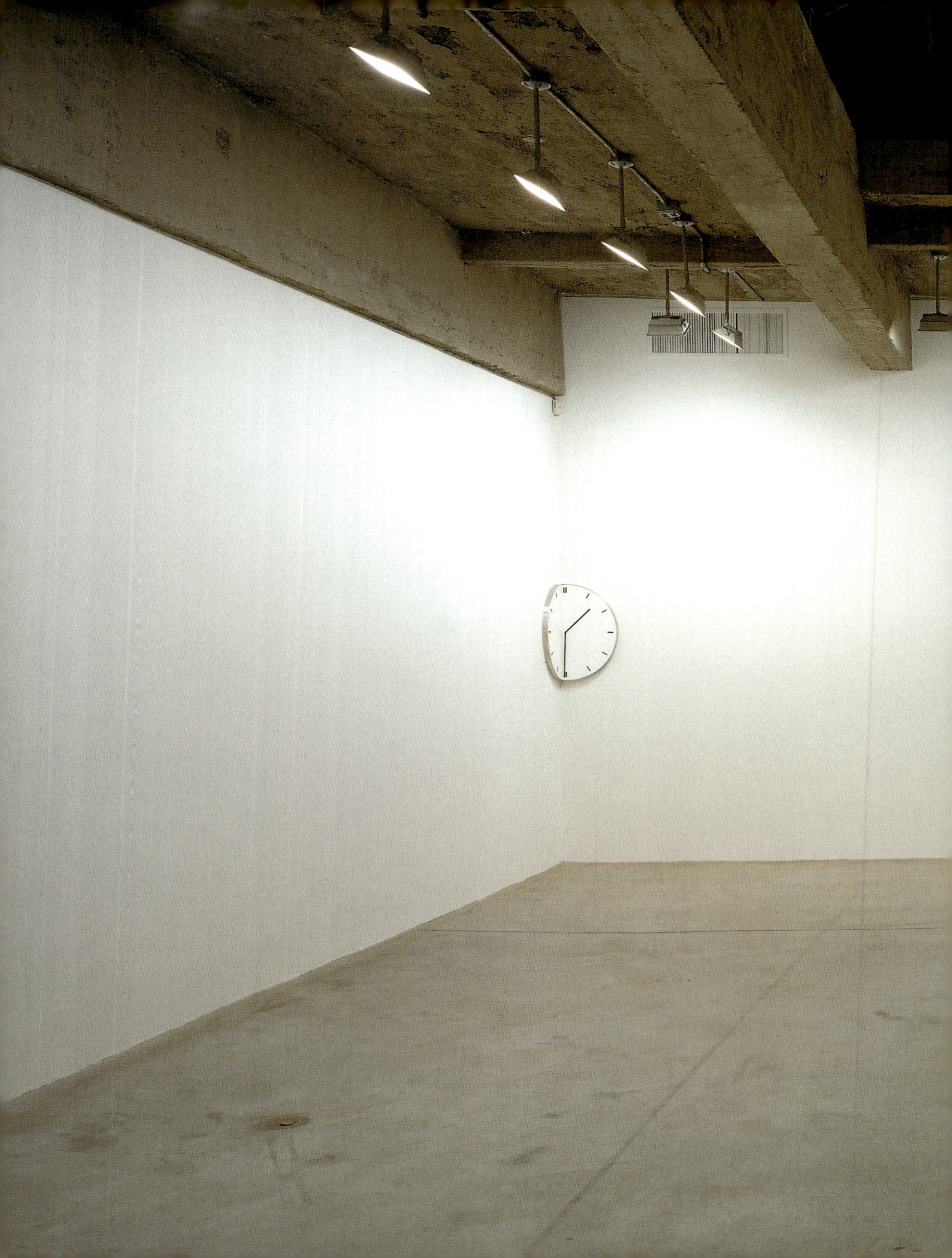

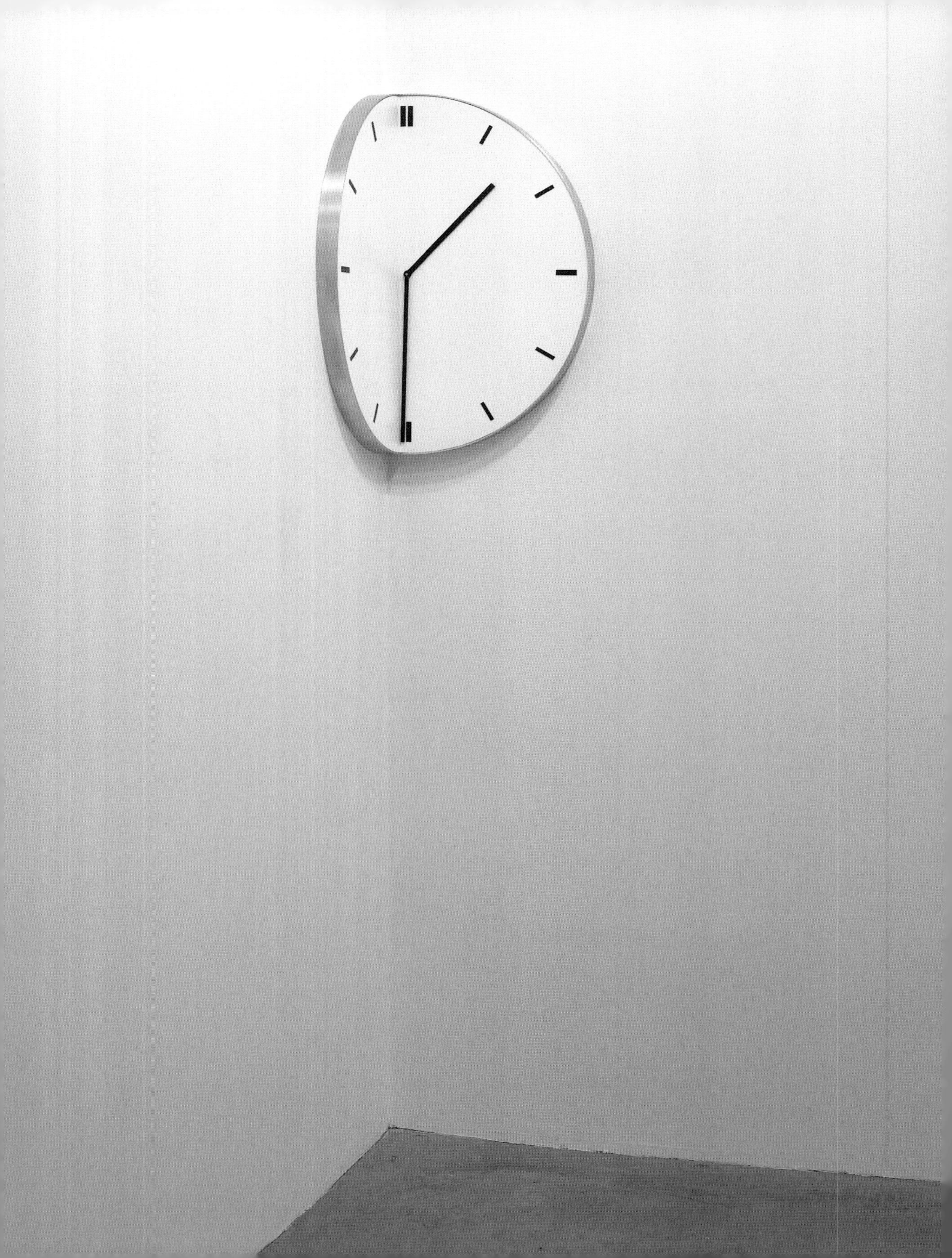

space, the response is connected both to the idealism implicit in the original premise and the inevitable disappointment in its results. Art attempts to take us somewhere else, the piece seems to say, but can only do so via our imaginations, leaving our physical self behind. The limits imposed by the physical world will always condition art's ability to propose a world in which such freedom knows no boundaries.
Although the visual confrontation with the diving-board-as-freedom and the window-as-obstacle seems to frame the work within the relatively straightforward limits of post-Duchampian irony, the underlying concerns of the "Powerless Structures" actually extend far beyond the traditional limits of the artwork within the world at large. As a gay couple working together in the tradition of Gilbert & George or Pierre et Gilles, Elmgreen & Dragset have been forced to confront the transformation of gay culture within the much larger field of social and cultural relationships, and have found themselves increasingly frustrated with what they have encountered. On the one hand, the apparent triumphs of the gay and lesbian movement have helped usher in a world where tolerance and respect for sexual differences is probably greater than at any other point in history. This is, of course, an important triumph for the civil rights movement and for the overall evolution of an open society. Partly as a result of these otherwise positive changes, however, the urgency that once propelled the creation and flowering of the international gay movement has greatly diminished, with the sole remaining need being the creation of public zones where gays can meet for sex and/or recreation. The primary exception to this rule has been those moments of crisis, such as the early years of the AIDS epidemic in the late 1980s and early 1990s, when societal homophobia contributed to many governments' slow response to the need to develop and make available appropriate medical treatment. Once these

die 1997 für eine Ausstellung im Louisiana Museum in Dänemark entstand, bringt die Intensität des selbstauferlegten Zwangs zu modernistischer Perfektion mit einem einfach formulierten »Ziel« zum Ausdruck: ein Sprungbrett, das den Betrachter einlädt, aus den Ausstellungsräumen des Museums in das kühle Wasser der nahe gelegenen Ostsee zu springen. Doch statt diese Konstruktion ganz innerhalb oder außerhalb der Grenzen des Ausstellungsraums zu platzieren, bringen sie die eine Hälfte drinnen und die andere draußen an. Wenn der Betrachter daher den geerdeten Teil des Sprungbretts sieht, der zum Fenster hinaufführt, während die andere Hälfte in einen unzugänglichen Raum hinausragt, so hat seine Reaktion sowohl mit dem Idealismus zu tun, der in den ursprünglichen Prämissen enthalten ist, als auch mit der unausweichlichen Enttäuschung über dessen Resultate. Die Kunst versucht, uns an einen anderen Ort zu führen, scheint diese Arbeit zu sagen, doch das kann sie nur auf dem Weg über unsere Einbildungskraft und indem sie unser physisches Ich hinter sich zurücklässt. Die Grenzen, die die materielle Welt uns setzt, werden stets die Fähigkeit der Kunst bestimmen, eine Welt zu entwerfen, in der solche Freiheit keine Grenzen kennt.
Auch wenn die visuelle Gegenüberstellung vom Sprungbrett-als-Freiheit und Fenster-als-Hindernis die Arbeit in die relativ klaren Grenzen einer post-duchampschen Ironie zu stellen scheint, reichen die tieferen Anliegen der »Powerless Structures« doch weit über die traditionellen Grenzen des Kunstwerks innerhalb der Welt hinaus. Als schwules Paar, das in der Tradition von Gilbert & George oder Pierre et Gilles zusammenarbeitet, mussten sich Elmgreen & Dragset mit dem Wandel der Schwulenkultur innerhalb des sehr viel größeren Feldes gesellschaftlicher und kultureller Beziehungen auseinander setzen, wobei sie zunehmend frustriert waren von dem, was sie sahen. Andererseits haben die scheinbaren Siege der Schwulen- und Lesbenbewegung dazu beigetragen,

eine Welt anzukündigen, in der sexuelle Unterschiede mehr toleriert und respektiert werden als zu irgendeinem anderen Punkt in der Geschichte. Das ist natürlich ein wichtiger Sieg für die Bürgerrechtsbewegung und für die Entwicklung einer offenen Gesellschaft überhaupt. Doch diese ansonsten positiven Veränderungen haben auch mit bewirkt, dass sich der Druck, aus dem heraus die internationale Schwulenbewegung einst entstanden und dann immer mehr erstarkt ist, sehr weit abgeschwächt hat und als einziges Bedürfnis nur noch die Schaffung von öffentlichen Bereichen übrig bleibt, in denen sich Schwule treffen können, um Sex zu haben und/oder sich zu vergnügen. Die wichtigste Ausnahme von dieser Regel stellte die Krise der ersten Zeit der AIDS-Epidemie Ende der achtziger und Anfang der neunziger Jahre dar, in der die Homophobie der Gesellschaft dazu führte, dass viele Regierungen nur sehr langsam auf die Notwendigkeit reagierten, eine geeignete medizinische Behandlungsmethode zu entwickeln und allgemein zugänglich zu machen. Als man sich dann in den Industrieländern endlich mit diesen drängenden Fragen befasste, schien sich nur ein sehr viel kleinerer Teil der Schwulen und Lesben für andere, ähnlich bedeutsame Probleme wie die gleichgeschlechtliche Ehe und die Adoption zu interessieren.

Das Image der Schwulenbewegung als einer immer zielloser werdenden Bewegung, der es an einem Auftrag fehlt, bildet eindeutig das Thema der Arbeit *Queer Bar/Powerless Structures, Fig. 21* (1998), die ursprünglich in Moss (Norwegen) und später in Vilnius (Litauen) gezeigt wurde. Dem allgemeinen guten Geschmack des Sprungbretts entsprechend, ist diese quadratische, queer (also seltsame oder Schwulen-)Bar ein gelungener Entwurf für einen transportablen oder begrenzten Raum, wobei die Höhe der Bar dazu benutzt wird, einen Eindruck von Größe zu erwecken und damit den Reiz zu erhöhen. Die wohl einzige Beschränkung, die diese Bar aufweist, besteht darin, dass niemand in das Innere des Vierecks hinein oder aus diesem heraus kann, womit sie für

urgent concerns were addressed in industrialized countries, equally momentous problems such as same-sex marriage and adoption seemed to be of interest to a much smaller segment of the gay and lesbians community.

The image of the gay movement as increasingly rudderless and lacking a mandate is the clear subject of Queer Bar/ Powerless Structures, Fig. 21 *(1998) originally presented in Moss, Norway, and later in Vilnius. Following the generic good taste of the diving board, the square-shaped queer bar is well conceived and constructed to suit a portable or confined space, using the bar height to lend an air of tallness, hence desirability. Probably the only inherent limitation to the bar is the fact that no one can get in or out of the interior, rendering it fully useless for an actual social situation. As a metaphor, the piece sums up the paradox represented by the very idea of a gay bar. On the one hand, it is a positive thing insofar as it enables gay men or lesbians to meet one another in an informal and gay-positive setting, just as one might find in a heterosexual bar. The drawback stems from the sense of discomfort that most non-gay people feel in a predominantly gay environment, which, coupled with the equal discomfort that most gay people feel letting their hair down in a predominantly heterosexual environment, produces a curious stalemate. Rather than demonstrating to the rest of society how gay people feel, think, and behave, the current situation serves to reinforce the comparative isolation in which many gay people live out that part of their lives in relation to the rest of society. Coming from a generation in which the val-ues of integration and expansion are prized above those of separatism and niche-marketing, Elmgreen & Dragset's have located the dilemma of how to be a fully realized gay person in an integrated society at the very center of their work. A very different perspective on integration is referred to in* Powerless Structures, Fig. 122 *(2000), consisting of two cornered doors connected by a security chain*

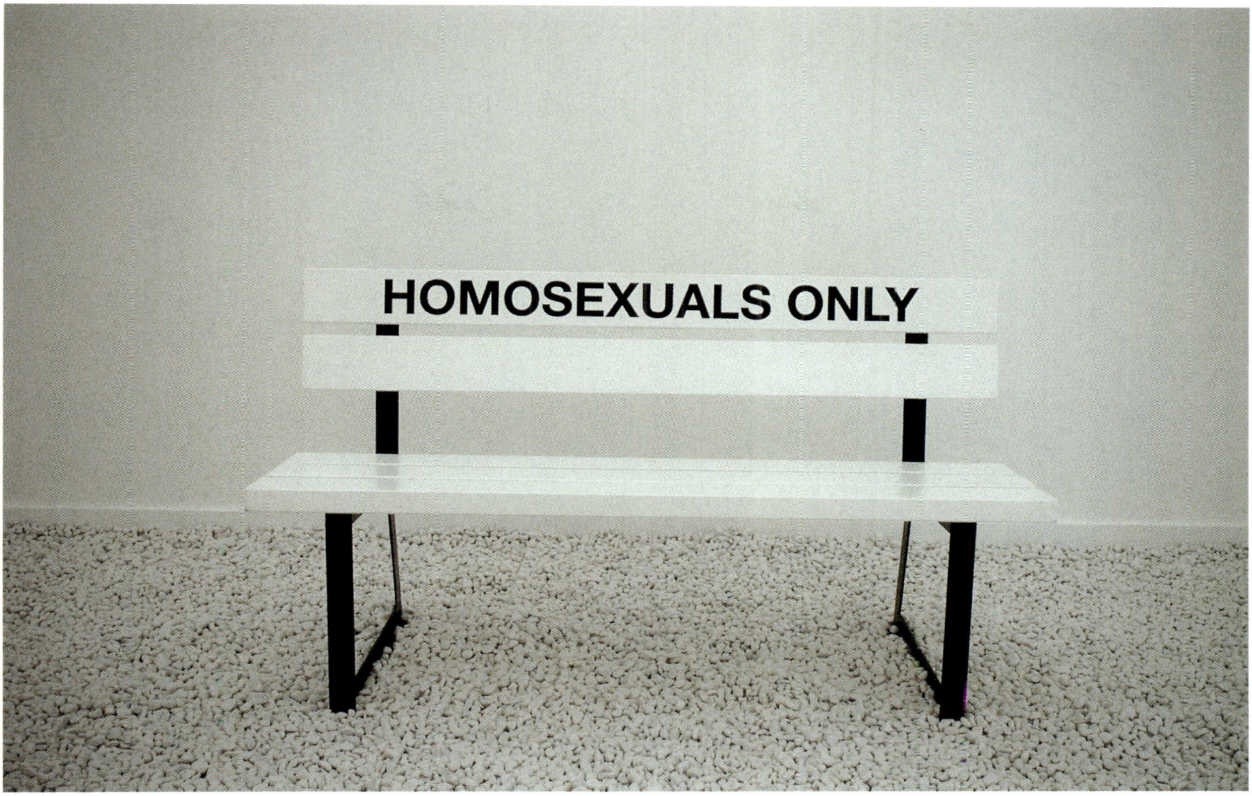
HOMOSEXUALS ONLY

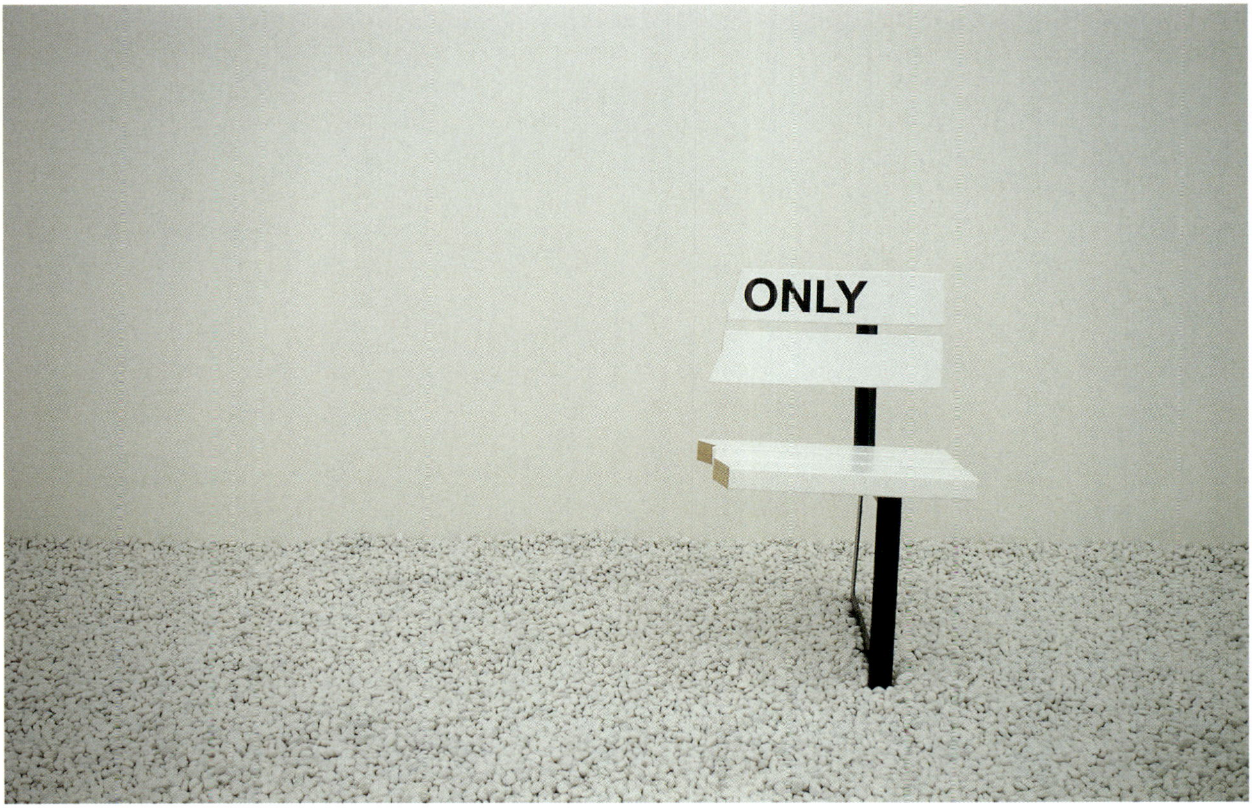
ONLY

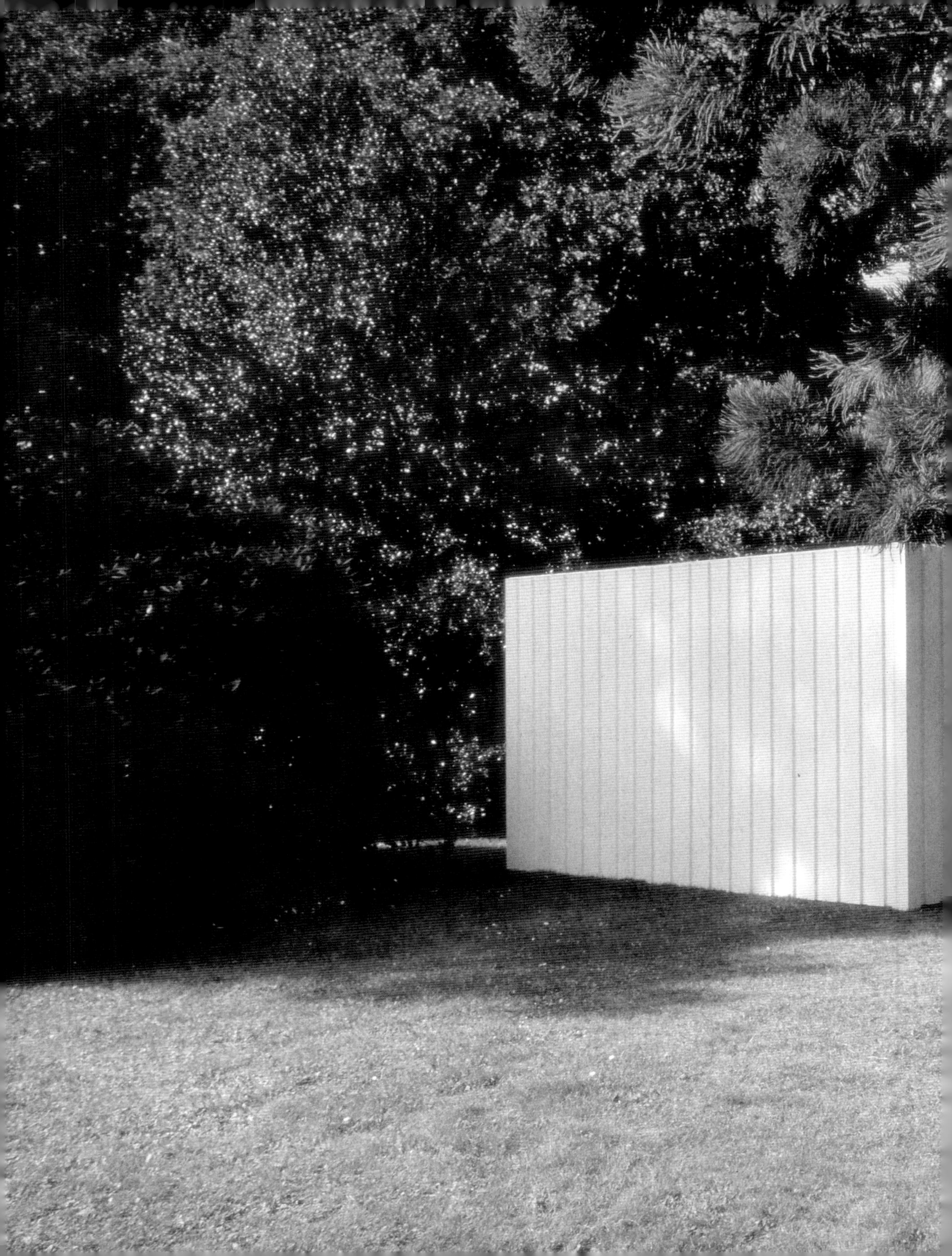

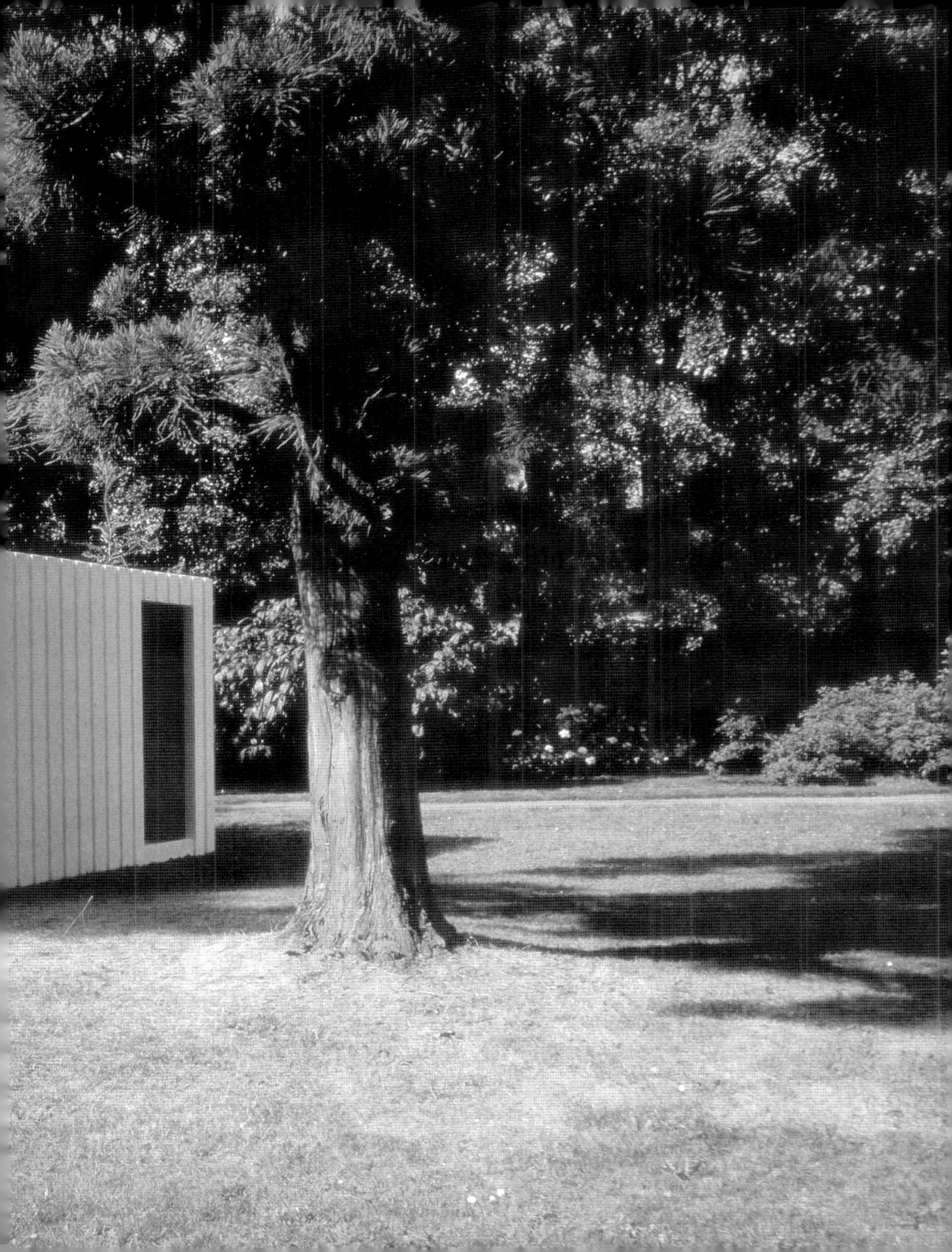

eine reale gesellschaftliche Situation völlig unbrauchbar wird. Die Arbeit ist eine Metapher für das Paradox, das die Idee einer Schwulenbar in sich trägt. Einerseits ist sie eine positive Sache, da sie es Schwulen oder Lesben ermöglicht, sich in einer lockeren, ihrer geschlechtlichen Ausrichtung wohlgesinnten Umgebung zu treffen, so wie Heterosexuelle in einer heterosexuellen Bar. Der Haken daran liegt in dem unbehaglichen Gefühl, das die meisten nicht-homosexuellen Menschen in einer vorwiegend homosexuellen Umgebung empfinden und das zusammen mit dem ähnlichen Unbehagen, das die meisten Homosexuellen empfinden, wenn sie in einer vorwiegend heterosexuellen Umgebung aus sich herausgehen, zu einem merkwürdigen Patt führt. Statt dem Rest der Gesellschaft zu zeigen, wie Homosexuelle fühlen, denken und sich verhalten, verstärkt die momentane Situation die relative Isolation, in der viele Homosexuelle im Vergleich zum Rest der Gesellschaft diesen Teil ihres Lebens zubringen. Als Vertreter einer Generation, in der die Werte der Integration und der Expansion über die des Separatismus und des Nischen-Marketings gestellt werden, haben Elmgreen & Dragset das Problem, wie man in einer integrierten Gesellschaft ein voll realisierter Schwuler sein kann, ins Zentrum ihrer Arbeit gestellt.

In einem ganz anderen Licht erscheint die Integration in *Powerless Structures, Fig. 122* (2000). Diese Arbeit besteht aus zwei übereck liegenden Türen, verbunden durch eine Sicherheitskette, die an den dafür vorgesehenen Schienen an beiden Türen befestigt ist und dazwischen schlaff herabhängt. Die Arbeit gehört zu einer größeren Serie von geplanten Skulpturen, in denen jeweils zwei Türen durch die inkorrekte Anbringung der Griffe, Schlösser und/oder Riegel unbrauchbar werden. Auch wenn diese Arbeiten die Implikationen der »Powerless Structures« sowohl vereinfachen als auch über rein subkulturelle Codes hinaus erweitern, so

which is attached to the lock of each one, the actual chain suspended limply in the air between the two. This work is from a larger series of proposed sculptures, each of which renders a pair of doors dysfunctional through the incorrect location of their knobs, locks, and/or bolts. Although these works both simplify and expand the references of the "Powerless Structures" so that they extend beyond purely subcultural codes, the state of futility or uselessness that they represent continues to have strong social undertones. By undercutting the premise of functionality or usefulness within a social environment, Elmgreen & Dragset explore the ways in which these same principles apply to individuals within societies. Each of us is powerless in a variety of ways, but some degree of powerlessness is invariably embraced by the individual, while the rest is imposed by outside forces. The paradox which the artists seem most interested in representing stems from cases in which external systems of order are applied incorrectly, so that the aspiration toward being useful and/or functional is effectively thwarted by circumstances beyond one's control. The adjacent doors, for example, may function well enough individually, so that their placement in relation to one another is what renders them unable to operate. Although the social metaphor may be more difficult to pin down in this work than in the previous examples, the sense of futility is more universally represented, making the effects of powerlessness shared, to a degree, by anyone who has a utilitarian expectation regarding the space in which they are displayed.

In these and other more recent examples, Elmgreen & Dragset seem increasingly engaged by the metaphor of power as it operates both within the framework of art and as part of the rules of social order. Each of us, as individuals, accepts our relative lack of power within the larger collective framework of society, yet we continue to cling to the possibility of

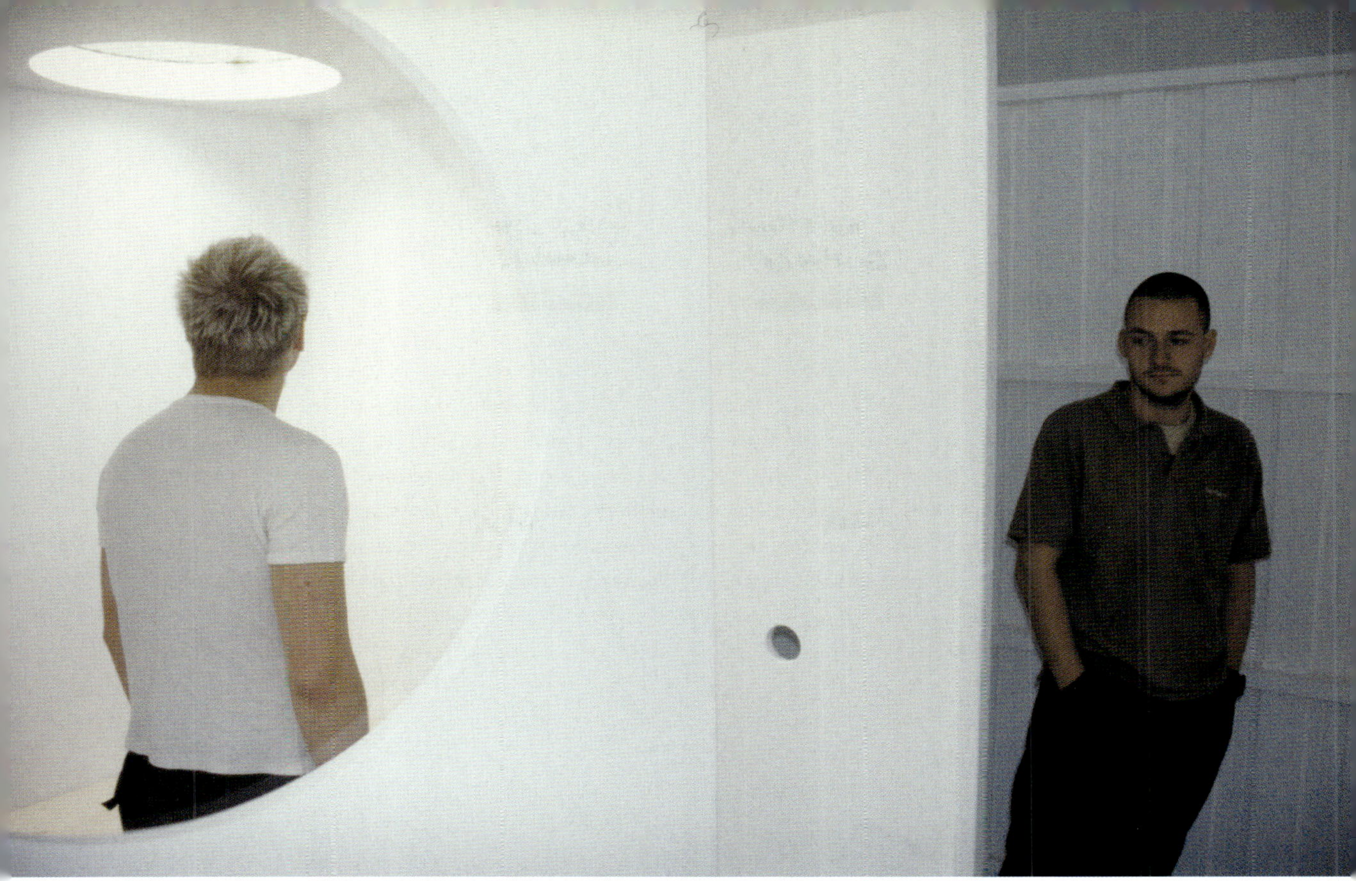

individual power as it relates to our ability to determine the outcome of our own lives. The power to create is, in effect, an extension of this latter possibility, and it illustrates the degree to which artists are expected to engage in a kind of free-play of assumed power, while simultaneously demarcating the zones in which their aspirations for power fall short. We tend to take for granted that artists do much of the creative work for the rest of the society, but we often see the limits of that creative power in terms of their control over their materials, or the context in which their work is experienced. By contrast, we do not always recognize that an equally important, if hidden, part of their role is to indicate the point at which their power—and by extension ours—terminates. By taking on the limits of power as the subject of their investigation, Elmgreen and Dragset choose not to restore any illusions regarding a sense of power, but continue to insist that the awareness of these limits is an extremely

hat doch der Zustand der Sinnlosigkeit oder Nutzlosigkeit, den sie darstellen, wiederum einen deutlichen gesellschaftskritischen Beiklang. Indem sie die Prämisse der Funktionalität oder Nützlichkeit in einem gesellschaftlichen Raum untergraben, untersuchen Elmgreen & Dragset, inwiefern diese Prinzipien auch für den Einzelnen innerhalb einer Gesellschaft gelten. Wir alle sind in vielerlei Hinsicht machtlos, doch ein gewisses Maß an Machtlosigkeit wird vom Einzelnen stets bereitwillig akzeptiert, während der Rest ihm von äußeren Mächten aufgezwungen wird. Das Paradox, das die Künstler am meisten zu interessieren scheint, entsteht dadurch, dass externe Ordnungssysteme inkorrekt angewandt werden, sodass das Bestreben, nützlich und/oder funktional zu sein, durch Umstände, über die man selbst keine Gewalt hat, wirkungsvoll vereitelt wird. So würde etwa jede der beiden übereck liegenden Türen für sich durchaus funktionieren; erst die Art, wie sie zueinander in Beziehung stehen, macht ihnen das Funktionieren unmöglich. Wenn die gesellschaftskritische Metapher in dieser Arbeit auch nicht so leicht dingfest zu machen ist wie bei den vorangehenden Beispielen, so ist das Gefüh der Sinnlosigkeit hier doch allgemeiner ausgedrückt, sodass die Auswirkungen der Machtlosigkeit bis zu einem gewissen Grad erfahrbar werden für jeden, der im Hinblick auf den Raum, in dem sie gezeigt werden, utilitaristische Erwartungen hegt.

In diesen und in anderen seitdem entstandenen Arbeiten scheinen sich Elmgreen & Dragset zunehmend damit zu befassen, wie die Macht im System der Kunst und als Teil der von der Gesellschaftsordnung vorgeschriebenen Regeln funktioniert. Als Einzelne akzeptieren wir unsere relative

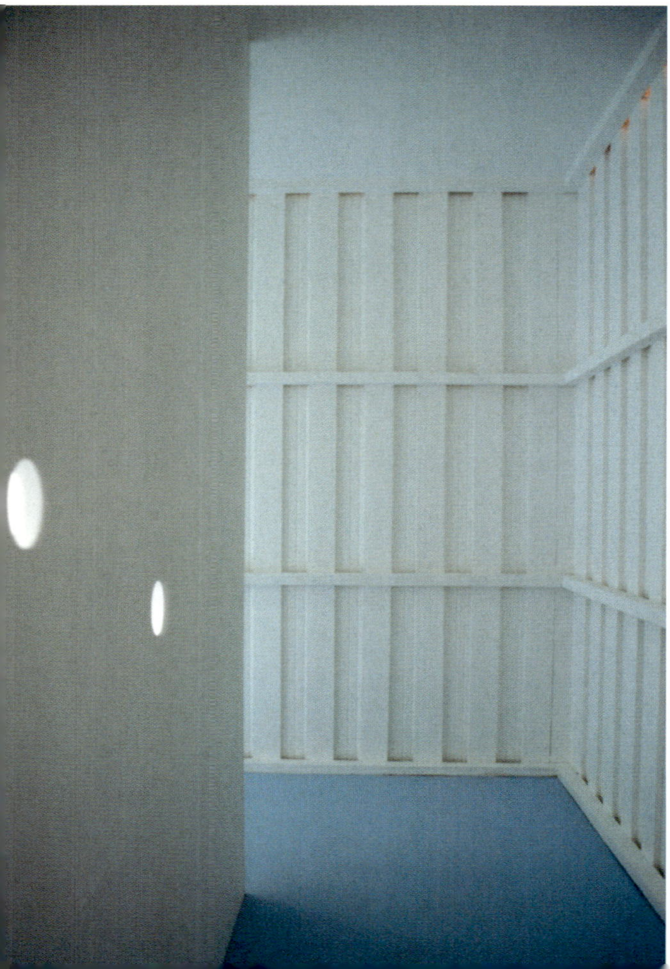

useful tool for the fully conscious citizen to have at hand. In fact, it is in the removal of the illusion of power that they enable their viewers to appreciate the possibility that individual actions can continue to operate at the precise margins where power and powerlessness meet, and perhaps even to convert the structures of containment into symbols of the restless and universal urge to venture beyond these limits. In other words, the exact spot where the illusion of power ends is where the seeds of hope for another kind of human interaction are sown.

Dan Cameron

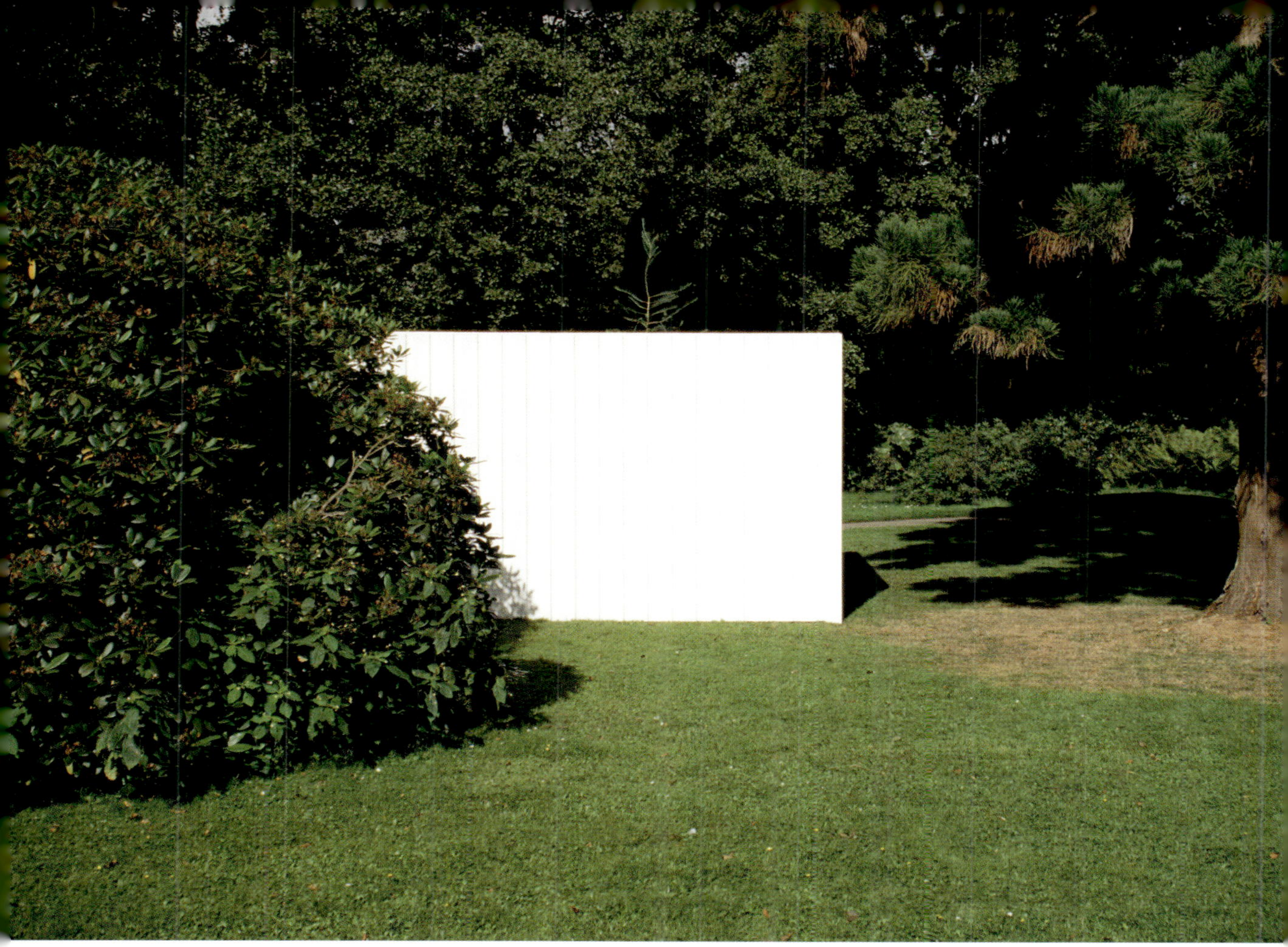

Machtlosigkeit in dem größeren, kollektiven System der Gesellschaft, und doch halten wir weiterhin an der Möglichkeit individueller Macht fest, wenn es um unsere Fähigkeit geht, das Ergebnis unseres eigenen Lebens zu bestimmen. Die Schöpferkraft ist letztlich eine erweiterte Form dieser Möglichkeit, und sie illustriert, bis zu welchem Grad von Künstlern erwartet wird, dass sie sich dem freien Spiel einer scheinbaren Macht widmen, während sie gleichzeitig die Bereiche abstecken, in denen ihr Anspruch auf Macht versagt. Wir neigen dazu, es für selbstverständlich zu halten, dass Künstler einen Großteil der kreativen Arbeit für den Rest der Gesellschaft übernehmen, aber oft werden uns die Grenzen dieser Schöpferkraft bewusst, wenn es um die Kontrolle, die die Künstler über ihr Material haben, geht oder um den Kontext, in dem ihre Arbeiten wahrgenommen werden. Dagegen machen wir uns oft nicht klar, dass ein ebenso wichtiger, wenn auch nicht offensichtlicher Teil ihrer Aufgabe darin besteht, auf den Punkt hinzuweisen, an dem ihre – und unsere – Macht aufhört. Indem sie die Grenzen der Macht zum Gegenstand ihrer Untersuchung machen, verzichten Elmgreen & Dragset darauf, irgendwelche Illusionen eines Machtgefühls zu nähren, und beharren stattdessen darauf, dass das Wissen um diese Grenzen für den bewusst lebenden Bürger ein äußerst nützliches Werkzeug ist. Tatsächlich kann der Betrachter bei ihnen gerade durch die Zerstörung der Illusion von Macht die Möglichkeit schätzen lernen, dass individuelle Handlungen weiterhin an den exakten Grenzen operieren können, an denen Macht und Machtlosigkeit zusammentreffen, und dass sie vielleicht sogar die Strukturen der Eindämmung in Symbole des rastlosen, allgemeinen Drängens, sich über diese Grenzen hinauszuwagen, verwandeln können. Mit anderen Worten: Der Punkt, an dem die Illusion von Macht endet, liegt genau dort, wo der Samen der Hoffnung auf eine andere Form von menschlicher Interaktion gesät wird.

Dan Cameron

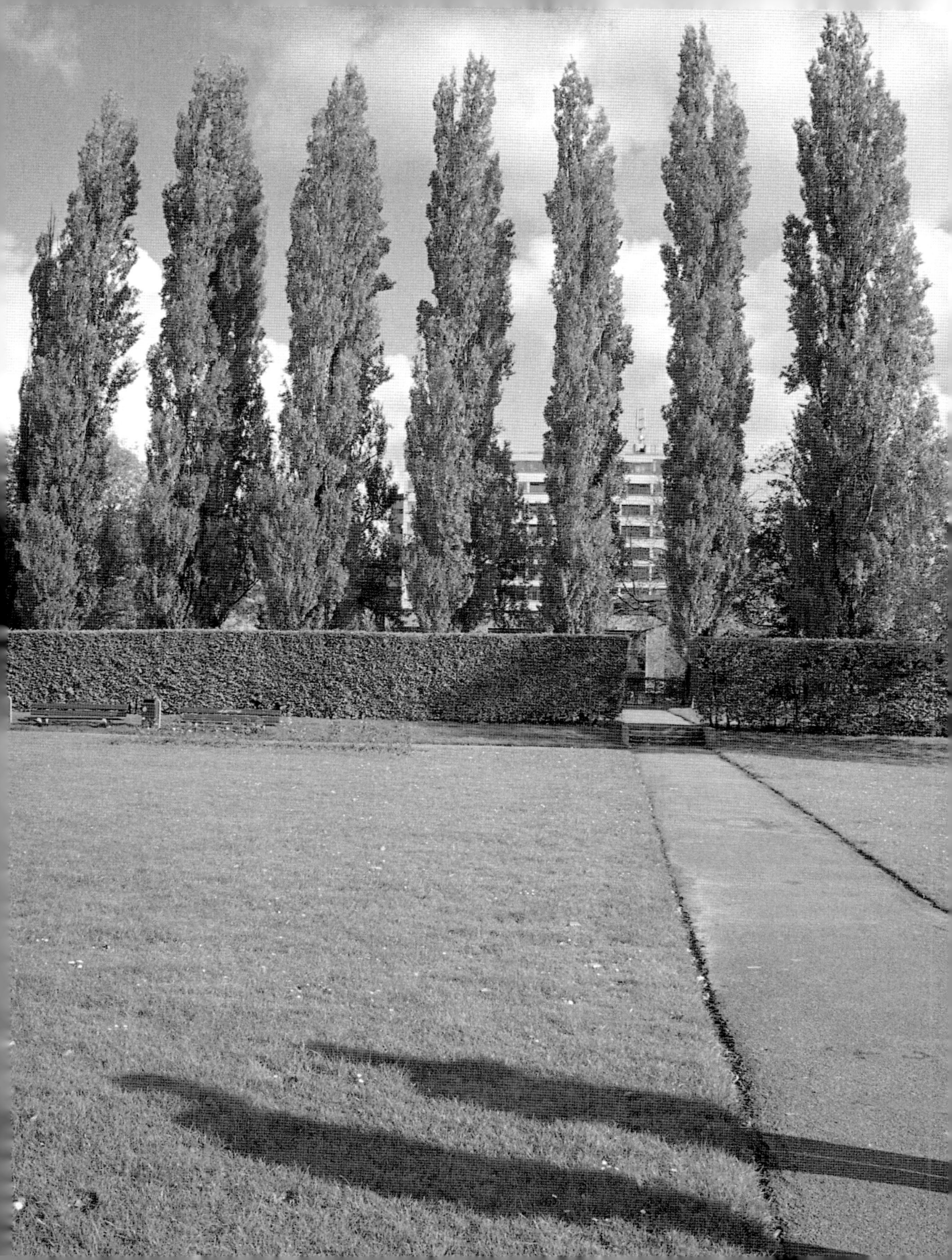

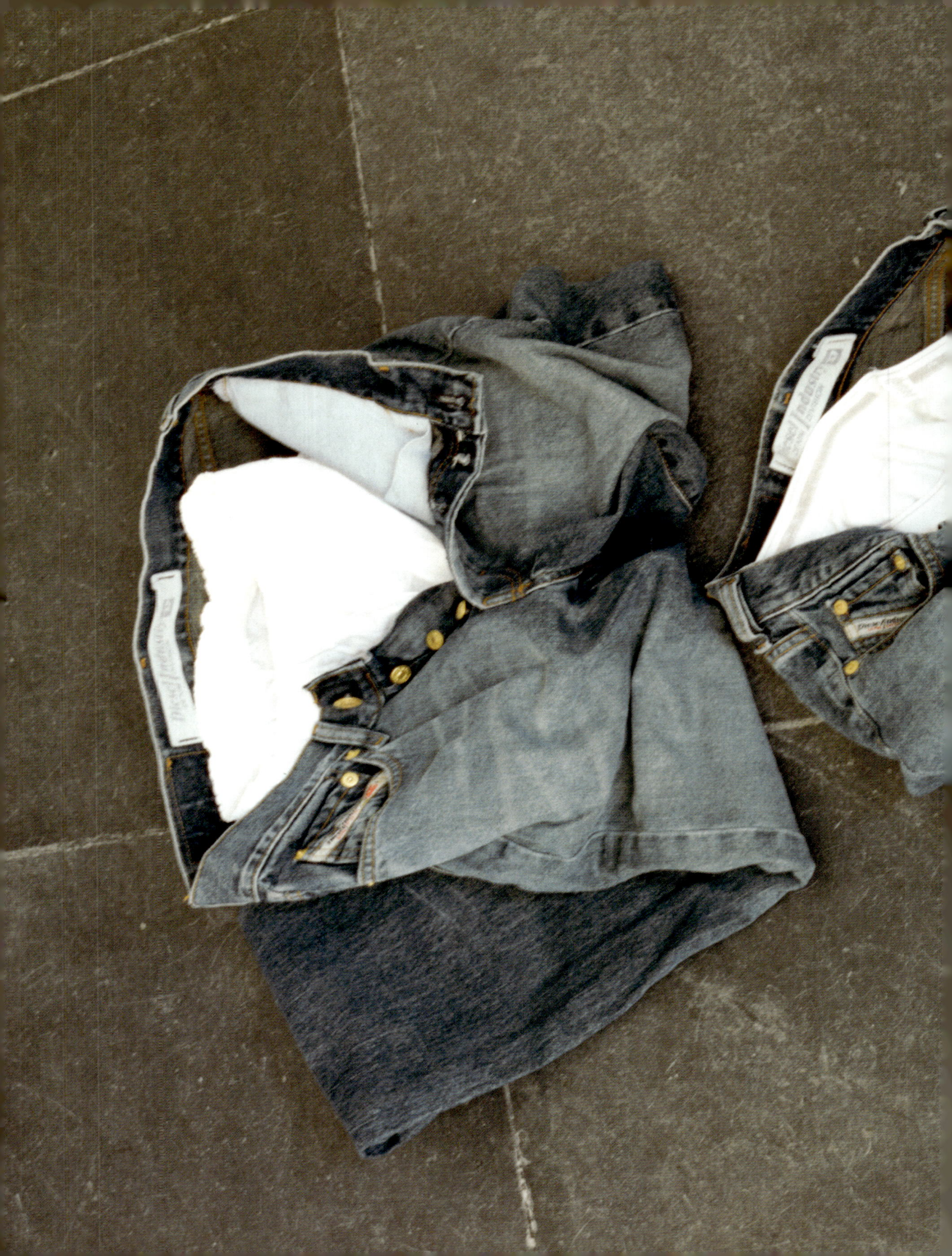

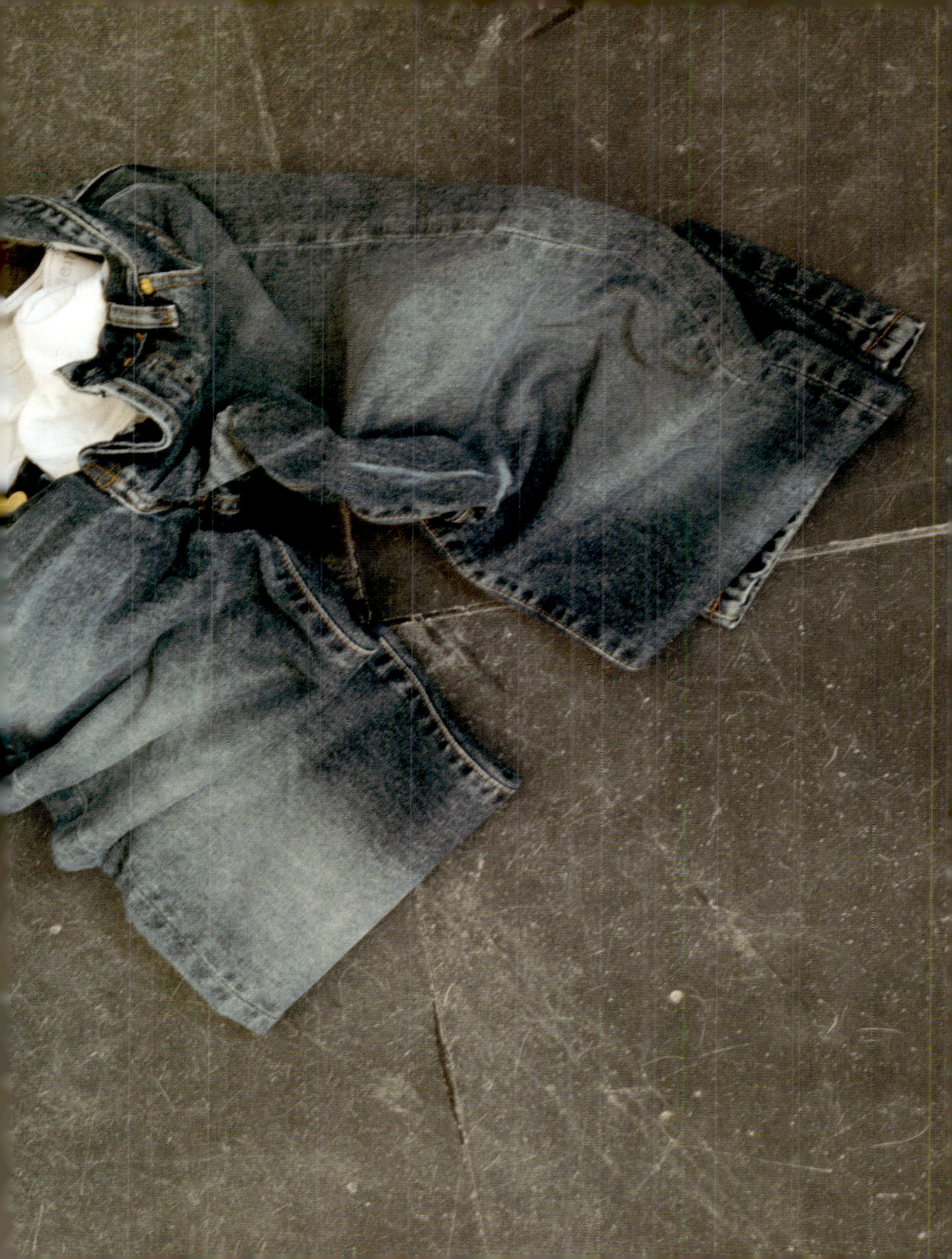

seite | page 108

Powerless Structures, Fig. 172, 2001

Malereimer aus Aluminium, Farbe, Schuh /
Aluminum paint bucket, paint, shoe
25 x 50 x 126 cm
Galleri Nicolai Wallner, Copenhagen
Photo: Bent Ryberg / Planet Foto
Courtesy Galleri Nicolai Wallner, København

seite | page 110–111

Powerless Structures, Fig. 11, 1997

MDF, Holz, Stahlleiter, Gummimatte /
MDF, wood, steel ladder, rubber matting
60 x 75 x 200 cm
Ausstellungsansicht / Installation view,
Louisiana Museum of Modern Art, Humlebæk
Photo: Bent Ryberg / Planet Foto
Sammlung / Collection: Louisiana Museum of Modern Art, Humlebæk

seite | page 113

Powerless Structures, Fig. 171, 2001

Malereimer aus Aluminium, Farbe /
Aluminum paint buckets, paint
240 x 50 x 60 cm
Galleri Nicolai Wallner, København
Photo: Bent Ryberg / Planet Foto
Sammlung / Collection: Charles J. Betlach, La Jolla, California

seite | page 114

Powerless Structures, Fig. 81, 1999

Stahlspüle, Teller, gefärbtes Wasser /
Stainless steel sink, plates, dyed water
180 x 100 x 65 cm
Galleri Nicolai Wallner, København
Photo: Bent Ryberg / Planet Foto
Sammlung / Collection: Thomas H. Bjarnason, Toronto

seite | page 115

Powerless Structures, Fig. 81, 1999

Detailansicht / Detail
Photo: Bent Ryberg / Planet Foto

seite | page 116–117

Queer Bar/Powerless Structures, Fig. 21, 1998

MDF, Farbe, Zapfhähne, Scheuerleisten, Fußstützen, Barhocker / MDF, paint, beer taps, skirting boards, foot rests, bar stools
120 x 300 x 300 cm
Ausstellungsansicht / Installation view,
Contemporary Art Centre, Vilnius
Photo: A. Kemezys
Sammlung / Collection: Axel Haubrok, Düsseldorf

seite | page 118–120

**Cornered Clock/
Powerless Structures, Fig. 244, 2001**

Aluminium, farbig besprühter Stahl /
Aluminum, spraypainted steel
71 x 41 x 37.5 cm
Ausstellungsansicht / Installation view,
Tanya Bonakdar Gallery, New York
Photo: Marc Lutrelle
Sammlung / Collection: Bernardo Nadal-Ginard and Laura Steinberg, Chestnut Hill, MA

seite | page 123

Powerless Structures, Fig. 117, 2001

Eisen, MDF, Farbe, Siebdruckschrift /
Iron, MDF, paint, silkscreened letters
80 x 120 x 40 cm, 80 x 50 x 40 cm
Witte de With, Rotterdam
Photo: Elmgreen & Dragset
Private Collection / Privatsammlung, Italia

seite | page 124–125

**Cruising Pavilion/
Powerless Structures, Fig. 55, 1998**

Holz, Farbe, Plexiglas, Gummimatten /
Wood, paint, perspex, rubber matting
230 x 400 x 400 cm
Ausstellungsansicht / Installation view
Marselisborg Forest, Århus
Photo: Bent Ryberg / Planet Foto
Courtesy Galleri Nicolai Wallner, København

seite | page 127–129

**Cruising Pavilion/
Powerless Structures, Fig. 55, 1998**

Marselisborg Forest, Århus
Photo: Elmgreen & Dragset
Courtesy Galleri Nicolai Wallner, København

seite | page 131

Rose Garden / Rosengarten, Rotterdam, 2001

Photo: Elmgreen & Dragset

seite | page 132–133

Powerless Structures, Fig. 19, 1998

Levi-Jeans, Calvin-Klein-Unterwäsche /
Levi's jeans, Calvin Klein underwear
Größe variabel / Dimensions variable
Frankfurter Kunstverein
Photo: Frankfurter Kunstverein
Sammlung / Collection: Medhi Chouakri, Berlin; Cosima von Bonin, Köln; Jacob Fabricius, København

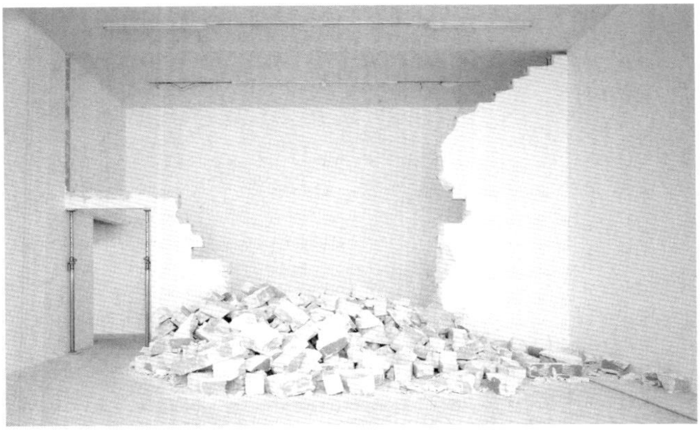
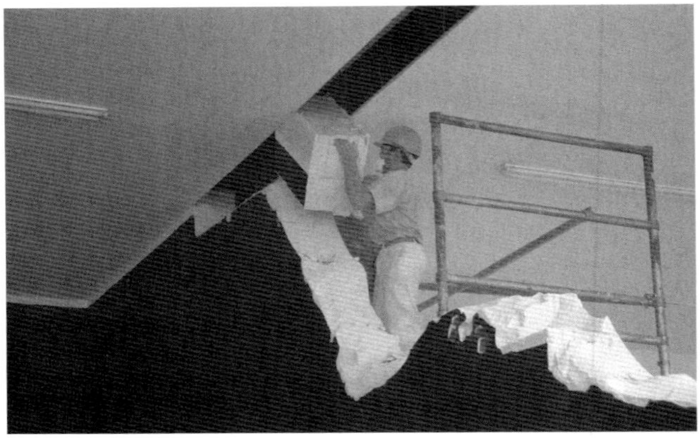
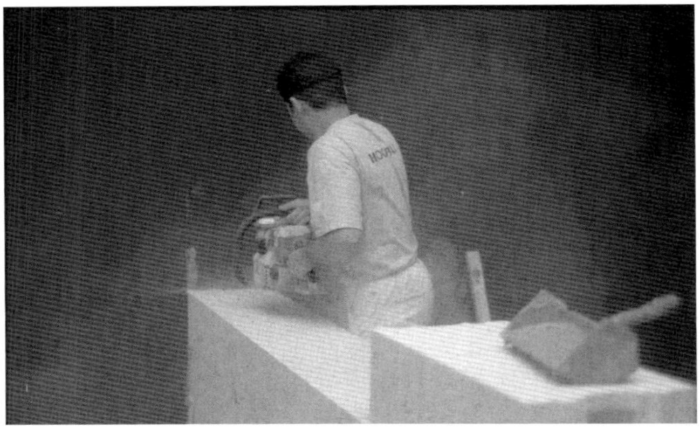
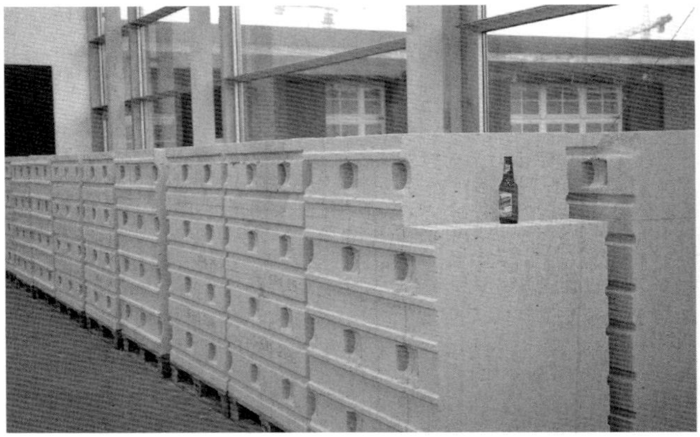
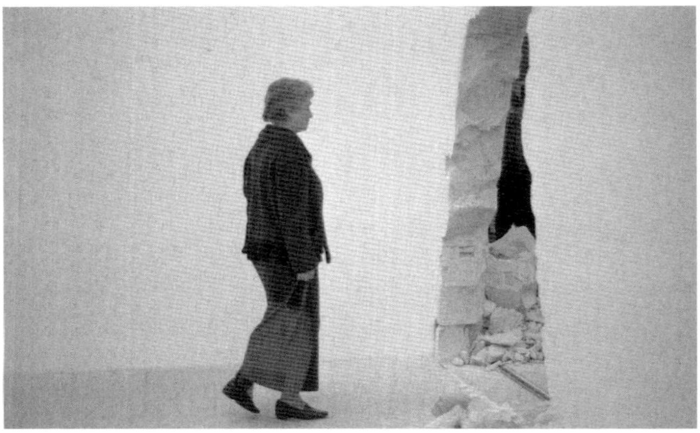
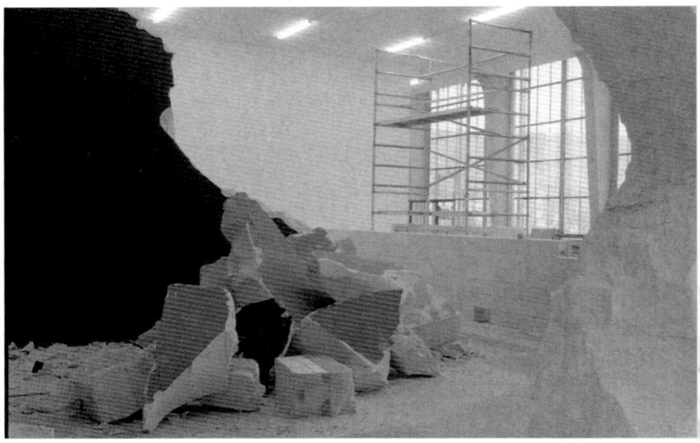
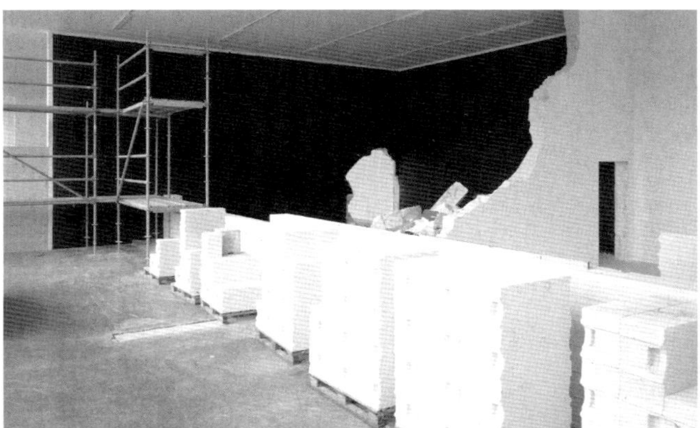
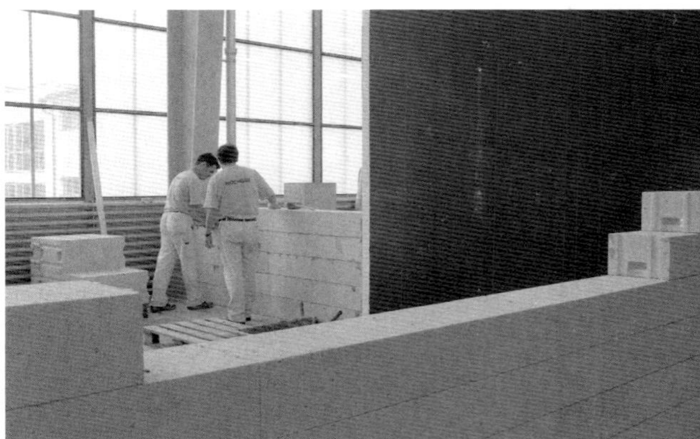

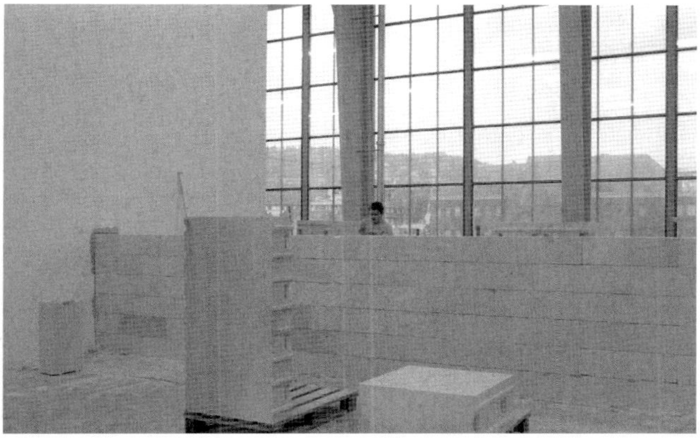
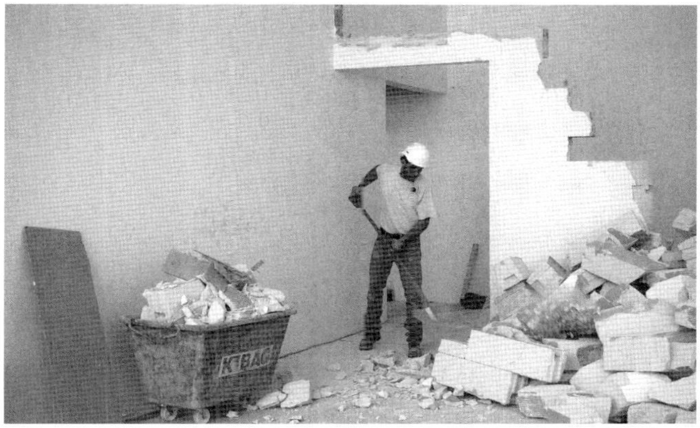
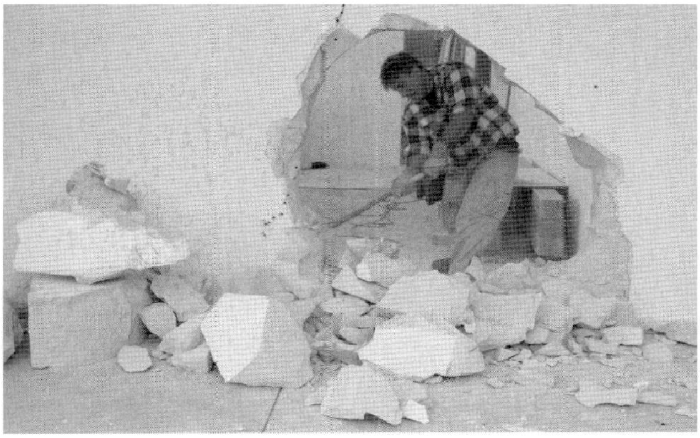
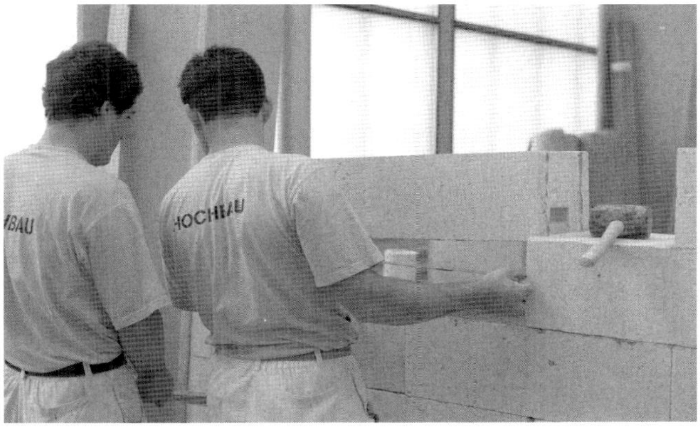
HOCHBAU
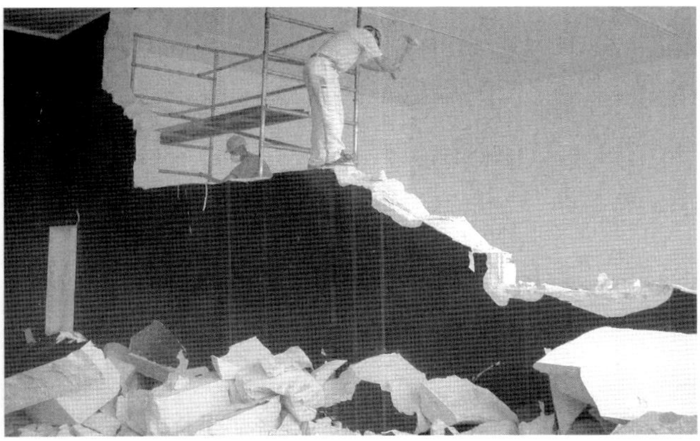
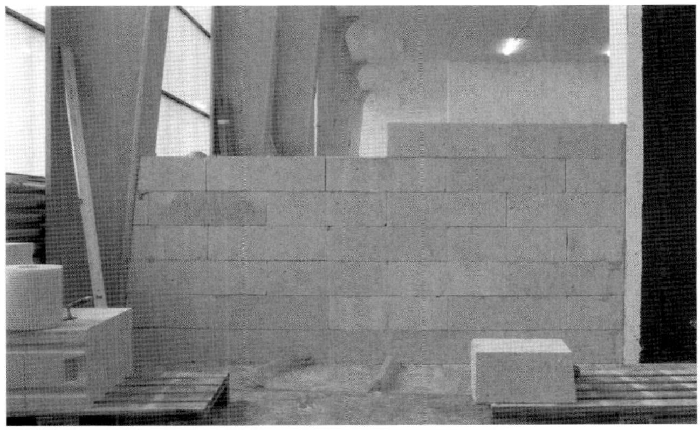
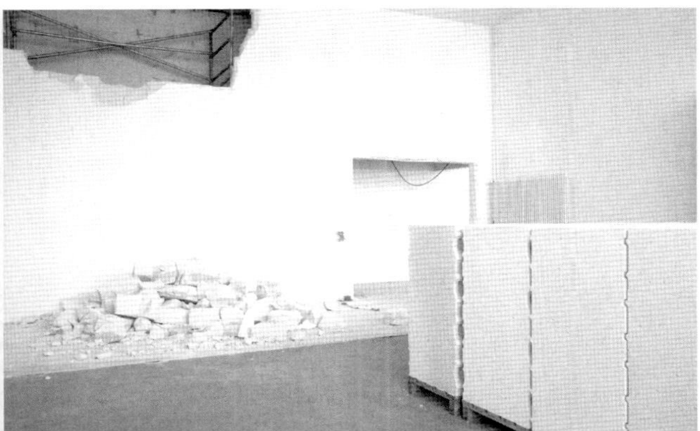
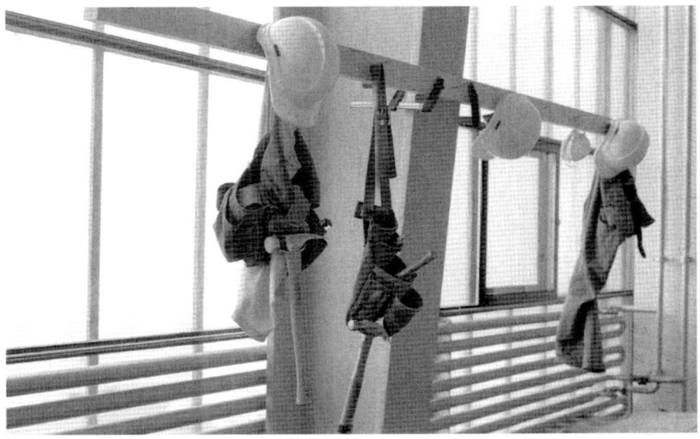

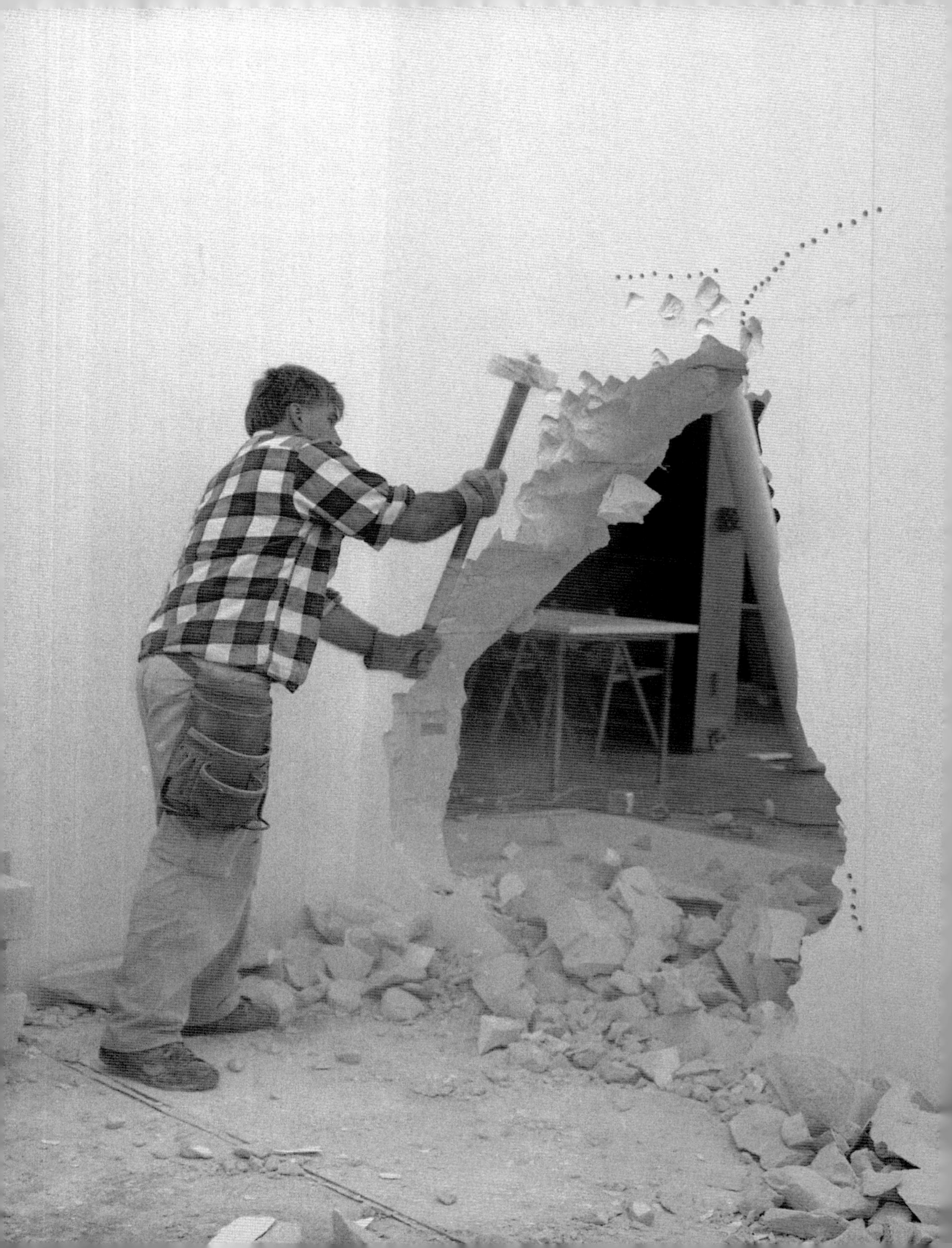

seite | page 136–141

Taking Place, 2001

Ortsbezogenes Projekt / Site-specific project:
Umbau der Ausstellungsräume /
Remodelling of the exhibition space
Kunsthalle Zürich
Photo: Carla Åhlander
Photo: Burkhard Meltzer
Courtesy Tanya Bonakdar Gallery, New York;
Klosterfelde, Berlin; Galleri Nicolai Wallner,
København

seite | page 143

Untitled, 1995

Performance, Kunstnernes Hus, Oslo
Courtesy Elmgreen & Dragset

umschlag-innenseite | inside cover

Powerless Structures, Fig. 188, 2001

Holz / Wood
300 x 225 x 100 cm
Galleria Massimo De Carlo, Milano
Photo: Giulio Buono / Studio Blu
Private Collection / Privatsammlung, Bozen

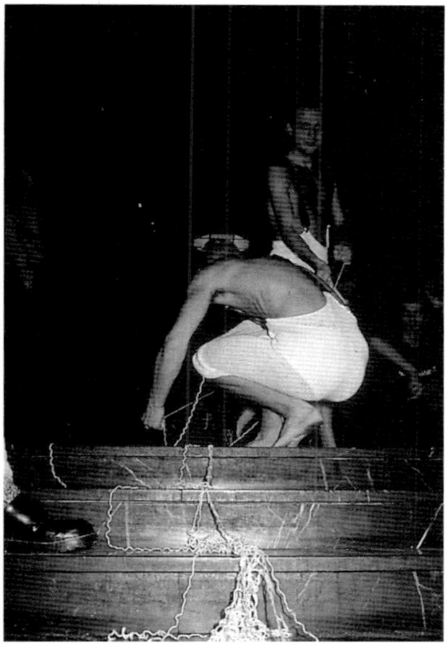

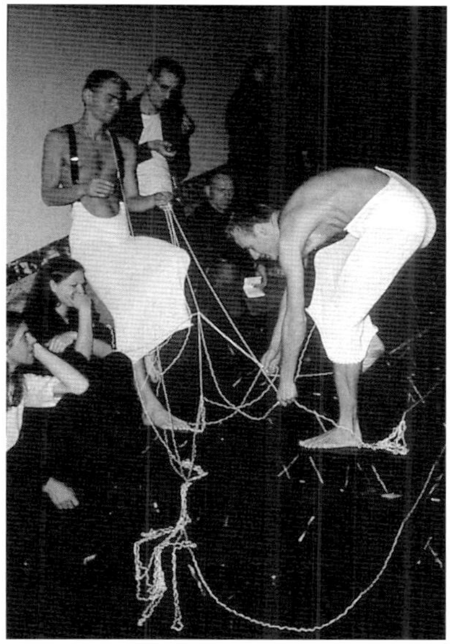

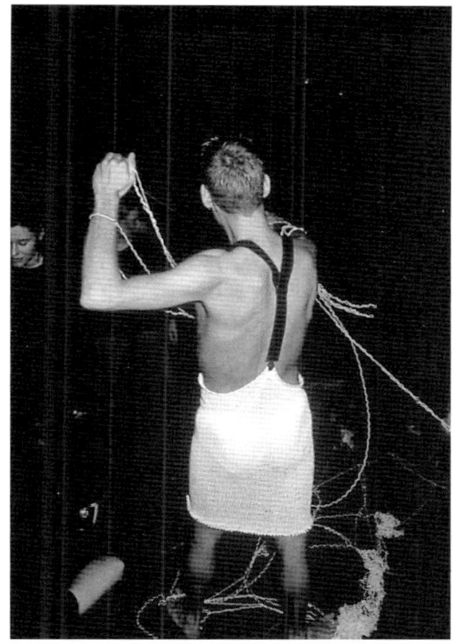

Dieser Katalog erscheint anlässlich der Ausstellungen
This catalogue is published to accompany the exhibitions

Michael Elmgreen & Ingar Dragset, Taking Place, Kunsthalle Zürich, 10 November 2001 – 20 January 2002
Michael Elmgreen & Ingar Dragset, Prison Breaking/Powerless Structures, Fig. 333, 25th São Paulo Biennial, São Paulo, 23 März / March – 2 Juni / June 2002

KATALOG / CATALOGUE
HERAUSGEBER / EDITOR: Beatrix Ruf, Kunsthalle Zürich; The Danish Contemporary Art Foundation, Copenhagen
KONZEPT / CONCEPT: Michael Elmgreen & Ingar Dragset
LEKTORAT / COPY EDITING: Karin Osbahr (Deutsch/German), Tas Skorupa (Englisch/English)
GESTALTUNG / DESIGN: superfantastic, Berlin
ÜBERSETZUNGEN / TRANSLATIONS:
Glen Garner, (Dänisch–Englisch / Danish–English)
Karen Lauer (Englisch–Deutsch / English–German)
John Southard (Deutsch–Englisch / German–English)

GESAMTHERSTELLUNG / PRINTED BY:
Dr. Cantz'sche Druckerei, Ostfildern-Ruit

Erschienen im/Published by:
Hatje Cantz Verlag
Senefelderstraße 12
73760 Ostfildern-Ruit
Deutschland/Germany
Tel. +49 711 44 05-0
Fax +49 711 44 05-2 20
www.hatjecantz.de

Distribution in the US
D.A.P., Distributed Art Publishers, Inc.
155 Avenue of the Americas, 2nd Floor
New York, N.Y. 10013-1507
Tel. +1 212 627 1999
Fax +1 212 627 9484

ISBN 3-7757-1156-2

Printed in Germany

Die Deutsche Bibliothek - CIP-Einheitsaufnahme
Ein Titeldatensatz für diese Publikation ist bei
Der Deutschen Bibliothek erhältlich

Die Deutsche Bibliothek - CIP Cataloguing-in-Publication-Data
A catalogue record for this publication is available from
Die Deutsche Bibliothek

Michael Elmgreen & Ingar Dragset möchten folgenden Personen für ihre Unterstützung und Mithilfe danken /
Michael Elmgreen & Ingar Dragset would like to thank for their contribution and help:

Dorthe Abildgaard, Carla Åhlander, Klaus Andersen, Teixeira Armenio, Emre Baykal, Walo Bertschinger, Daniel Birnbaum, Spela Bizjak, Thomas H. Bjarnason, Dany Boller, Tanya Bonakdar, Markus Brüderlin, Troels Bruun, Camilla Carlberg, Raoul da Silva, Helga de Alvear, Massimo de Carlo, Nikola Dietrich, Werner Dubach, Jesper Dyrehauge, Tanja Elsgest, Jacob Fabricius, Stephen Friedman, Andreas Fuhrimann, Coco Fusco, Lars Grambye, Gabrielle Hächler, Jeppe Hein, Fernando Alves Henriques, Jens Hoffman, Peter Hubacher, Marjory Jacobsen, Martin Klosterfelde, Boris Kremer, Annette Kulenkampff, Lars Bang Larsen, Konrad Leiser, Maria Lind, Peter Lindner, Peter Lütje, Tommy Lund, Bettina Marbach, Ivo Mesquita, Aasa Nacking, Alfonso Negri, Konrad Oehler, Henrik Olesen, Attila Panczel, Adriano Pedrosa, Agustin Perez Rubio, Paula Perissinotto, Kirsten Pieroth, Sean Reynard, Martin Rinderknecht, Kathrin Rhomberg, Kirstine Roepstorff, Beatrix Ruf, Pietro Sanguineti, Ethan Sklar, Marianne Torp, Carlos Urroz, Charlotte von Koerber, Nicolai Wallner

AUSSTELLUNG IN ZÜRICH/EXHIBITION IN ZURICH
AUSSTELLUNG / EXHIBITION: Beatrix Ruf
ASSISTENZ / ASSISTANCE: Bettina Marbach
TECHNIK / TECHNICAL ASSISTANCE: Attila Panczel, Reto Lütscher

Kunsthalle Zürich
Limmatstraße 270
8005 Zürich
Schweiz / Switzerland
Tel: +41 1 272 15 15, Fax +41 1 272 18 88
E-mail: info@kunsthallezurich.ch
Internet: www.kunsthallezurich.ch

Dank / Acknowledgments: The Danish Contemporary Art Foundation, Copenhagen; Walo Bertschinger AG, Zürich

DÄNISCHE REPRÄSENTATION / THE DANISH REPRESENTATION, 25TH BIENNIAL DE SÃO PAULO 2002
AUSSTELLUNG / EXHIBITION: Dorthe Abildgaard
ASSISTENZ / ASSISTANCE: Karin Francke, Paula Perissinotto, Helle Qvistgaard
TECHNIK / TECHNICAL ASSISTANCE: Troels Bruun, André Vainer

The Danish Contemporary Art Foundation
3–5 Kongens Nytorv
1050 Copenhagen K
Dänemark/Denmark
Tel: +45 33 70 74 70, Fax +45 33 70 74 80
E-mail: dca-cdb@dca-cdb.dk
Internet: www.dca-cdb.dk

DCA
DAN SH CONTEMPORARY ART FOUNDATION

Dank / Acknowledgments:
Royal Danish Consulate in São Paulo, Consul-General Henrik Petersen, Troels Bruun, Ivo Mesquita, Adriano Pedrosa, Paula Perissinotto, Susanne Skjoldager, André Vainer